A GUIDE TO
ROYAL
LONDON

A GUIDE TO
ROYAL
LONDON

edited by Christopher Hibbert

adapted from *The London Encyclopædia*
edited by Ben Weinreb and Christopher Hibbert

MACMILLAN
LONDON

First published 1987 by
MACMILLAN LONDON LIMITED
4 Little Essex Street London WC2R 3LF
and Basingstoke

Associated companies in Auckland, Delhi,
Dublin, Gaborone, Hamburg, Harare, Hong
Kong, Johannesburg, Kuala Lumpur, Lagos,
Manzini, Melbourne, Mexico City, Nairobi,
New York, Singapore and Tokyo

Design by Robert Updegraff
Picture research by Juliet Brightmore

Typeset by Wyvern Typesetting Ltd, Bristol

Printed in Hong Kong

British Library Cataloguing in Publication Data
Hibbert, Christopher
  Royal London.
  1. London (England)——Description——1981–
  ——Guide-books 2. Great Britain——Kings
  and rulers——Dwellings 3. Pageants——
  England——London 4. Great Britain——
  Kings and rulers
  I. Title
  914.21'04858   DA679

ISBN 0-333-42506-5

CONTENTS

Editor's Note

This book contains all those entries in the *London Encyclopædia* that deal with buildings and land which belong or belonged to the Crown or which have peculiarly royal connections. Many of the entries have been revised, new entries have been included, and opening times have been added so that *Royal London* may serve as a guide book as well as an encyclopædia.

Names of buildings which have been demolished or otherwise destroyed are printed in funereal Gothic – as, for instance, 𝔅𝔯𝔦𝔡𝔢𝔴𝔢𝔩𝔩.

A few subjects, such as Statues, are grouped together. There are also various special subject entries including Ceremonies.

Cross references are indicated by SMALL CAPITALS in the body of the entry.

In a book such as this the debt to previous writers is, of course, prodigious; but it has been considered impracticable to enumerate the very many works that have been consulted. We are deeply grateful to the authors and editors of them all. A list of contributors to the *London Encyclopædia* upon which this book is based is given below. The editor is also most grateful to his friend, Ben Weinreb, who conceived the *London Encyclopædia*; to Michael Alcock, the director at Macmillan who was responsible for it; to Brenda Stephenson and Katrina Whone for bringing *Royal London* into being; to Juliet Brightmore who has collected and chosen the illustrations; to Robert Updegraff who has designed the book; to Tracy Florance who has been responsible for its production; to Dawn Marriott who has helped in the extension and revision of some of the entries; to the staff of the London Tourist Board; and to Ralph Hyde of the Guildhall Library, who has made his unrivalled knowledge available to us all.

Contributors to *The London Encyclopædia* R. D. Abbott, Ann Arnold, Phyllis Auty, Keith Bailey, Victor Belcher, Josephine Birchenough, Mervyn Blatch, Mary Boast, Richard Bowden, Jane Bowen, Nicholas Boyarsky, Bromley Local History Society, James Bull, Hilary Burr, R. M. Burton, W. F. Bynum, Andrea Cameron, Mary Clark, Nancy Clark, Peter Clark, Patricia Clarke, Paul Clayden, Peter Clayton, Peter A. Clayton, J. A. R. Clench, Paul Clifford, Douglas Cluett, Cecil Clutton, J. T. Cooper, John W. Collier, C. A. Cornish, Mary Cosh, Ann Cottingham, Jeremy Cotton, A. H. Cox, Margaret Cox, A. D. Croft, B. R. Curle, Lucy Dargue, Marie P. G. Draper, Ann Ducker, Edmonton Hundred Historical Society, Esther Eisenthal, Julia Elton, Brian D. Evans, R. F. Farmer, Keith Fletcher, Jacqueline Fortey, Caroline Francis, Kenneth Gay, W. H. Gelder, Laurence Gillam, Colin Glover, J. S. Golland, Sarah Good, Edwin Green, J. W. Green, Erica Griffiths, Michael Hallett, Gabrielle Harris, C. W. Harrison, A. N. Harrisson, Jennifer Hartley, T. O. Haunch, Frances Hawes, Winifred M. Heard, E. G. Heath, Gerald Heath, Geoffrey Hewlett, Jennifer Hewlett, Christopher Hibbert, Edward Hibbert, Kate Hibbert, Susan Hibbert, Paul Hodges, Geoffrey Hollingworth, Valerie Hope, Peter Hounsell, James Howgego, Penny Howman, James Howson, Cecilia Hull, Richard Jeffree, Patricia M. Jenkyns, Colm Kerrigan, Jane Kimber, Sonia Kinahan, Henry Law, James Leasor, Vivienne McAuliffe, Phyllis McDougall, Margaret Mair, Eric de Maré, Dawn Marriott, Hester Marston-Smedley, A. L. J. Matthews, D. J. Montier, James Mosley, Margaret Mundy, Paddy Musgrove, Norman H. Nail, Stanley Newens, B. N. Nunns, Bernard Nurse, Robert Oakley, C. B. O'Beirne, Mary O'Connor, Archie Onslow, David Owen, M. A. Pakenham-Walsh, D. O. Pam, K. R. Pearce, Angela Perkins, Alan Piper, Francis Pollen, Thérèse Pollen, C. W. Plant, Patricia Pratt, John A. Prichard, Ruislip, Northwood and Eastcote Local History Society, Jan Reid, R. N. G. Rowland, Donald Rumbelow, Fiona Rutherford, Frank Sainsbury, A. J. Salmon, Jane Salmon, Alicia Salter, Ann Saunders, R. A. M. Scott, Clare Segal, John Selmon, Anthony Shaw, J. C. M. Shaw, Philip Shelbourne, Francis Sheppard, Joanna Sheppard, Margery M. Smith, Bob Smyth, Stanmore and Harrow Historical Society, Ann Strawson, Veronica Steel, Edmund Street, Tessa Street, Allyce Tessier, John Turner, E. E. Vella, Vestry House Museum, Walthamstow, Heather Waddell, Hugh Walker, Priscilla Waller, Julian Watson, Ben Weinreb, Joan Weinreb, B. T. White, Gordon White, Godfrey Whitelock, F. J. Whyler, Gwen Wilcox, Michael Wilcox, Audrey Wild, E. J. Willson, Emma Woodcraft, Ron Woollacott, Priscilla Wrightson, Humphrey Wynn, George Wynne Willson.

Queen Victoria and Prince Albert at the opening of the Great Exhibition of 1851.

Albert, Prince Consort   (1819–61). Born near Coburg, Germany, the Prince of Saxe-Coburg-Gotha married the young QUEEN VICTORIA in the CHAPEL ROYAL, ST JAMES'S PALACE in 1840. At first neither the Queen nor Parliament encouraged him to take any part in politics. In 1850 he presided over the Royal Commission which was set up to raise money for the Great Exhibition of 1851, a project in which he was intensely interested and to which he gave great encouragement. It was he who suggested that the profits from the Exhibition should be used to buy land on which Cromwell Road, Exhibition Road and Queensgate were built, the names of which he chose.

Albert had hoped that a Hall of Arts and Sciences would be built in London, but he died before it was even begun. However, when the ROYAL ALBERT HALL was constructed it was named after him. On the steps of the Hall stands his statue by Joseph Durham, and opposite, in KENSINGTON GARDENS, is the imposing ALBERT MEMORIAL. At the southern end of Exhibition Road is the museum of fine and applied art named after the Queen and the Prince Consort, the VICTORIA AND ALBERT MUSEUM.

Albert Hall   *see* ROYAL ALBERT HALL.

Albert Memorial   *Kensington Gardens, SW7.* In 1862 a public meeting was convened at the Mansion House by the Lord Mayor, William Cubitt, to

7

The memorial to Prince Albert which was erected in Kensington Gardens in 1872.

discuss the raising of funds for a national memorial to Prince Albert. Queen Victoria was asked to choose the design of the memorial. She formed a committee to advise her, on which sat the Earl of Derby, the Earl of Clarendon, Sir Charles Eastlake and Lord Mayor Cubitt. They rejected the first idea of a memorial obelisk and asked several architects to submit plans. George Gilbert Scott, James Pennethorne, T. L. Donaldson, P. C. Hardwick, M. Digby Wyatt, Charles Barry and E. M. Barry competed. The Queen chose Scott's design. The Royal Society of Arts (the Prince had been their president) collected small subscriptions from all over the country. In 1863 Parliament voted £50,000 towards the memorial. Gladstone delayed its construction by haggling over the cost which did not go unnoticed by the Queen. The Irish refused to subscribe and did not carry out their contract for granite.

The Queen took a close interest in the enterprise. On 1 July 1872 she inspected the memorial which was now completed except for the central statue of the Prince. She did not express an opinion, but Scott was knighted. On 3 July the hoardings were removed and the public admitted. There was no official unveiling ceremony.

In 1876 the 14 ft high statue of the Prince by John Foley was erected. The delay had been caused by the death of the first sculptor, Baron Marochetti, whose 1867 model had proved unsatisfactory. The memorial is 175 ft high and cost £120,000. The Gothic canopy is inlaid with mosaics, enamels and

8

polished stone and is topped by an inlaid cross. There are no less than seven tiers of statuary ascending from the base. The outer corners are marked by massive marble groups of 'Asia', sculpted by J. H. Foley, 'Europe', by Patrick Macdowell (Gibson had refused the commission), 'Africa' by William Theed and 'America' by John Bell. On the corners of the podium are 'Agriculture' by Calder Marshall, 'Manufactures' by Weekes, 'Commerce' by Thornycroft and 'Engineering' by Lawlor, all in marble. Around the base of the memorial is a white marble frieze, with 169 life-size figures, by H. H. Armstead and J. B. Philip: on the east side, painters; on the north, architects; musicians and poets on the south; and sculptors on the west. Philip was responsible for 87 of them.

Enshrined above is the mighty bronze statue of Prince Albert, seated and holding the catalogue of the Great Exhibition. On the pillars of the memorial are bronze statues by Philip of 'Astronomy', 'Chemistry', 'Geology' and 'Geometry'; and above, in niches, 'Rhetoric', 'Medicine', 'Philosophy' and 'Physiology' by Armstead. Mosaics in the arches are by Salviati's and show 'Poetry', 'Painting', 'Architecture' and 'Sculpture'. In niches on the spires are gilt bronze figures designed by J. Redfern of 'Faith', 'Hope', 'Charity' and 'Humility', with 'Fortitude', 'Prudence', 'Justice' and 'Temperance' at the corners. Above them are eight gilt bronze angels designed by Philip.

The memorial was initially acclaimed but towards the end of the century a reaction set in. Modern opinion tends to equivocation.

UNDERGROUND *High Street, Kensington, Knightsbridge.* BUS ROUTES *9, 33, 49, 52, 52A, 73.*

Anne, Princess (*b. 1950*). The second child and only daughter of Princess Elizabeth and the Duke of Edinburgh was born at CLARENCE HOUSE, her parents' London house. (On her mother's accession as QUEEN ELIZABETH II in 1953, the royal family's London home became BUCKINGHAM PALACE.) In 1973 Princess Anne and Captain Mark Phillips were married in WESTMINSTER ABBEY. In 1974 a kidnap attempt was made on her as she was being driven back to BUCKINGHAM PALACE along The Mall. She and Captain Phillips have two children, Peter, born in 1977, and Zara, born in 1981. Since 1981 she has been Chancellor of London University, a position in which she succeeded her grandmother, QUEEN ELIZABETH, THE QUEEN MOTHER.

Anne, Queen (*1665–1714*). Born at ST JAMES'S PALACE, the daughter of James, Duke of York, afterwards JAMES II. As Princess Anne she lived from 1691–6 at Campden House, Kensington. She succeeded her brother-in-law WILLIAM III in 1702. In 1710 a general election swept to power a High Church Tory Government, which celebrated its victory by bringing in an Act for the building of fifty new churches in or near London. This number proved too ambitious to fulfil but several fine churches were completed, six of them –

9

including St George's, Bloomsbury, and St Mary Woolnoth – by Christopher Wren's pupil, Nicholas Hawksmoor. Wren's St Paul's Cathedral, having taken 35 years to build, was also completed during her reign.

In 1683 Anne married the kindly, asthmatic, hard-drinking and dull Prince George of Denmark, of whom her uncle, CHARLES II, observed, 'I have tried him drunk, and I have tried him sober and there is nothing in him.' She had seventeen children by him, most of them born at KENSINGTON PALACE, but only one survived infancy and he died shortly after his eleventh birthday. She died, the last of the Stuart monarchs, at KENSINGTON PALACE and was buried in Henry VII's chapel at WESTMINSTER ABBEY.

Banqueting House   *Whitehall, SW1.* The only remaining part of the old WHITEHALL PALACE above ground. Designed by Inigo Jones and completed in 1622, it was the first purely Renaissance building in London. The first known Banqueting House at Whitehall was a temporary structure of wood and canvas, built in 1572. In 1581 Elizabeth I erected a more permanent building on the same site for the entertainment of the envoys who had come to negotiate a marriage between the Queen and the Duke of Alençon. It also was made from wood and canvas, but with 292 glass windows and richly painted. James I considered this to be an 'old, rotten, slight-builded shed' and in 1606 it was pulled down. Its replacement was 'very strong and statlie, being every way larger than the first'. It was 120 ft by 53 ft and set out as a theatre. On its opening, in January 1608, Ben Jonson's *The Masque of Beauty* was performed. It was burnt down in 1619.

The new Banqueting House by Inigo Jones was faced with Portland stone and cost £15,653 3s 3d in all. Horace Walpole wrote of it, 'It is so complete in itself that it stands as the model of the most pure and beautiful taste.' It has a gallery, with a stone balustrade, from which the King's subjects could watch him dine. The ceiling, commissioned by Charles I, is painted by Rubens, and celebrates the benefits of wise rule. It is on a vast scale, each cherub being more than 9 ft high. The building was much admired. In 1655, for example, a foreign visitor described it as looking 'very stately, because the rest of the Palace is ill-built, and nothing but a heap of Houses, erected at divers times, and of different Models.'

It was opened in 1622 with a performance of Jonson's *Masque of Angers*, but after the installation of the Rubens ceiling in 1635, masques were performed in a new wooden building nearby, lest the lamp smoke should damage the paintings.

The Banqueting House was used for a variety of state and court ceremonies, including the reception of foreign embassies, the traditional Maundy Thursday observances, the St George's Day dinner for Knights of the Garter, and the 'touching' for King's Evil (scrofula).

On 30 January 1649 King Charles I walked for the last time across the Banqueting House, and out through a window (there is a controversy as to

10

The execution of Charles I outside the Banqueting House in 1649.

which) on to the scaffold. Here he made a brief speech, declaring himself 'the Martyr of the People', before he was beheaded. Charles II celebrated his Restoration in the hall in 1660. The building also formed the background to the Glorious Revolution: James II added a weather vane to the north end to warn him of a 'Protestant wind' which might carry his son-in-law over the sea from Holland, and it was in this hall too that William and Mary were offered the joint sovereignty by the assembled nobility and commons on 13 February 1689.

The fire of 1698 marked the end of the ceremonial significance of the Banqueting House. It was converted by Wren into the CHAPEL ROYAL, as the old chapel had been burnt. In 1809 it became the Chapel of the HORSE GUARDS. It remained their chapel until 1829 when it was restored and again used as the Chapel Royal until 1890. In 1890 it was granted as a museum to the Royal United Services Institute. In 1963 it was redecorated in its original colours and opened to the public.

It can be seen from 1000 to 1700 from Tuesday to Saturday and from 1400 to 1700 on Sundays. It is closed on Mondays except on public holidays.

UNDERGROUND *Charing Cross, Embankment, Westminster.* BUS ROUTES *3, 11, 12, 24, 29, 53, 77, 77A, 88, 109, 159, 170, 184, 196.*

Beefeaters   The Yeoman Warders of the TOWER OF LONDON. Their Tudor uniform is similar to that of the QUEEN'S BODYGUARD OF THE YEOMEN OF THE GUARD. They were originally appointed by Edward VI. Their popular name may well have been derived from their fondness for roast beef, but it has also been suggested that it comes from the French *buffetier*. 'Eater' was once a synonym for servant, and is used in this sense in Jonson's *Epicoene, or The Silent Woman* (1609). The Old English *hlaf-oeta* (loaf-eater) meant a menial servant.

Blue Coat School   *see* CHRIST'S HOSPITAL.

Bridewell   A royal palace built in 1515–20 for Henry VIII on the banks of the Fleet River. It was named after a holy well nearby dedicated to St Bride. The building was a large rambling brick structure round three courtyards. In 1522 Charles V, the Holy Roman Emperor, was entertained here with pageants, music, tennis and feasts. A wooden footbridge was built across the Fleet so that the Emperor could reach his lodgings in Blackfriars Monastery. In 1525 Henry VIII installed Henry Blount, his illegitimate son, here as Earl of Nottingham and Duke of Richmond and Somerset. It was here that preliminary conferences took place with the papal legate on the King's divorce in 1528. And on 30 November 1529 Catherine of Aragon probably last saw her husband when they dined together here.

Between 1531 and 1539 the palace was leased to the French Ambassador. In 1553 it was the scene of Holbein's painting *The Ambassadors*. In that same year Edward VI gave the palace to the City for the reception of vagrants and

An early 19th-century reconstruction of Bridewell Palace c. 1660.

12

homeless children and for the punishment of petty offenders and disorderly women. Queen Mary Tudor confirmed Edward VI's charter in 1556 and the City took possession, turning the palace into a prison, hospital and work-rooms. There were other Bridewells in London: one at Westminster and another at Clerkenwell, besides several hundred others throughout the country. Orphans of Freemen of the City and later destitute children were also accommodated here and apprenticed to tradesmen for seven years.

Most of the old buildings were destroyed in the Great Fire and rebuilt in 1666–7, and in 1833 the entire prison was brought under state control before being closed in 1855 when prisoners of both sexes were transferred to Holloway. The buildings were demolished in 1863–4 except for the Gateway built in 1802. The rest of the site was first covered by de Keyser's Royal Hotel and since 1931 has been occupied by the Unilever Building.

Buckingham House (The Queen's House) *St James's Park*. Built in 1702–5 for John Sheffield, 1st Duke of Buckingham and Normanby, by William Winde. The Duke had previously lived at Arlington House but, dissatisfied with both building and site, he had that house demolished and his new red-brick house built partly on land of which he owned the freehold and partly on land which he held on lease from the Crown. A few weeks after its completion, Macky described Buckingham House as 'one of the great beauties of London, both by reason of its situation and its building. It is situated at the west end of St James's Park, fronting the Mall and the great walk; and behind it is a fine garden, a noble terrace (from whence, as well as from the apartments, you have a most delicious prospect) and a little park with a pretty canal.' The Duke died in 1721 and his widow, who claimed to be an illegitimate daughter of James II by Catharine Sedley, entered into negotiations for the disposal of the property to the Prince of Wales (after-wards George II). Nothing came of these negotiations, however, and it was to be George III who bought the property for £28,000 in 1762 from the Duke's illegitimate son, Sir Charles Sheffield. Furniture and pictures were taken here from HAMPTON COURT and KENSINGTON, and the King and Queen slept here for the first time in September. In 1775 the house was transferred to the Queen for life in exchange for SOMERSET HOUSE which had been made over to the newly founded Royal Academy of Arts. It was here that Dr Johnson had his celebrated meeting with George III in the library. From time to time extra rooms were added to house the King's growing collections; and the Queen's House became more of a palace than the family home that the King had originally intended to possess. In 1800 James Wyatt built a new grand staircase with a main and two branching flights which swept majestically up to the first floor beneath ceilings painted by Laguerre. After the Queen's death in 1818, her eldest son, by then Prince Regent, determined to build a larger and even grander house on the site; this eventually became BUCK-INGHAM PALACE.

Buckingham House, the home of George III and Queen Charlotte, also known as
The Queen's House, on whose site George IV built the present palace.

Buckingham Palace   *SW1*. Soon after he came to the throne, King George IV announced that CARLTON HOUSE was no longer a sufficiently grand and imposing residence for a King of England. He decided that it would have to be demolished and a new palace built to replace BUCKINGHAM HOUSE, his parents' London house where all his brothers and sisters had been born. The Government's intention that the old house merely be repaired and improved was no deterrent to the King who was determined to have something entirely new built of Bath stone. John Nash was employed as architect. He retained the shell of the earlier house and a good deal of the plan, but what gradually emerged was much larger and much more expensive than the Government had envisaged. By the time the original estimate of £252,690 had been increased to £331,973, the work was far from completed; and all manner of costly building materials had arrived on the site, including 500 massive blocks of veined Carrara marble.

The basic design was a three-sided court open at the east, in front of which was to stand the MARBLE ARCH as the main entrance into the forecourt. But the ornamentations seemed to most observers, as they seemed to Thomas Creevey, who sallied forth to see the alterations in February 1827, the 'devil's own'.

In 1828 Wellington became Prime Minister. Nash went to see him with a proposal that the wings, which did not meet with the King's approval, should be pulled down and rebuilt, to which the Duke replied crossly, 'If you expect me to put my hand to any additional expense, I'll be damned if I will.' But the work, once begun, could not very well be abandoned; and month after month it went on, mounting towards an ultimate total of £700,000, excluding the cost of the MARBLE ARCH.

The King did not live to see the palace finished. His brother, William IV, never lived there either; and when Queen Victoria came to the throne in 1837 it was scarcely habitable. The drains were faulty; there were no sinks for the chambermaids on the bedroom floors; few of the lavatories were ventilated; the bells would not ring; some of the doors would not close; and many of the thousand windows would not open. After Nash's dismissal in 1830, Edward Blore was appointed architect and it was he who finished the building, replaced Nash's dome by an attic and, in 1847, enclosed the courtyard by adding the east front – the front facing the Mall, which is the one familiar to the public today – an operation which involved the removal of the MARBLE ARCH to its present position at the top of Park Lane. In 1853–5 the ballroom block was added by Sir James Pennethorne.

By then the Queen had grown fond of the palace. So, too, did her son, Edward VII (who was born and died here), once he had cleared out the jumble of unwanted objects with which the Queen had filled it during her

Queen Victoria's sitting room at Buckingham Palace in 1848. She was the first monarch to live in the Palace.

long life, had had it redecorated and had rearranged the furniture and pictures. In the time of George V, though the official receptions were as grand as ever, the atmosphere of the palace became much more domesticated. To their eldest son, indeed, it became positively stuffy. 'The vast building,' he wrote in his memoirs after he had become Duke of Windsor, 'with its stately rooms and endless corridors and passages, seemed pervaded by a curious, musty smell that still assails me whenever I enter its portals. I was never happy there.' As King he was once seen jumping out of a window and running away across the garden to avoid an unwelcome confrontation with his private secretary. His brother George VI, who shared most of their father's tastes and was innately and unalterably conservative, liked the palace much better and was deeply distressed when it was bombed in the war and the chapel, in his own words, was 'wrecked'.

Since the war the palace has once again been renovated and redecorated. And whatever adverse criticisms may be made of the work of both Nash and Blore concerning the interior of the building – whose east front was replaced in 1913 by the present Portland stone façade designed by Sir Aston Webb – there are several rooms of surpassing grandeur.

There are some 600 rooms in all in the Palace, including those used by the staff as offices for the various members of the Royal Household and the domestic quarters. The rooms occupied privately by the Royal Family are few in number. The Queen and the Duke of Edinburgh have a suite of about 12 rooms on the first floor of the north wing overlooking GREEN PARK. On the

Buckingham Palace in the 1840s, showing Marble Arch in its original position.

second floor, overlooking the Mall, there are rooms for the Duke and Duchess of York, Prince Edward, and for Princess Anne, whose offices are here. The Prince of Wales also has an office in the Palace, and there is a sitting-room for the Ladies-in-Waiting. On the north side is the covered swimming-pool.

The gardens of the palace, landscaped by W. T. Aiton, extend to Hyde Park Corner and cover some 45 acres. They are graced by expansive lawns, a lake, and a wide variety of flowers and trees including one of the mulberry trees planted by James I in what was then the Mulberry Garden. Here in the summer garden parties are held, usually three each year for about 8,000 guests. The south wing of the palace contains the QUEEN'S GALLERY.

The forecourt of the palace is patrolled by sentries of the Brigade of Guards in full dress uniform. On most mornings the ceremony of CHANGING THE GUARD takes place here. When the Queen is in residence the Royal Standard, her personal flag, flies at the palace's masthead.

The palace and gardens are not open to the public.

UNDERGROUND *St James's Park, Victoria, Green Park.* BUS ROUTES *2, 2B, 10, 11, 14, 16, 19, 22, 24, 25, 29, 30, 36, 36B, 38, 39, 52, 52A, 55, 70, 73, 74, 76, 137, 185, 500, 507.*

Carlton House *Pall Mall.* Built at the beginning of the 18th century for Henry, Lord Carlton, it was purchased in 1732 by Frederick, Prince of Wales, whose widow, Augusta, George III's mother, continued to live there until her death in 1772, considerably enlarging it and adding to it the house next door which was bought from George Bubb Dodington. George III granted the use of the house to his eldest son, provided he undertook 'all repairs, taxes and the keeping of the garden'. The gardens, which stretched as far down as MARLBOROUGH HOUSE and had been laid out by William Kent, were particularly attractive; but the house was unremarkable and in poor repair. The Prince of Wales instructed Henry Holland, whose work at Brooks's Club he had much admired, to reconstruct it. Work began in the early autumn of 1783 and was to continue intermittently for nearly 30 years at a cost which the inordinately extravagant Prince was himself to admit was 'enormous'. Adjoining houses were bought and demolished to make way for new wings; a fine Corinthian portico was added; inside a splendid hall, decorated with Ionic columns of brown Siena marble, led to an octagon and a graceful double staircase. Above were the state apartments, the Prince's exotic bow-windowed bedroom, his dressing-room and bathroom. Beyond the music room there was a drawing-room decorated in the Chinese taste for which agents were sent to China to buy furniture; the mercer's bill alone came to £6,817 and £441 was spent on lanterns. All the rooms in the house were as expensively decorated and furnished, many of them with exquisite pieces from France, several of which are now at BUCKINGHAM PALACE.

The entrance hall of Carlton House, the Prince Regent's palace in Pall Mall, converted for him by Henry Holland and later by John Nash.

It was the scene of several extraordinarily grand receptions and balls, notably a splendid fête on 19 June 1811 to celebrate the inauguration of the Prince's Regency, an entertainment which Thomas Moore thought more magnificent than any ever given, and an equally wonderful fête given for 2,000 guests in 1814 as a tribute to Wellington, for which special buildings, designed by John Nash – who was responsible also for new Corinthian rooms in the house – were erected in the beautiful gardens. The Regent's only child, Princess Charlotte, was born here in 1796 and married here in 1816. Splendid as the house was, however, when the Regent came to the throne as George IV he decided that it was not fine enough for his new dignity. Another large palace would, therefore, have to take its place. It was demolished and a terrace of houses, Carlton House Terrace, was built upon its site and in the garden. Its columns were used in the portico of the National Gallery; several of its fireplaces and doors were removed to BUCKINGHAM PALACE and Windsor Castle; and some of the armorial stained glass from the conservatory was incorporated in the windows at Windsor. But little else remains of a residence which Horace Walpole, during its reconstruction, described as likely to be 'the most perfect palace' in Europe.

18

Ceremonies   One of London's oldest ceremonies, apart from the CORONA-
TION of the sovereign, is the distribution of the Royal Maundy on Maundy
Thursday. Although it is now held in a different place each year, and in the
Middle Ages took place wherever the monarch was in residence, it was, and
still is, often held in London – at GREENWICH PALACE, the BANQUETING
HOUSE, St Paul's Cathedral or WESTMINSTER ABBEY. The custom originated in
the 12th century when Henry I's 'good Queen Maud' washed and kissed the
feet of the poor at Westminster in memory of Jesus at the Last Supper.
Elizabeth I had the feet washed before she performed the token ceremony
and changed the custom of presenting the royal gown into a gift of money.
William III was the last monarch to kiss the feet, and during the 18th and
19th centuries the monarch ceased to attend. The custom was revived by
George V and the Queen has taken a keen interest and nearly always
distributes the Royal Maundy herself.

Ceremony for the Accession is well established. On the death of the
sovereign the Heralds assemble on the Friary Court Balcony of ST JAMES'S
PALACE and after a fanfare by the State Trumpeters, the Garter King of Arms
proclaims the successor. This is repeated at Charing Cross and then at
Temple Bar, which is ceremonially closed. Behind the Bar stand the Lord
Mayor, Aldermen and high officers of the City, and the City Marshal
challenges Her Majesty's Officers of Arms. After the Proclamation has been
made, the Lord Mayor declares, 'Admit the cavalcade' and they proceed into
the City and read the Proclamation at the corner of Chancery Lane and on
the steps of the Royal Exchange.

The distribution of the Royal Maundy in the Banqueting House of the 1770s.

19

Temple Bar is also ceremonially closed when the monarch enters the City in state. She is met by the Lord Mayor who presents the City's Pearl Sword. It used to be the custom to surrender the sword, but when Charles I entered the City in 1641 the sword was returned immediately, and now the Queen merely touches the hilt. The Lord Mayor then carries the sword before her.

Some of our rulers are commemorated by annual ceremonies. Every 30 January, the anniversary of his execution, there is a service by Charles I's statue in Trafalgar Square and a wreath-laying ceremony at the BANQUETING HOUSE. Charles II is remembered on Oak Apple day at the CHELSEA HOSPITAL early in June. His statue is decked with oak branches and the CHELSEA PENSIONERS parade, in their uniforms, wearing oak leaves. They give three cheers for 'Our Pious Founder' and three cheers for the sovereign.

On 6 January, in a 700-year-old ceremony during the Royal Epiphany Gifts service at the CHAPEL ROYAL, ST JAMES'S PALACE, officials of the Royal Household offer up gifts of gold, frankincense and myrrh in the name of the sovereign whose personal participation lapsed in the time of George II. The frankincense is afterwards given to an Anglican church where incense is used; the myrrh to Nashdom Abbey; and the gold is returned to the Bank of England and its cash equivalent spent on charitable purposes.

On 21 May representatives of Henry VI's foundations, Eton College and King's College, Cambridge, meet at Wakefield Tower in the TOWER OF LONDON, where he was murdered on that day in 1471. Lilies from Eton and roses from King's are placed on the spot where he was slain.

Special annual church services with ceremonies include the Bridewell Service at St Bride's, Fleet Street, on the second Tuesday in March, to commemorate Edward VI's foundation of the BRIDEWELL ROYAL HOSPITAL in 1553 (see also CHANGING THE GUARD, SWANS ON THE THAMES and TROOPING THE COLOUR. For Ceremony of the Keys see TOWER OF LONDON).

Changing the Guard   The ceremony of Changing the Guard is performed on the forecourt of Buckingham Palace every day in summer and on alternate days in winter at 1130.

The main residence of the Court when in London moved from WHITEHALL PALACE to ST JAMES'S PALACE at the end of the 17th century, and from that time the duty of providing a guard for the Sovereign has belonged to the Guards Division. Although the Changing of the Guard now takes place at Buckingham Palace, the Headquarters of the Captain of the Queen's Guard is still at St James's, and that is where the Colour is lodged. The five regiments of Foot Guards take it in turns to mount guard outside the two Palaces, CLARENCE HOUSE and the TOWER OF LONDON, wearing ceremonial tunics in summer and greatcoats in winter, and bearskins. The bearskins were adopted for wear after the Battle of Waterloo; they have been in use for ceremonial purposes since 1832. The Guards Regiments fulfil their ceremonial duties for a set time, and later return to operational duties. The

The Grenadier Guards mounting guard at St James's Palace, c. 1820.

different regiments can be identified by the plumes that they wear. The Grenadier Guards wear a white plume on the left side of their bearskins; the Coldstream Guards a red plume on the right side; the Welsh Guards a green and white plume on the left; the Irish Guards a blue plume on the right, and the Scots Guards no plume at all. If the regiment concerned in the ceremony is celebrating the anniversary of one of its victories in the field of battle, the Colour will be ornamented by a wreath.

The Old Guard, who have been on duty for the previous twenty-four hours, assemble for inspection at Buckingham Palace and at St James's Palace at 1100. The Detachment from St James's Palace, bringing the Colour, march up the Mall, led by the Corps of Drums, to join the Buckingham Palace Detachment. Together they await the arrival of the New Guard. Accompanied by a Regimental Band and its Corps of Drums, the New Guard marches from Wellington Barracks, arriving through the North Centre Gate of the Palace at 1130. The Band plays the traditional slow march of the Regiment, while the Guard advances in slow time and forms up opposite the waiting Old Guard. The Captains of each Guard touch left hands, to symbolise the handing over of the keys of Buckingham Palace. Once the sentries of the New Guard have been posted, the Old Guard returns to Barracks, with the Band and the Corps of Drums, while the New Guard, leaving the Buckingham Palace Detachment on duty, marches off to its duties at St James's, where it lodges the Colour in the Guard Room.

A similar ceremony, called the Queen's Life Guard, takes place at the HORSE GUARDS in Whitehall at 1100 each weekday and at 1000 on Sundays. When the King lived in WHITEHALL PALACE, he was guarded by a mounted Guard, whose Royal guardroom was in the Horse Guards building, just across Whitehall from the Palace. After the Court moved, the Household Cavalry remained in Whitehall to guard the Horse Guards Arch, at that time the only access, other than on foot, to the Royal Park of St James. This arch still remains the official entrance to the Royal Palaces, and the Household Cavalry are there to guard it. The Guard is now mounted by two regiments: the Life Guards and the Blues and Royals, both operational armoured units, whose officers and men can be posted for a spell to ceremonial duties in London, with a special ceremonial unit called the Household Cavalry Regiment. Each morning the New Guard rides through the Park to the HORSE GUARDS. The ceremony normally takes place in the courtyard, between the sentry boxes and the clock tower in winter, and on HORSE GUARDS PARADE in summer. The horses of the New and Old Guard line up facing each other; the standards are saluted and the sentries posted. Dismounted sentries guard the archway and the outside of the guardroom. The two mounted sentries, facing out across Whitehall, are known as boxmen; they are relieved every hour and are on duty from 1000 to 1600. The foot sentries change every two hours and are on duty day and night. After the Ceremony, the Old Guard returns along the Mall back to barracks.

Chapel of St John, *in the* **Tower of London**   see ST JOHN'S CHAPEL.

Chapel Royal   *St James's Palace, SW1.* The Chapel Royal and the imposing gatehouse are the main surviving parts of the Tudor Palace built by Henry VIII. The Chapel is famous chiefly for being the nursery of church music. It employed the finest English church musicians and numbered amongst those who served in it such talented organists as Thomas Tallis, William Byrd and Henry Purcell. It was Queen Anne who moved the choral foundation from the BANQUETING HOUSE in Whitehall to ST JAMES'S PALACE. Although much of the building itself dates from the time of redecoration in about 1836, the ceiling, decorated with names and cyphers of William IV and Queen Adelaide, matches the original ceiling of 1540 which commemorated the short-lived marriage of Henry VIII and Anne of Cleves. Charles I received here the Sacrament of Holy Communion on 30 January 1649 before crossing the park to his execution in Whitehall. Happier occasions were the marriage of Queen Victoria and the Prince Consort in the chapel in 1840 and that of George V (then Duke of York) and Princess May of Teck in 1893.

Chapels Royal   Developed from the priests and choirs, their vestments and chalices, which used to accompany the peripatetic households of the early medieval kings. When the King's court became more settled they were

The marriage of Queen Victoria to Prince Albert in the Chapel Royal, St James's Palace. The Prime Minister, Lord Melbourne, is holding the Sword of State.

established as oratories in his palaces. Although commonly referred to as such, not all royal chapels are Chapels Royal. The Chapels Royal in London are those at HAMPTON COURT PALACE, ST JAMES'S PALACE and the TOWER (the CHAPELS OF ST JOHN and ST PETER AD VINCULA). There are also royal chapels at BUCKINGHAM PALACE and in the Strand (*see* SAVOY CHAPEL). The Dean of the Chapels Royal has offices in ST JAMES'S PALACE.

Charles I (*1600–49*). Son of JAMES I and Anne of Denmark, he succeeded his father in 1625. Born at Dunfermline, he did not come to England until he was nearly four years old. After the breakdown of negotiations for his marriage to the Spanish Infanta, within three months of his accession King Charles married Henrietta Maria, daughter of Henry IV, King of France, and Denmark House (now SOMERSET HOUSE) became her London home. WHITE-HALL PALACE, the King's residence, was graced by his discerningly chosen art collection, much of which was later dispersed. Although it had been Charles's intention to rebuild the whole Palace, only the BANQUETING HOUSE, by Inigo Jones, was completed.

After the disagreements between the King and Parliament had resulted in the outbreak of the Civil War in 1642, the King fled from London and set up his headquarters in Oxford, while London became the headquarters of the Parliamentarian Army. In 1646 the King surrendered. He faced trial in

23

WESTMINSTER HALL, during which he refused to plead, denying the right of such a court. He spent the last night of his life in ST JAMES'S PALACE, whence on 30 January 1649 he was led to his execution on a black-draped scaffold erected outside the BANQUETING HOUSE in Whitehall. The equestrian statue of the King in Trafalgar Square is by Hubert Le Sueur.

Charles II (*1630–85*). Son of CHARLES I, he was born at ST JAMES'S PALACE and christened in St Martin-in-the-Fields. From 1644, after the sharp decline of the Royalist cause in the Civil War, he lived in exile, returning to London for the Restoration of the monarchy in 1660. He was welcomed at Blackheath, was received by the Lord Mayor and Aldermen in St George's Fields, Southwark, then rode over London Bridge, through the City and by Charing Cross to Whitehall where both Houses of Parliament awaited him, and where the Restoration was celebrated in the BANQUETING HOUSE. As the Crown Jewels had been dispersed during the Commonwealth a new collection was made for his coronation.

Out-of-doors London owes much to King Charles. He it was who made GREEN PARK into a Royal Park; he enclosed HYDE PARK; he got Louis IV's gardener, André Le Nôtre, to landscape ST JAMES'S PARK, to which he added 34 acres, and also to design the gardens at HAMPTON COURT, a palace of which he was particularly fond. He used to play a croquet-like game called pall mall in the Park, and that is the origin of the name of the street we now know as Pall Mall.

Van Dyck's portrait of Charles II, c. 1638, when he was eight years old.

It was to HAMPTON COURT that he retired when the Great Plague was raging in 1665, returning to ST JAMES'S PALACE eight months later. Further disaster struck in 1666 with the outbreak of the Great Fire. The Monument by Wren and Robert Hooke was raised to mark the place where the Fire broke out. On the west panel is a bas-relief by Caius Gabriel Cibber depicting the King in Roman costume.

In the winter of 1683–4 Charles visited the great Frost Fair on the Thames; the river was frozen over and there were booths and entertainments on the ice. The next winter he died at Whitehall and was buried in the Henry VII Chapel in WESTMINSTER ABBEY.

Charles, Prince of Wales   (*b. 1948*). Eldest son of QUEEN ELIZABETH II and PRINCE PHILIP, DUKE OF EDINBURGH, he was born at BUCKINGHAM PALACE. The Queen created him Prince of Wales in 1958. In 1981 he married Lady Diana Spencer, third daughter of the eighth Earl Spencer, and, like her husband, a descendant of JAMES I, in St Paul's Cathedral. They have two sons, both born in St Mary's Hospital, Paddington: Prince William of Wales in 1982, and Prince Henry of Wales in 1984.

Chelsea Hospital   *Royal Hospital Road, SW3*. Founded by Charles II for veteran soldiers, an idea inspired by the Hôtel des Invalides in Paris and by a similar hospital for the Irish Army. It stands on the site of an unsuccessful College of Theology established in 1618 by Dr Sutcliffe, Dean of Exeter. Archbishop Laud called it 'Controversy College'. After 40 years it closed and the government took over the building for Dutch and Scottish prisoners of war who were supervised here by John Evelyn. In 1666 it was granted to the Royal Society, but it was too dilapidated for them to use. In 1681, Sir Stephen Fox, the first Paymaster General, outlined the idea of the hospital to Charles II. The next year Christopher Wren was appointed architect and the King laid the foundation stone. 476 old pensioners were admitted in 1689. The building was finished in 1692. It was constructed around three courtyards, the centre one opening to the south, the side ones to the east and west respectively. In the centre one a statue of Charles II was erected (*see* STATUES). The building remains more or less unchanged except for minor alterations made by Robert Adam in 1765–82 and the stables which were added to the west by Sir John Soane in 1814. Carlyle called the hospital, 'quiet and dignified and the work of a gentleman'. The main north block contains the Central Saloon flanked by the Hall and Chapel. The hall is panelled and in it hangs a large painting of Charles II on horseback by Antonio Verrio. In 1807 General Whitelock was cashiered here after his court martial for surrendering the fortress of Monte Video. In 1852, from 10 to 17 November, the Duke of Wellington lay in state. So many people filed past his coffin that two of them were killed in the crush. The Chapel is also panelled and decorated with flags captured in battle. Over the altar is a

A view from the river of Chelsea Hospital in 1746.

painting of the *Resurrection* by Sebastiano Ricci. The east and west wings are dormitories. At the southern end of the west wing is the Governor's House. The State Room is panelled and has a fine limewood carving over the fireplace by William Emmett. Royal portraits line the walls, among them those of Charles I and his family by Van Dyck, Charles II by Lely, and William III by Kneller. To the west of the hospital is the infirmary. The original one was the home of Sir Robert Walpole in 1723–43. It was destroyed by a landmine in 1941 and rebuilt with 80 beds in 1961. East of the Hospital is a small museum illustrating the hospital's history. Every May the Chelsea Flower Show is held in the grounds. The granite obelisk was erected in the grounds in 1853 in memory of the men who died at Chilianwalla in 1849. To the south-west of the hospital is the National Army Museum (*see also* CHELSEA PENSIONERS).

The hospital is open from Monday to Saturday from 1000 to 1200 and from 1400 to 1600, and on Sundays from 1400 to 1600.

UNDERGROUND *Sloane Square.* BUS ROUTES *11, 19, 22, 39, 137.*

Chelsea Pensioners   The Royal Hospital, CHELSEA, more familiarly known as CHELSEA HOSPITAL, was founded by Charles II as a home for veteran soldiers. The in-pensioners, about 420 in number, are divided into six companies. Men over 65 (55 if unable to earn a living) are boarded, lodged, clothed, nursed when ill, and receive a small weekly allowance. Their uniform, navy blue in winter and light scarlet in summer, dates from the 18th century. A three-cornered hat is worn on special occasions such as Oak Apple Day (29 May) when pensioners parade in the central quadrangle, in honour of their royal founder's birthday (*see* CEREMONIES). On this occasion oak foliage decorates the large statue of Charles II (*see* STATUES) and sprigs are carried by pensioners. In autumn a Harvest Festival parade takes place.

Christ's Hospital   *Newgate Street.* Founded in 1553 by Edward VI ten days before his death, as a hospital for orphans. The distinctive long blue coats and yellow stockings, which the boys still wear, date almost from this time. The colour of the stockings is said to have been chosen to keep away the rats from the boys' ankles. The hospital was given the old Greyfriars Monastery buildings. 380 children were collected but 'many of them, taken from the dunghill, when they came to swete and cleane keping and to pure dyett,

Christ's Hospital, with the steeple of Christchurch, Newgate, in the background.

dyed downe righte.' Before long there was a school attached, with a grammar master, writing master, music master, two other teachers and a matron for the girls who became fewer and fewer as time went on. The school was, and is, also known as the Blue Coat School, because of the uniform. In the 17th century the children were often hired out as mutes for funerals. In 1666 many of the buildings were burnt in the GREAT FIRE. Most were rebuilt under the superintendence of Wren. The actual work appears to have been carried out by Hooke and Oliver. Wren began work on designs for the writing school, which were completed by Hawksmoor. New buildings for the girls were opened at Hertford in 1704. Coleridge and Charles Lamb came to the school in 1782 and Leigh Hunt in 1791.

Clarence House   *Stable Yard Road, St James's Palace, SW1.* Prince William, Duke of Clarence, third son of King George III, was allocated as lodgings when he came of age a series of rambling apartments between the Great Kitchen and the Stable Yard at the back of ST JAMES'S PALACE. After his marriage, he suggested to his brother, George IV, that a more suitable residence should be provided for him. 'I earnestly request,' He wrote to the King's Privy Purse, 'for the sake of the amiable and excellent Duchess, you will . . . represent the wretched state and dirt of our apartments.' He got his way; and in 1825 John Nash submitted to the Board of Works plans for the construction of a gracious, stuccoed house on the site of the Prince's old lodgings. It was finished in 1828. In 1830 William became King and, because BUCKINGHAM PALACE was not finished, he continued to live here. He tried ST JAMES'S PALACE for a time, but found there was so little room that he and his Queen had to move all their books and letters out of the rooms before levées. So a passage to connect the palace with Clarence House was built. On King William's death in 1837 Princess Augusta, George III's daughter, took the house until her own death three years later. In 1840–61, Clarence House was the home of Queen Victoria's mother, the Duchess of Kent; and from 1866 to 1900 it was the official residence of Prince Alfred, Duke of Edinburgh. Another storey was added in 1873. In 1900–42 it was used by Queen Victoria's third son, the Duke of Connaught. During the remainder of the 2nd World War it was the headquarters of the Red Cross and the St John Ambulance Brigade. In 1947–50 it was the home of Princess Elizabeth before her accession. Princess Anne was born here. In 1953 the Queen Mother moved here with Princess Margaret, who now lives at KENSINGTON PALACE. Although twice remodelled and enlarged, and restored after bomb damage in the 2nd World War, three storeys remain of Nash's building as well as a number of ceilings and mantelpieces of the same period. The house contains many valuable paintings from the Queen Mother's private collection. When she is in residence her personal standard flies over Clarence House, and a guard is always on duty, outside.
It is not open to the public.

The College of Arms, Queen Victoria Street, was rebuilt after the Great Fire.

College of Arms   *Queen Victoria Street, EC4.* The fine 17th-century home of the royal heralds. Part of the royal household from Edward I's reign or earlier, they were granted their first charter by Richard III in 1484 and were also given Coldharbour, a house in Upper Thames Street. When Richard lost his throne in 1485 Henry VII ousted them. Mary I granted them another charter in 1555 and gave them Derby Place which was built on the present site for Thomas Stanley, Earl of Derby, in the late 15th century. This was burned down in the Great Fire but the heralds' charters, rolls and records were saved. In 1671–8 the College was rebuilt to the designs of Maurice Emmett, Master Bricklayer to the Office of Works. The building was preserved from fire in the heavy bombing of May 1941 by a change in wind. The wrought iron gates and railings, which had formerly stood at Goodrich Court, Herefordshire, were presented to the College in 1956 by an American benefactor. The College is still very active, examining and recording pedigrees and granting armorial bearings. The Earl Marshal (a title always held by the Duke of Norfolk) arranges State occasions such as CORONATIONS, STATE OPENING OF PARLIAMENT and proclamations in England, Wales and Ulster. Under him the chief officers are the Kings of Arms (Garter, Clarenceux, and Norray and Ulster King of Arms); the heralds, York, Richmond, Windsor, Somerset, Lancaster and Chester; and the Pursuivants Portcullis, Rouge Dragon, Rouge Croix and Bluemantle. Each has his own room.

The College is open from 1000 to 1600 from Monday to Friday.

UNDERGROUND *Blackfriars.*   BUS ROUTES *45, 63, 76, 109, 141, 184.*

An attempt on Queen Victoria's life on Constitution Hill in 1840 when a 'feeble minded youth', Edward Oxford, fired a pistol at her coach.

Constitution Hill   *SW1*. A pleasant avenue dividing GREEN PARK from the walled gardens of BUCKINGHAM PALACE. It is still lined with trees and old lamp posts, despite recent attempts to remove them. Nobody knows how it got its name. One theory is that Charles II took constitutional walks here. He was said to have been walking here one day when his brother, the Duke of York (later James II), returned from hunting on Hounslow Heath accompanied by a large party of guardsmen. Surprised to see the King walking with so few attendants, the Duke 'thought His Majesty exposed himself to some danger'. 'No kind of danger, James,' the King replied. 'For I am sure no man in England will take away my life to make you King.' Constitution Hill was, however, the site of three attempts made on Queen Victoria's life – in 1840, 1842 and 1849. In 1850 Sir Robert Peel was fatally injured when thrown from his horse by the wicket gate leading into GREEN PARK after calling at the Palace.

Coronations   The coronation ceremony is over 1,000 years old. It was first planned by St Dunstan, Archbishop of Canterbury, for the crowning of King Edgar at Bath in 973. Since 1066 every coronation has taken place in WESTMINSTER ABBEY. In that year two kings were crowned – Harold in January, and on Christmas Day the victorious William I, whose coronation

30

was marred because the Norman soldiers on guard outside the Abbey thought the shouts of acclaim were a sign of rebellion and began killing the Saxons. Throughout the centuries some sovereigns have had ill omens at their coronations. A bat swooped round the head of Richard I as he assumed the crown. Richard II lost a shoe as he left the Abbey. Charles I wore white, which many said was unlucky. James II's crown wobbled and nearly fell during the procession to Whitehall. (This Catholic King heard mass at ST JAMES'S PALACE but submitted to Anglican rites at his coronation.) George IV was determined to have a magnificent ceremony and Parliament voted £243,000 for it. It was indeed magnificent, even though it was held on an exceptionally hot July day and the king appeared 'distressed almost to fainting' in his full robes and heavy wig during the five-hour service. Lady Cowper said he looked 'more like the victim than the hero of the fête'. Once revived with sal volatile he recovered sufficiently to wink at Lady Conyngham until the sternly admonitory sermon of the Archbishop of Canterbury induced a more serious mood. Meanwhile his rejected Queen Caroline was trying to force her way into the Abbey, but all doors were barred against her.

William IV thought the ceremony 'a pointless piece of flummery' in the words of his biographer, Philip Ziegler; and looked comical rather than regal, and 'very infirm in his walk'. There was great splendour for Victoria's coronation procession in June 1838. The bewildered Turkish Ambassador

The coronation of King George VI in Westminster Abbey in 1937, which, after chaotic rehearsals, was carried off without mishap.

31

The coronation of King James II in 1685. A Roman Catholic, he had heard mass at St James's Palace before the Anglican ceremony in the Abbey.

kept muttering: 'All this for a woman!' Victoria arrived at the Abbey 30 minutes late, but despite her youth (she was 18) 'performed her part with great grace and completeness'. Other participants did not do so well. Peers, generals and maids-of-honour scrabbled inelegantly for coronation medals tossed about by the Treasurer, and the Queen's ladies proved utterly incompetent to cope with their own trains and manage hers. Lord Rolle tripped and fell down the stairs of the throne, and the congregation cheered as he shakily picked himself up and climbed again towards the Queen's outstretched hand. There was confusion over the presentation of the Orb; and the ruby Ring, designed for her little finger, was painfully forced on to the fourth. Once the Bishop of Bath accidentally turned over two pages at once and nearly ended the service prematurely.

Edward VII was to have been crowned in June 1902 but the coronation was postponed until August because of his serious illness. When the ceremony took place the ancient Archbishop of Canterbury caused great confusion. He almost fell over with the Crown, was only just prevented from putting it on the wrong way round, and had to be helped up after paying homage to the King on behalf of the church. In consequence of past mishaps, there were careful preparations for George VI's coronation in May 1937, but even so rehearsals in the Abbey were chaotic, with the Archbishop of Canterbury wandering about crying 'Where is the Lord of the Manor of Worksop?' (who had the right to present an embroidered glove). There was dismay when the Orb was lost, until the six-year-old Princess Margaret was found playing with it on the floor. The King recorded his own worries, particularly over the reading, and whether his Crown would be the right way round; but despite some anxious moments all went well.

Queen Elizabeth II's coronation in June 1953 was well rehearsed, dignified and well ordered, thanks to the calm organisation of the Archbishop of Canterbury and the Earl Marshal. The only adverse factor was the weather, but the pouring rain could not diminish the enthusiasm of the huge crowds. It was the first coronation to be televised. The coronation of her father, George VI, had been the first 'to be recorded by cinematography' and the first coronation photographs were taken at that of her grandfather, George V, in 1911.

The order of service closely followed the *Liber Regalis* written and illustrated in the 14th century and kept in WESTMINSTER ABBEY. In it the parts to be played by the various dignitaries and officials in the rite are carefully laid down. The Queen walked into the Abbey at the end of a procession of 250, pausing first at the area, between the Choir and the Sanctuary, known as the Theatre. There were the three chairs used during the ceremony by the Sovereign – the Chair of State; the Throne; and King Edward's Chair, holding the Stone of Scone which was first used for the coronation of Edward II in 1308. In the rite, known as the Recognition, the Archbishop presented the Queen to the congregation and asked if they were willing to do homage and service. All cried 'God Save Queen Elizabeth' and the trumpets sounded. The Oath followed and the Presentation of the Bible, and then the Communion Service began. After the Creed the Queen took her place in King Edward's Chair, clad in a simple white gown, for the Anointing. She was invested with the royal robes and ornaments: the Jewelled Sword, the Armils (gold bracelets of sovereignty and wisdom), the Orb and Sceptre and the Coronation Ring. Then everyone in the Abbey rose as the Archbishop of Canterbury, having dedicated St Edward's Crown, raised it on high and solemnly lowered it on to the Queen's head. All shouted 'God Save the Queen', the trumpets sounded and the guns of the TOWER OF LONDON fired a Royal Salute. The enthronement followed and then the Queen received the homage of the Princes and Peers. After the Homage the drums beat and the trumpets sounded and all cried 'God Save Queen Elizabeth, Long live Queen Elizabeth, May the Queen live for ever.' The Queen and Prince Philip then retired to St Edward's Chapel where the Queen was arrayed in her Royal Purple Robe and the weighty St Edward's Crown was replaced by the lighter Imperial State Crown. Finally the newly crowned Queen moved with her great procession through the Abbey to the West Door to the sounds of the National Anthem and the pealing of bells.

A Coronation Banquet used to be held in WESTMINSTER HALL, where the Barons of the Cinque Ports carried the canopy over the King's head and the King's Champion rode in full armour into the Hall and challenged to mortal combat any who might dispute his right to the title. At James II's Coronation Banquet the Champion fell in full armour as he dismounted to kiss the King's hand, while at George III's banquet, although the Champion did well, one of his companions, Lord Talbot, could not prevent his horse from entering the Hall backwards. All went well at the last Challenge in 1821, when, after no one had taken up the Gauntlet, George IV drank to the Champion from a gold cup which, having drunk from it himself, the Champion took away with him as his rightful trophy. The peers enjoyed an excellent meal, while their wives and children, who were allowed to watch from the rows of seats above, looked on hungrily – though it is good to be able to record that one thoughtful peer tied a cold capon in his handkerchief and tossed it up to his family.

Crown Jewels, *see* TOWER OF LONDON.

George IV's magnificent coronation which cost the equivalent of almost £5,000,000.

The column erected in Waterloo Place as a memorial to the Duke of York.

Duke of York Column *Waterloo Place, SW1.* A memorial to Frederick, second son of George III. It is 124 ft from base to head, of a sufficient height, so it was suggested, to keep the Duke – whose debts amounted to £2,000,000 at his death – out of the way of his creditors. Its cost (about £25,000) was met largely by stopping one day's pay from every soldier in the Army, in which, hitherto, the Duke – an admirable Commander-in-Chief for all his faults – had been a popular figure. The column, designed by Benjamin Wyatt, is of the Tuscan order. Above its capital there are a square balcony, a drum and a dome. The bronze statue of the Duke surmounting all is by Sir Richard Westmacott (1834). After lengthy discussions about which way the statue should face, it was decided that it should look towards the War Office in Whitehall.

UNDERGROUND *Piccadilly Circus.* BUS ROUTES *3, 6, 9, 12, 13, 14, 15, 15A, 19, 22, 38, 53, 55, 88, 159.*

Edward I *(1239–1307).* An excellent soldier and administrator, he succeeded his father, HENRY III, in 1272. His so-called Model Parliament, which assembled at WESTMINSTER HALL in 1295, was the first representative Parliament. Edward was born in the PALACE OF WESTMINSTER. When his coronation procession left the TOWER for WESTMINSTER ABBEY, the conduits flowed with wine, as did the conduits at either end of Cheapside, the great market, when he first brought his Queen, Eleanor of Castile, to London. There were similar celebrations to mark the birth of his son, the Black Prince.

Though he spent much of his reign away from London, subduing Wales and Scotland, Edward continued his father's work of repairing and fortifying the TOWER, and he started the rebuilding of St Stephen's Chapel in the Palace of Westminster after it had burned down in 1298. He is believed to be the first king to have kept hawks in mews in what is now Trafalgar Square. In the forecourt of Charing Cross Station stands the Eleanor Cross, a replica (designed by A. S. Barry in 1863) of the cross the King ordered to mark one of 20 places where the funeral cortège of his much-loved Queen rested on the way from Harby in Nottingham, where she died, to her tomb in WESTMINSTER ABBEY. He, too, is buried in the Abbey, his tombstone inscribed 'Eduardus primus, Scotorum malleus, hic est.'

Edward II (*1284–1327*). Son of EDWARD I and his first wife, Eleanor of Castile, born at Caernarvon Castle in Wales. At the age of 17 he was the first of the line of eldest sons of the monarch or heirs apparent to be created Prince of Wales and, in 1308, the first English King to be crowned on the Stone of Scone, the 'stone of destiny' upon which the Scottish kings had been crowned until EDWARD I captured it in 1296 in his wars with Scotland.

Thoroughly incompetent as both ruler and soldier, in January 1327 in WESTMINSTER HALL Edward was forced to abdicate and his 14-year-old son was there chosen to succeed him. Eight months later Edward was murdered in Berkeley Castle, where he had been held prisoner since his deposition.

Edward III (*1312–77*). Son of EDWARD II and his Queen, Isabella of France. He acceded at the age of 14 in 1327 on the deposition of his father. He was virtually kept prisoner in the TOWER during his minority, when his mother and her lover, Roger Mortimer, Earl of March, governed. Three years later he banished his mother and had Mortimer arrested. Mortimer was hanged, drawn and quartered at Tyburn Elms. The Jewel Tower of the TOWER OF LONDON was built for King Edward. There he kept his treasure, jewels, clothes and furs.

War was waged throughout his reign, first with the Scots, and then with France in a war to be known as the Hundred Years' War. Edward died at Shene Palace, later renamed RICHMOND PALACE.

Edward IV (*1442–83*). First of the only two kings of the House of York, he was the son of Richard, Duke of York, who had been Protector of England during the minority of HENRY VI. He and King Henry were both the great great grandsons of EDWARD III. Edward won the crown after defeating the Lancastrians in 1461 during the Wars of the Roses (the intermittent civil war of 1455–85), and entered London in triumph.

As a result of popular discontent, caused partly by his licentiousness and by the almost limitless honours bestowed on the Queen's family, in 1470 he was driven into exile. The night he returned to London the deposed King Henry VI was murdered in the TOWER. In 1478 Edward had his brother, the Duke of Clarence, committed to the TOWER, where he was murdered – tradition has it drowned in a butt of Malmsey wine. Regicide and fratricide though he was, court life was lively and pleasurable during his reign.

Edward V (*1470–83*). Son of EDWARD IV, he was born in Westminster Sanctuary. On the death of his father on 9 April 1483 his uncle, Richard, Duke of Gloucester, became Lord Protector. While awaiting his coronation (which never took place) the 13-year-old King and his brother, the 11-year-old Duke of York, were lodged in the TOWER. Three months later Gloucester usurped the throne and was crowned RICHARD III. The princes are believed – though not by his champions, the Richard III Society – to have been secretly murdered by order of the usurping King; and, according to Sir Thomas More, the corpses were buried at the foot of the stairs in the Garden Tower. The skeletons of two boys were discovered in just such a place in the reign of CHARLES II, who, believing that they were indeed the princes' remains, had them re-interred in the Henry VIII chapel in WESTMINSTER ABBEY.

A Victorian artist's impression of Edward V and his brother in the Tower.

An anti-papal allegory of 1548 depicting Henry VIII on his death-bed, pointing to his successor, Edward VI, at whose feet the Pope lies stunned by a Bible.

Edward VI (*1537–53*). Son of HENRY VIII and Jane Seymour. He was born at HAMPTON COURT, where he spent much of his life and where he met his stepmother Catherine Parr, of whom he became very fond. Edward succeeded his father in 1547, and, as was customary, spent the days before his coronation in the TOWER. It was he who appointed the first BEEFEATERS, the Yeomen Warders of the Tower of London who guard it to this day. The hospital at BRIDEWELL and CHRIST'S HOSPITAL were his foundations. He also refounded St Thomas's Hospital, which had been closed at the Dissolution of the Monasteries. On the north wing of St Thomas's are two statues of the King, one by Thomas Cartwright and the other by Peter Scheemakers. In April 1553 Edward left the PALACE OF WESTMINSTER by state barge for GREENWICH PALACE, where he died in July of tuberculosis, having been persuaded to name the LADY JANE GREY his successor. He was entombed in Henry VII's Chapel, WESTMINSTER ABBEY.

Edward VII (*1841–1910*). Eldest son of QUEEN VICTORIA and Prince Albert (later ALBERT, PRINCE CONSORT). On the death of Queen Adelaide, QUEEN VICTORIA asked Parliament to assign MARLBOROUGH HOUSE for the use of the Prince of Wales when he reached the age of nineteen. In 1863 he married the Danish Princess Alexandra, to whom he was unremittingly unfaithful while treating her always with the utmost respect. She arrived in London by train at Southwark, where huge crowds had gathered to see her. The bedecked carriage route was over London Bridge, down the Strand, through Pall Mall, St James's Street, Piccadilly and HYDE PARK to Paddington, whence she and the Prince of Wales travelled by train to Windsor Castle for their wedding. They went to live at MARLBOROUGH HOUSE, where the Princess suffered a serious bout of rheumatic fever which left her with a permanent limp. Among the guests they entertained at MARLBOROUGH HOUSE were the Tsarevitch and his family and, reluctantly, Kaiser Wilhelm II. In 1869 the Prince founded the MARLBOROUGH CLUB, all of whose members were known to him personally. In 1871 he nearly died of typhoid fever; and on his recovery there was a carriage procession to St Paul's for a service of thanksgiving. His interest in medicine led him to suggest the foundation of a Hospital for Officers which, in 1903, was named the KING EDWARD VII'S HOSPITAL FOR OFFICERS. When he succeeded Queen Victoria in 1901, he took possession of BUCKINGHAM PALACE where shortly afterwards he was operated on for perityphlitis, because of which his coronation had to be postponed. On his death at BUCKINGHAM PALACE there was a ceremonial procession to WESTMINSTER HALL, where the King lay in state for four days before burial at Windsor, when Big Ben tolled for the first time for the funeral of a monarch.

King Edward VII, Queen Victoria's successor, in his coronation robes, c. 1902.

Edward VIII *(1894–1972)*. Born at WHITE LODGE, RICHMOND PARK, the home of his grandparents the Duke and Duchess of Teck, he was the son of the Duke and Duchess of York, later to become GEORGE V and Queen Mary. His childhood London home was with his parents at York House (now LANCASTER HOUSE), ST JAMES'S PALACE, but on the death of QUEEN VICTORIA in 1901, EDWARD VII gave MARLBOROUGH HOUSE to the Duke of York and thereafter that was the Prince's boyhood home in London.

In 1910, just before he was 16 years old, he marched in procession with his father, following the coffin of his grandfather, EDWARD VII, from WESTMINSTER HALL to Paddington for burial at Windsor. George V and his family moved to BUCKINGHAM PALACE. On the Prince's sixteenth birthday he was created Prince of Wales. After the 1st World War he was given his own establishment. York House became his London home until the death of his father in 1936 when, as King Edward VIII, he moved again to BUCKINGHAM PALACE, a place he thoroughly disliked. He did not spend more time there than he had to, and left finally in December 1937 when he abdicated to marry the divorced Wallis Simpson. He was created Duke of Windsor and thereafter lived abroad.

Edward, Prince *(b. 1964)*. Born at BUCKINGHAM PALACE, the London home of his parents, he is the third son of QUEEN ELIZABETH II and PRINCE PHILIP, DUKE OF EDINBURGH. After taking his degree at Cambridge University he joined the Royal Marines. He was the supporter of his brother, the DUKE OF YORK, at his wedding in WESTMINSTER ABBEY in 1986.

Elizabeth I *(1533–1603)*. Daughter of HENRY VIII and Anne Boleyn. Before she was three years old her mother was executed on Tower Green, and when she was only eight and a half her third stepmother, Catherine Howard, of whom she was very fond, was also executed at the same place. Elizabeth's reluctance to marry is hardly surprising. She and her elder half-sister MARY and her half-brother EDWARD VI spent much of their childhood at Elsyng House, Enfield. After her father's death and her brother's accession she lived at Chelsea Manor House with her father's widow, Catherine Parr.

At QUEEN MARY's accession Elizabeth met her at Wanstead and they rode into London together; but six months later a rebellion broke out with the object of deposing the Roman Catholic Queen in favour of the Protestant Princess. Elizabeth was brought in a litter from the country to Whitehall, where she was constantly questioned for three weeks as to her knowledge of the plot, and was then confined for two months in the TOWER. For much of her sister's reign she was kept captive at HAMPTON COURT, where, after her accession, she always kept Christmas. GREENWICH PALACE, her birthplace, was her principal summer residence, and she also used WHITEHALL PALACE and Nonsuch Palace. When she kept Court at ST JAMES'S PALACE she hunted in ST JAMES'S PARK. She hunted, too, in the Forest of Middlesex, part of which is now REGENT'S PARK, in Epping Forest, and in what is now HYDE PARK, where she inaugurated military reviews.

In 1581 Elizabeth knighted Francis Drake in his ship, the *Golden Hind*, in which he had circumnavigated the globe; and in 1588 she reviewed the army assembled at Tilbury against the expected invasion by the Spanish Armada, in the defeat of which Sir Francis played so large a part. There was a magnificent procession to St Paul's for a thanksgiving service for the victory. In it the Queen rode in an open chariot with a canopy in the form of a gilded crown. The cortège started from SOMERSET HOUSE, up Fleet Street and under Temple Bar, then up Ludgate Hill to the Cathedral.

The death of her favourite, the Earl of Leicester, and the execution for treason of her other great favourite, the Earl of Essex, deeply saddened her. She spent the last two months of her life at RICHMOND PALACE. Her Secretary of State, Robert Cecil, greatly concerned for her, said, 'Madam, to content the people you must go to bed.' She replied 'Little man, little man, the word *must* is not to be used to princes.' She died on 25 March. She had a funeral of great splendour, and over her tomb, which is beside her sister's in WEST-MINSTER ABBEY, her successor JAMES I erected an imposing monument. Her pearls are set in the Imperial Crown of State which is kept in the Jewel Tower in the TOWER OF LONDON.

Queen Elizabeth I, towards the end of her reign, is carried in procession by courtiers and preceded by Knights of the Garter.

George VI and Queen Elizabeth with their daughters, the Princesses Elizabeth and Margaret, having tea at the Royal Lodge, Windsor, in 1950.

Elizabeth II (*b. 1926*). Elder daughter of the Duke and Duchess of York who later became KING GEORGE VI and QUEEN ELIZABETH (now THE QUEEN MOTHER). She was born at 17 Bruton Street, the London home of her grandfather, the Earl of Strathmore. Her childhood was spent, when in London, with her parents at 145 Piccadilly until her father's accession when she was 11 years old; thenceforth they lived at BUCKINGHAM PALACE. After she and PRINCE PHILIP married in WESTMINSTER ABBEY in 1947 they had apartments in BUCKINGHAM PALACE while CLARENCE HOUSE was being converted for them. CLARENCE HOUSE was their London home from 1949 until the Queen succeeded. In 1953 her accession was proclaimed at ST JAMES'S PALACE in accordance with custom, and there she gave her first speech as sovereign at the Accession Council. She was crowned six months later with St Edward's Crown in WESTMINSTER ABBEY. No coronation ceremony had been televised before. In June 1978 she drove in procession to St Paul's for the service of thanksgiving for her Silver Jubilee, after which she and PRINCE PHILIP walked among the crowds.

Queen Elizabeth, The Queen Mother (*b. 1900*). Lady Elizabeth Bowes-Lyon, youngest daughter of the fourteenth Earl of Strathmore, was married to the Duke of York in WESTMINSTER ABBEY in 1923. Their first home was White Lodge, RICHMOND PARK. Their elder daughter, Princess Elizabeth, was born at the London home of the Duchess's parents, 17 Bruton Street, in 1926. Later 145 Piccadilly became their London home. After the death of her husband, during whose reign as GEORGE VI they lived at BUCKINGHAM PALACE, the Queen adopted the title of Queen Elizabeth, the Queen Mother. She moved to MARLBOROUGH HOUSE, where her younger daughter, Princess Margaret, lived with her until her marriage in 1960. She now lives in CLARENCE HOUSE.

Eltham Palace *SE9*. At the time of the Domesday survey of 1086 the manor of Eltham was in the hands of Odo, Bishop of Bayeux and was held for him by Haimo, sheriff of the county, from whose heirs it passed to the Clare family; then, in 1278, to the de Vesci family; and in 1295 to Antony Bek, Bishop of Durham, who seems to have extensively rebuilt the manor house before presenting both house and manor to Edward, Prince of Wales, son of Edward I and later Edward II. The buildings were again extended by Edward II for Queen Isabella who spent much time here. Edward III was also a frequent visitor and it was here that he received the captive King John II of France.

The improvements to the palace were continued in the reign of Richard II under the supervision of Geoffrey Chaucer, the clerk of works. Among these improvements was a stone bridge, the predecessor of the 15th-century bridge across the moat which still survives. Further additions were made to the palace in the reign of Henry IV, who was married by proxy here to Joan of Navarre in 1402, and in that of Henry VI. The great hall, the most splendid surviving part of the palace, with the third largest hammerbeam roof in England, was constructed in about 1479 and a new chapel (excavated in 1976) was built in the reign of Henry VIII who was often at Eltham in his early years and issued from here the Statutes of Eltham, those regulations of the Royal Household which were drawn up in 1525 by Wolsey who had been installed as Lord Chancellor in the chapel 10 years before. The timbered Chancellor's Lodging was probably built at this time.

Towards the end of his reign Henry rarely came to Eltham, and Elizabeth I even less often. In 1576 Lambard wrote, 'This house by reason of its nearness to Greenwich hath not been so greatly esteemed.' And when Parliament took possession of it after the execution of Charles I it was reported as being 'much out of repair'. It was sold to Colonel Nathaniel Rich who began to pull it down. After a visit in 1656 John Evelyn wrote, 'Both the palace and chapel in miserable ruins, the noble wood and park destroyed by Rich, the Rebel.' When the manor was leased to Sir John Shaw in 1663 he chose to leave the palace in ruins and, appointing Hugh May his architect, rebuilt the manor lodge in the park which survives as Eltham Lodge, the clubhouse of the Royal Blackheath Golf Club. The Great Hall was used as a barn.

When a lease was granted in 1931 to Stephen Courtauld, however, the restoration of the Hall began and was completed by 1937. Courtauld built a new house, designed by Seely and Paget, and redesigned the gardens. The Courtaulds lived at Eltham Palace until shortly before the end of the 2nd World War, when the lease was acquired by the War Department.

The great hall and forecourt are open on Thursdays and Sundays from April to October from 1030 to 1215 and from 1415 to 1800. From November to March they are closed at 1600. They are also closed on Christmas Day.

BRITISH RAIL *Eltham or Mottingham.* BUS ROUTES *21, 61, 108, 124, 126, 132, 160, 161, 228, B1.*

George I (*1660–1727*). First monarch of the House of Hanover. The strongest claimant to the throne was Prince James Edward Stuart, son of JAMES II, known as the Old Pretender, but he was debarred because he was a Roman Catholic. On the death of QUEEN ANNE the Elector of Hanover, great-grandson of JAMES I was invited to accede. On landing in England (without a word of the language, which he never troubled to learn) he was rowed in the royal barge up the Thames to GREENWICH PALACE in dense fog. He was very taken with HAMPTON COURT, where he kept a Court of stupefying rigidity, and he spent much of his time at KENSINGTON PALACE, where he annoyed Londoners by increasing the size of the park at the expense of HYDE PARK. He died in his coach on his way for a visit to Hanover.

George II (*1683–1760*). On the accession of his father GEORGE I in 1714, he was declared Prince of Wales. He succeeded in 1727 and thereafter KENSINGTON PALACE became his principal residence. His wife, Caroline of Anspach, was interested in landscape gardening and had the Serpentine created in 1730. Early in the reign the Broad Walk and the Round Pond were made in KENSINGTON GARDENS; the King gave permission for 'respectfully dressed people' to visit the Gardens on Saturdays. Every summer between 1728 and 1738 he went stag-hunting and coursing at HAMPTON COURT, and was the last monarch to live there. The Dutch House at Kew was a favourite home (*see* KEW PALACE), and in nearby RICHMOND PARK he built the Palladian villa White Lodge. He also contributed towards the building of Marble Hill House at Twickenham for his mistress, Henrietta Howard. At the battle of Dettingen King George was the last British King to command an army in the field. He died in his water-closet at KENSINGTON PALACE in 1760.

George III (*1738–1820*). Born at Norfolk House, St James's Square, which was rented by his father, the Prince of Wales, who predeceased him. He succeeded his grandfather, GEORGE II, in 1760. For his coronation the Gold

State Coach was made and has been used for every subsequent coronation. In 1761 he married Princess Charlotte of Mecklenburg-Strelitz in the CHAPEL ROYAL, ST JAMES'S PALACE. The following year he bought BUCKINGHAM HOUSE which became the principal royal residence. He never lived at HAMPTON COURT, and he allowed KENSINGTON PALACE to fall into disrepair. On his mother's death he took possession of the small White House at Kew and of the adjacent Dutch House, where the elder royal children were lodged, as the White House was too small for his large family (*see* KEW PALACE). In 1765, while living at Kew, he suffered his first attack of porphyria, which led to a loss of reason. He recovered after treatment but after further attacks he relapsed into permanent insanity in 1811 when the Prince of Wales (later GEORGE IV) undertook the King's duties as Prince Regent. George III died nine years later at Windsor Castle.

George IV (*1762–1830*). Eldest of the fifteen children of GEORGE III. Prince of Wales from the first week of his life, he became Prince Regent on his father's derangement in 1811, acceding on his father's death in 1820. He was born at ST JAMES'S PALACE and baptised there in the Queen's drawing room. His childhood was spent at The Queen's House (BUCKINGHAM HOUSE) in London, and in the country at Richmond Lodge and at the Dutch House at Kew (*see* KEW PALACE). At the age of 23 he secretly married Maria Fitzherbert, a Roman Catholic widow six years his senior, in her house in Park Street. The marriage, contracted without the consent of GEORGE III, was invalid

Caricatures by Gilray of George III and the Prince Regent satirise the penuriousness of the King's Court at Windsor and the luxuriousness of his son's life at Carlton House.

under the Royal Marriages Act, and later the Prince denied that it had ever taken place. When the Prince was 21 the King granted him the use of CARLTON HOUSE in Pall Mall. It was a large house with extensive grounds but he determined to make it far grander and more imposing, sparing no expense either on the building or on the furnishings and works of art. In 1811 he gave a magnificent fête here to celebrate his inauguration as Regent. Regent Street was laid out by the Prince's favourite architect, John Nash, from 1813 to connect CARLTON HOUSE with Marylebone Park, later named after him, REGENT'S PARK.

The Prince of Wales's marriage to Princess Caroline of Brunswick, which took place in the CHAPEL ROYAL, ST JAMES'S PALACE, was a disaster from the start. He was so reluctant a bridegroom that on their wedding night, which was spent at St James's, he was very drunk and fell into the fireplace where his bride let him remain all night. Their only child, Princess Charlotte, who was later to die in childbirth, was born at Carlton House nine months later.

At his coronation, an occasion of the utmost splendour, Queen Caroline was refused entry into WESTMINSTER ABBEY. Within three weeks she died. On King George's accession he decided he must have a palace of even greater magnificence than Carlton House. Parliament having reluctantly voted a huge sum of money, the King was able to build BUCKINGHAM PALACE on the site of BUCKINGHAM HOUSE. Carlton House was demolished and on its site and in its garden was built Carlton House Terrace to the design of Nash. The King died at Windsor Castle before the Palace was finished.

Like one of his predecessors, CHARLES I, he was a great art collector and connoisseur, and added considerably to the royal collection. He and other collectors and connoisseurs, by persuading the government to purchase 38 important pictures, were instrumental in the foundation of the National Gallery, the portico of which came from the demolished Carlton House.

The King had many faults, but with them went many varied virtues. As the Duke of Wellington said of him, 'he was the most extraordinary compound of talent, wit, buffoonery, obstinacy and good feeling'. He was also, the Duke added, 'the most magnificent patron of arts in this country and in the World.'

George V (*1865–1936*). Born at MARLBOROUGH HOUSE, he succeeded his father EDWARD VII in 1910. In 1893 the Duke of York, as he then was, married his distant cousin, Princess Victoria Mary of Teck in the CHAPEL ROYAL, ST JAMES'S PALACE. MARLBOROUGH HOUSE was their London home until their accession, when they went with their family to live at BUCKINGHAM PALACE. A week after their coronation they attended a thanksgiving service at St Paul's. In 1917, during the 1st World War, the King 'deemed it desirable' that members of the royal family should relinquish their German surname. He chose instead the surname Windsor, though he was unaware that EDWARD III had been styled 'Sir Edward de Windsor, King of England'. Early in his

George V, who is said to have believed 'implicitly in God, in the invincibility of the Royal Navy and in the essential rightness of whatever was British'.

reign he revived the Royal Maundy ceremony, which no monarch had attended since WILLIAM III. In 1910 he bought the Glass State Coach to be used for royal weddings. Eight months after the Silver Jubilee service in St Paul's the king died. He lay in state for four days and nights in WESTMINSTER HALL before his funeral at Windsor. The widowed Queen Mary went to live again at MARLBOROUGH HOUSE, where she died in 1953, shortly before her granddaughter's coronation.

George VI *(1895–1952)*. The second son of GEORGE V came to the throne in 1936 on the abdication of his brother, EDWARD VIII. In 1923 when he and the Lady Elizabeth Bowes-Lyon were married in WESTMINSTER ABBEY the Glass State Coach was used for the first time. The Duke and Duchess of York lived for the first few years of their married life in his mother, Queen Mary's, childhood home, White Lodge, RICHMOND PARK, and later at 145 Piccadilly. Their coronation in 1937 was the first to be broadcast, a project to which the King, despite his speech impediment, gave his full support.

On his accession he and the Queen and the two Princesses lived at BUCKINGHAM PALACE. On the outbreak of war the Princesses were sent into the country but the King and Queen remained in London, visiting the bombed areas, including the East End which was particularly badly hit. BUCKINGHAM PALACE itself was bombed twice within three days, and nine times in all. When the war in Europe ended in 1945 the King and Queen drove in state through London for a service of thanksgiving in St Paul's, where they attended another thanksgiving service in 1948 in celebration of their silver wedding. From the steps of the same Cathedral in 1951 the King opened the Festival of Britain.

In January 1952 King George saw the Princess Elizabeth off on an overseas visit at London Airport, Heathrow, and a week later he died in his sleep at Sandringham.

Green Park *SW1*. So called because of its verdure of grass and trees, it comprises about 53 acres between Piccadilly and Constitution Hill, bounded in the west by Duke of Wellington Place and in the east by QUEEN'S WALK. It is said to have been the burial ground of the lepers from the hospital of St James's (*see* ST JAMES'S PALACE), which is supposedly why there are no flowers here as there are in adjoining ST JAMES'S PARK.

It was enclosed by Henry VIII; and at the time of the Restoration, the land between the wall of ST JAMES'S PALACE and the Reading Road (which is now Piccadilly) was still meadowland and untended waste ground. King Charles II turned the area into a Royal Park, 'having purchased several fields which ran up to the road and as far as Hyde Park, now enclosed with a brick wall'. The King laid out walks and built a snow-house. For this, a pit was dug and filled with snow and ice; on top of this was laid a thick layer of straw and bracken, and the house was used in summer for cooling wines and other drinks. The remains of this snow-house were to be found in the Park until early in the 19th century; and the mound where it stood can still be seen opposite No. 119 Piccadilly, surmounted by one of the Park's fine plane trees.

In 1730, Queen Caroline, wife of George II, had a private walk laid out along the eastern boundary of the Park, so that she and other members of the Royal Family could take the air protected from the public gaze. Part of the north–south path that runs on the eastern side of the Park is still known as 'Queen's Walk'. The Queen had a little pavilion built beside the Walk; it was usually known as her 'Library'. One winter's morning in 1737 she walked up there to take her breakfast, caught a severe chill, and died ten days later. After her death the pavilion fell into disrepair.

Great firework displays were held in Green Park to celebrate events such as the signing of the Treaty of Aix-la-Chapelle in 1749, which was directed by a group of Italian pyrotechnists and accompanied by music composed for the occasion and conducted by George Frederick Handel. Another firework display was held for the 1814 celebrations, when there was also a spectacular

The rococo Temple of Peace, erected in Green Park as part of a musical and firework display in 1749 to celebrate the treaty that ended the war with France.

ascent from Green Park when Windham Sadler's balloon 'sprang into the air with its usual velocity and Mr Sadler, who had taken up with him a vast number of programmes of the jubilee . . . flung them down again from the sky with much industry and profusion.' Six years after this event Charles Green ascended in his balloon, decorated with the Royal Arms and inscribed 'George IV, Royal Coronation Balloon', from the Park, made a successful ascent to a height of 11,000 ft and flew northwards as far as Barnet.

The Broad Walk which cuts across the park from Piccadilly to the eastern end of Constitution Hill is part of the design for the QUEEN VICTORIA MEMORIAL. The ornamental iron gates at the southern end were given by the Dominions, while those at the Piccadilly end were formerly outside Devonshire House and were erected here in 1921.

The park is open every day from dawn to dusk.

Greenwich Palace *SE10.* A favourite residence of the Tudor monarchs. It was built by Humphrey, Duke of Gloucester, brother of Henry V, on the banks of the Thames in 1427. Bella Court, as he called it, was one of the finest houses in England, with, as was usual at that time, a moat and battlements. In 1445 he lent the house, for their honeymoon, to Henry VI and Margaret of Anjou who, after Gloucester's arrest in 1447 and sudden death five days later, took it over and renamed it Placentia – the pleasant place. In 1465

49

Elizabeth Woodville gave birth here to Elizabeth of York, the future wife of Henry VII. In 1466 Edward IV settled the house on his Queen for life. In 1480 Edward IV granted a piece of land for a monastery to Franciscan friars who were given permission by the Pope 'to build a house with church, low bell tower, bell, cloister, frater, dorter, gardens and other necessary offices for the perpetual use and habitation of the friars in Greenwich'. In 1490 Henry VII made Elizabeth Woodville a virtual prisoner at Bermondsey Abbey and took over the palace. The next year his son, the future Henry VIII, was born here. In 1501 his elder brother, Prince Arthur, married Catherine of Aragon in the palace. Arthur died soon afterwards and was succeeded by Henry.

The palace became Henry's favourite residence. In his day it was a complex of buildings round three quadrangles. The main entrance was from the river through a massive gatehouse which led to the central court. Henry added armouries, a banqueting hall designed by William Vertue and a large tilt yard. In 1515 Princess Mary, his sister, the widow of Louis XII, married Charles Brandon, Duke of Suffolk, at Greenwich in front of the whole court. In February 1516, Henry's daughter, the future Mary I, was born at Greenwich and baptised in the friars' church. Wolsey was godfather. From 1529–31 Catherine of Aragon was kept prisoner in the palace for refusing to acknowledge the invalidity of her marriage. In 1533 Anne Boleyn gave birth here to Elizabeth I. After the suppression of the monastery in 1536, 200

The view across Greenwich Park from the Observatory, showing the Queen's House before the colannade was built in 1810, and the Royal Hospital.

monks were thrown into prison where they remained for several years until Sir Thomas Wriotheseley interceded for them and they were allowed to go to Scotland or the Continent. In 1536, at the May Day tournament Anne Boleyn is said to have dropped her handkerchief as a signal to a lover. Henry left early and that night Anne's brother and four of his friends were taken to the TOWER, followed the next day by Anne herself. Henry signed her death warrant at Greenwich, and it was here in 1540 that he was married by proxy to Anne of Cleves. In April 1553 the sickly Edward VI was sent to Greenwich for his health's sake, but he died here in July.

Soon after her accession, his sister, Mary I, invited the Franciscan friars to return. She rarely came to Greenwich herself. On one of her rare visits a cannon ball, fired in salute, came through the wall of her apartment, 'to the great terror of herself and her ladies', but nobody was hurt. In 1558 Elizabeth I became Queen and soon after banished the Franciscans for ever. She made Greenwich her principal summer residence. It was here that Ralegh put his cloak over a puddle so that she would not get her shoes dirty. In 1573 the Queen revived here the Maundy Ceremony in which she washed the feet of 39 pauper women (having had them washed by three other people first) and gave them food and money.

Elizabeth's successor, James I, settled Greenwich on his Queen, Anne of Denmark, for whom the QUEEN'S HOUSE was designed by Inigo Jones. In 1652 the Parliamentarians tried to sell the palace but no buyers could be found; it was stripped of its paintings and furniture and turned into a biscuit factory. Dutch prisoners of war were kept here in 1653–4. At the Restoration of 1660 Charles II decided to rebuild the palace rather than restore it. Three new blocks, designed by John Webb, were planned but only the western one had been completed by the time of the King's death. William and Mary preferred the royal palaces at KENSINGTON and HAMPTON COURT, and the remains of the building were demolished to make way for the ROYAL NAVAL COLLEGE.

Greenwich Park SE10. Burial mounds suggest that Bronze Age tribes settled here. A Roman built his villa on the east side of the park and many silver and bronze coins dating from 35 BC to AD 425 have been found. A Roman road ran through the park down to Greenwich, which was then probably a fishing village. In 1427 Humphrey, Duke of Gloucester, brother of Henry V, built himself a house on the river, the forerunner of GREENWICH PALACE. He enclosed a mile-long rectangle of land stretching from the Thames to Greenwich Hill. In 1433 Henry VI gave him permission to enclose 200 acres of pasture, wood, heath and gorses, the area of the present royal park. On the hill he built a watch-tower. From 1515 deer have been kept in the park, originally to provide game for the royal hunt.

Under Henry VIII Greenwich reached the height of royal favour. Henry loved 'to go a-maying' in the park. On the flat ground at the bottom of the hill tilting, shooting at butts, wrestling, fighting with spears and swords, and casting the light and heavy bars took place. In 1526 Henry rebuilt the castle on the hill for younger members of his family and his mistresses.

In 1558, soon after Elizabeth's accession, the City of London provided a spectacular entertainment for her in the park. In 1572 she reviewed companies of 1,400 men raised by the City after the Duke of Norfolk's plot. A mock battle then took place 'which had all the appearances of a regular battle except for the spilling of blood'. In 1619 James I enclosed the park with a brick wall costing £2,000. At the Restoration Charles II had the park laid out anew by Le Nôtre, Louis XIV's landscape gardener. The QUEEN'S HOUSE was made the focal point, with tree-lined avenues converging on it. During the 1660s many elms and Spanish chestnuts were planted under the direction of Sir William Boreman, and in 1675 Sir Christopher Wren built the ROYAL OBSERVATORY on the hill on the site of Duke Humphrey's castle. Charles Sackville, Earl of Dorset and Middlesex, was appointed in 1690 as first Ranger of the park with the right to live in the QUEEN'S HOUSE.

Since the 18th century the park has been open to the public.

In 1855 a steamboat service between Greenwich and London began and a year later the first London railway between Deptford and London

Bridge opened. Two years later the line was extended to Greenwich. As a result Greenwich became the playground of Londoners at bank holidays and the existing fair was expanded. In 1859 the fair was described as 'little more than a confusion of unwashed and shabbily dressed people, presenting a mobbish appearance'. In 1870 the Metropolitan Board of Works suppressed the fair as a nuisance to local residents. During 1848–78 a tunnel was made under the park to extend the railway to Charlton, Woolwich and Gravesend.

In 1930 the statue of General Wolfe was erected and in 1935 the statue of William IV from the City was re-erected here (*see* STATUES). During the period 1948–57 the Royal Observatory moved to Herstmonceux in Sussex and the buildings have since been opened as a branch of the National Maritime Museum. The view from Greenwich Hill is famous, giving a panorama of London with the QUEEN'S HOUSE, the ROYAL NAVAL COLLEGE and the Thames in the foreground. The bronze, *Standing Figure and Knife Edge*, is by Henry Moore (1979).

The park is open daily from 0700 to dusk.

Grey, Lady Jane (*1537–54*). Shortly before the death of EDWARD VI, the Duke of Northumberland arranged the marriage of his son, Lord Guildford Dudley, to the unwilling Lady Jane, the grand-daughter of HENRY VII, and persuaded the dying King to name her his successor. She was living with her husband at Syon House when news was brought to her of her accession. Nine days later MARY I claimed the crown, and Lady Jane and Dudley were tried for high treason in Guildhall. They were imprisoned in the TOWER and later executed, he on Tower Hill and she on Tower Green. They are buried in the Tower chapel of ST PETER AD VINCULA.

Hampton Court Gardens The 50 acres are a blend of Tudor, French, Italian and Dutch gardening styles. Cardinal Wolsey created the original garden with flower-beds, galleries, arbours and a 'mount' on a base of 256,000 bricks, with a three-storeyed summerhouse on top. The Maze, constructed for William and Mary, is a version of Wolsey's labyrinth: the shape is triangular and originally consisted of hornbeam, cypress and flowering shrubs, but holly and privet have now been added. In the Tilt Yard, where knights once jousted, is a rose garden, and to the south side of the Palace lie the formal Tudor gardens, with a knot garden planted from old patterns. The long herbaceous border was laid out by William Robinson who disliked formal gardens and developed a style known as 'wild gardening' with flowers appearing throughout the year. The Great Vine, planted in 1769, is now controlled to produce a third of the original 2,200 bunches of grapes each season. The gardens also contain Wren's Chestnut Avenue and Broad Walk; the Wilderness; and the Great Fountain, Pond and Privy Gardens. (*See also* HAMPTON COURT.)

A bird's-eye view of Hampton Court at the beginning of the 18th century.

Hampton Court Palace   *Middlesex*. On the banks of the THAMES some 15 miles south-west of London, contains some of the finest Tudor architecture in Britain, as well as buildings of great splendour designed by Sir Christopher Wren. Its clean air, pure water, spacious woods and grounds, and the opportunity it offered for the laying out of gardens, arbours and tree-lined walks, made it the favourite country home, hunting lodge and pleasure palace of successive generations of English monarchs. Their personal tastes and the genius of their artists, architects and designers can still be seen in the buildings and gardens and in the art treasures which fill its rooms, galleries and halls.

Thomas Wolsey bought the site in 1514 from the Order of St John of Jerusalem, a year before he became Cardinal and Lord Chancellor of England. The private residence he projected rapidly assumed the proportions and grandeur of a royal palace, with 280 rooms for guests and a staff of nearly 500. The magnificence of his hospitality and entertainments were the wonder of Europe. When Wolsey fell from favour, he presented Hampton Court to Henry VIII in a vain attempt to regain his position; but in 1529 all his goods and lands were declared forfeit to the Crown. Henry moved in at once and began to enlarge the buildings and efface, where possible, traces of its former owner. New courtyards, kitchens, galleries, a new library and guard room were added during his reign. The famous Astronomical Clock, designed by Nicholas Oursian in 1540, was set in Wolsey's great gateway, redecorated and named after Anne Boleyn, Henry's second Queen. Wolsey's arms over the entrance, defaced by Henry, are now restored, and the clock, removed in 1840, was repaired and replaced in 1879, and is still in working order. Henry took great interest in the gardens, planting trees and shrubs, and, a keen huntsman, saw that the estate was well stocked with game. Towers, turrets, a Water Gallery and an elaborate summer house were put up on the south side between the palace and the river, and a complex of buildings leading to the water-gate which Henry used when he came to Hampton Court by barge. He refurbished the Chapel, part of Wolsey's original Palace, giving it a fan vault; his son, the future King Edward VI, was christened here. The Tudor ceiling is still in place. The Chapel was redecorated by Wren; the classical reredos is by Grinling Gibbons. Henry brought five of his six wives to live at Hampton Court. Anne Boleyn's badges and initials can still be seen among the carvings and tracery of the Great Hall which Henry built to replace Wolsey's smaller one, though Jane Seymour, who died in the palace having given birth to Henry's only son, Edward VI, had taken her place before the work was finished.

Edward VI spent most of his short life here, and it was here that his successor, Mary Tudor, received Philip II's proposal of marriage, spent her honeymoon, and passed many sad months during the remaining four years of her life, hoping vainly for a child.

Edward VI, Henry VIII's son and heir, who spent most of his short life at Hampton Court, painted in 1547, in the first year of his reign when he was ten years old.

Elizabeth first came to live at Hampton Court in 1559, a year after her accession to the throne. She had often stayed there, and, for some weeks in the early part of Mary's reign, had been kept under guard in the Water Gallery, suspected of intriguing to usurp her sister's crown. Her alterations to the palace included a three-storey building to the south-east of Wolsey's lodgings, which still bears her initials and the date 1568; and on the north side of the Great Hall a large room, known as the Horn Room, was converted for the display of a collection of horns and antlers. Elizabeth kept up and improved her father's gardens, working there herself every morning, in the words of a contemporary, 'briskly when alone', but when others were present, 'she, who was the very image of majesty and magnificence, went slowly and marched with leisure.' Rare plants were brought back from distant lands by Hawkins, Ralegh and Drake for her hot-houses and flower beds, including the tobacco plant and the potato. She kept great pomp and ceremony at Hampton Court, conducting both state and private business here; it was here that her Council debated and decided the fate of Mary, Queen of Scots; and here also that a succession of foreign ambassadors came to suggest husbands for her. She always celebrated Christmas here, lavishly entertaining hundreds of guests in great merriment and pageantry, with banquets, masques, balls, masquerades, plays, music and dancing, tennis

Queen Elizabeth I dances with courtiers in the athletic manner she so enjoyed.

in the covered court built by her father (and still in use), and, out-of-doors, shooting, stag-hunting, tilting and coursing. The Great Hall, where plays were presented, is the oldest surviving Elizabethan theatre in England. Armies of carpenters, tailors, silk and buskin weavers, haberdashers and upholsterers were employed to make costumes and scenery; ingenious lighting effects were invented, and even artificial snow fell when required. The Duke of Württemberg, visiting in 1590, recorded in his diary: 'Now this is the most splendid and most magnificent royal palace of any that may be found in England, or indeed in any other Kingdom' and went on to describe one of the Queen's apartments 'in which she is accustomed to sit in State' with its tapestries encrusted with gold and precious stones, the inlaid tables, fine paintings, musical instruments and ornaments.

James I took his Danish Queen to stay at Hampton Court a few weeks after his accession in 1603, and was determined to maintain the festive atmosphere which had been so marked a feature of Elizabeth's reign. Anne was an enthusiastic actress, and her first Christmas saw the royal party producing and acting in a masque commissioned from Samuel Daniel, with the young Inigo Jones designing and building the scenery. Thirty other plays were acted that Christmas by the visiting King's Companie of Comedians, Shakespeare among them. Soon afterwards, in January 1604, James arranged a Conference of Divines in an attempt to resolve fundamental differences between the Puritans and the Established Church. In this he was not successful, but out of that Conference came the Authorised Version of the Bible. After the Queen's death, in 1619, James visited the palace mainly to indulge his great love of hunting and hawking, and closely supervising, with Inigo Jones, his Surveyor, the management of the estate.

James died in 1625 and his son Charles I, recently married to the sister of Louis XIII, spent his honeymoon there and made it his home for many months during the new few years. The State Rooms were redecorated, the gardens redesigned, Charles being responsible for new ornamental lakes, ponds and fountains. He had a wide channel cut 11 miles long to bring water to feed them, and to supplement the domestic supply installed by Wolsey, making himself in the process very unpopular with his neighbours for despoiling their land. Charles was a great art collector: a catalogue of 1639 shows that nearly 400 pictures, as well as ivories, crystal, porcelain and sculpture, were at Hampton Court. The pictures included the nine canvases by Mantegna, *The Triumph of Caesar*, now cleaned and hung in their own gallery. Charles used the palace as a refuge during the troubled years 1633–42, and five years later, after the Civil War, was held prisoner there for some months by the victorious Parliamentarians. In his absence, Puritan zeal had been at work desecrating the Chapel and destroying 'popish and superstitious pictures and images'. And two years later, a few months after the King's execution, the new Parliament put Hampton Court up for sale: the proceeds were to be used to pay the royal debts and 'for the benefit of the Commonwealth'. But in 1651 the sale was stopped and Cromwell moved in with his family and lived here until his death in 1658. After the Restoration, Charles II applied himself to redecorating and repairing the palace and bringing back many of the tapestries, pictures and articles of furniture sold during the Commonwealth. The gardens in the Home Park were completely redesigned on models he had admired during his exile in France and Holland; the avenues of lime trees radiating from the east front of the State Rooms were replanted or restocked; new fountains and cascades were added. Charles spent his honeymoon at the Palace, visited it constantly to walk and picnic in the parks, entertained a stream of guests from England and abroad, and found the extensive lodgings well suited to housing his many mistresses. Evelyn and Pepys were frequent visitors, Lely came to paint the Court ladies, fashionable Londoners took refuge here from the Great Plague in 1665, and a year later Charles stored valuable paintings there while the Great Fire raged. Charles's brother, James II, who succeeded him, never lived at Hampton Court, but after the Revolution in 1688 and the accession of William and Mary, the second great rebuilding of the palace began. Taste had moved on, the apartments were 'old-fashioned and uncomfortable' and Sir Christopher Wren, appointed by Charles II as Architect and Surveyor of Works, was now charged with creating something more in keeping with modern ideas. Originally he intended to demolish the whole palace, except for Henry's Great Hall, and to build 'a new Versailles' in its place, but Mary's early death in 1694, halfway through the first phase, and then a growing shortage of money, forced William to abandon the plan, and only Henry's State Apartments were pulled down. Four splendid new ranges in the classical French Renaissance style were built round the new Fountain Court. Antonio Verrio, Grinling Gibbons, Jean Tijou and Louis Laguerre were among the many notable artists commissioned to decorate the interior and design the intricate wrought-iron and stone work on the outside, on the terraces, and in the gardens. The King and Queen were keenly involved at every stage, virtually living on the site, but after Mary's death work slowed down and the new palace was not ready until 1699, when William moved in. Much had still to be done, and in the next three years William supervised the arrangement of the art treasures he had inherited and augmented, including Mary's collection of fine china, made further changes in the gardens and parks and conducted most of his official business and entertaining here. The Banqueting House near the site of the old Water Gallery dates from this time and incorporates some of the brickwork Wren was instructed to rescue and use 'in lieu of new materials' when the old buildings were demolished.

Work already begun continued during the 12 years of Anne's reign. The Chapel was redecorated by Wren, with carvings, including the great classical reredos, by Grinling Gibbons; and the Queen's Drawing Room and other rooms on the east front were painted with murals by Verrio, Thornhill

Queen Mary II's state bedchamber as it appeared after alterations in 1817.

and others. Many of the rooms were not finished until after her death. Anne increased the size and importance of the Hampton Court Stud, and enjoyed the hunting. In her last years, crippled by gout and dropsy, she devised a method of hunting in a one-horse chaise. She had the parks drained and levelled and special 'chaise-ridings' made, and here she drove in pursuit of the stag, according to Swift 'furiously like Jehu', on one occasion 'no less than forty miles'. But in spite of these prodigious feats, Anne's social life was restricted by her health, and by the heavy debts she had inherited from William for work on the new palace and gardens. The days of costly royal hospitality were already past. The palace lodgings, occupied by Court and other officials, and increasingly by unauthorised persons, had become popular for private entertainments, one of which is said to have been Pope's *Rape of the Lock*.

It was not long before Anne's successor, George I, discovered the charms of Hampton Court. Unpopular and ill-at-ease among an alien people, he retreated there, whenever he could, to enjoy the rigid etiquette of his small German Court and the company of his mistresses, always travelling ceremoniously by the State barges. He took no part in the work of embellishing and finishing the new palace, which continued throughout his reign. His prolonged absences in Hanover gave his son, while Prince of Wales, freedom to invite his friends for river parties and other junketings, but the fun stopped when the King returned and the royal family settled once more into dull domesticity. By 1720 they had left the palace in the hands of caretakers and retired to London. George II brought his own family there in 1728, a year after his accession, and came every summer for the next ten years for stag-hunting and coursing, conducted, according to Mrs Howard, the King's mistress, 'with great noise and violence'. William Kent and Sir John Vanbrugh were engaged to decorate or alter parts of Wren's palace, including the ornate white marble chimneypiece and doorways in the room where the King and Queen dined in public. George II was the last English monarch to reside at Hampton Court. George III's decision not to use it came, according to his son, from having had his ears boxed by his grandfather in the State Apartments while he was still a boy. After his accession in 1760, the palace was managed by a staff of 40, among them 'Capability' Brown, who planted the Great Vine in 1769. George III solved the age-old problem of illegal tenants by his system of 'Grace and Favour' lodgings for needy and deserving people, which is still in existence.

In ensuing years Hampton Court continued to attract the interest and concern of its royal owners. George IV, keenly devoted to the turf, extended and improved the Royal Stud; his successor, William IV, renovated and repaired dilapidated buildings and brought back many of the art treasures for display in the State Rooms. Queen Victoria declared it open to the public 'free and without restriction' on certain days of the week, and in 1851, re-established the Stud which had been entirely sold 15 years earlier. At this time the administration was transferred from the Crown to the Government. The Department of the Environment now superintends the restoration, repairs and decoration, and the care of parks and gardens.

The Royal Mews at Hampton Court consists of two buildings: on the left is the King's New Stable, built for Henry VIII in 1536; this has a characteristic Tudor archway with stables and coach-houses. On the right are the stables built for Elizabeth I, consisting of two barns and a coach-house. The Horse Rangers Trust has its headquarters in the Royal Mews. They are not open to the public.

The palace and gardens are open from 0930 to 1800 from Monday to Saturday (and from 1100 to 1800 on Sundays) from April to September, and from 0930 to 1700 from Monday to Saturday (and from 1400 to 1700 on Sunday) from October to March.

BRITISH RAIL *Hampton Court.* BUS ROUTES *111, 131, 216, 267.* GREEN LINE *461, 713, 715, 716, 718, 726.* RIVER TRIPS *from Westminster Pier, Kingston and Richmond.*

Henry I (*1068–1135*). The only one of the four sons of WILLIAM I, the Conqueror, to be born in England, traditionally at Selby. On the death of his brother, WILLIAM II, he seized the royal treasure in the absence of his elder brother, Robert, Duke of Normandy, and was then chosen king by the Witan, the council of the Anglo-Saxon kings. He waged almost constant warfare in Normandy, and there he died, having named his daughter Matilda his successor.

Henry II (*1133–89*). The second son of the Empress Matilda by her second husband, Geoffrey Plantagenet, Count of Anjou, he was the first of the Plantagenet kings. He landed in England in 1153 and made a treaty with KING STEPHEN by which Henry was named as Stephen's successor. King Henry was crowned at WESTMINSTER ABBEY the following year. His reign is noteworthy for the great legal reforms which were enacted.

Henry III (*1207–72*). Son of KING JOHN, he succeeded his father in 1216, the year after John had been forced by the barons to sign Magna Carta at Runnymede. Like his father, Henry incurred the displeasure of the barons by misrule and extortion. Matters came to a head in 1264 with the outbreak of the Barons' War in which the King was captured. Simon de Montfort, leader of the barons, governed through a reformed Parliament until his death at the battle of Evesham in 1266. (Before de Montfort's day Parliament had consisted of an assembly of barons from the shires meeting only at the monarch's pleasure.)

In spite of disaffection and civil war, Henry's reign was a great time of building. In 1220 a Lady Chapel was built as an addition to WESTMINSTER ABBEY and in 1245 the reconstruction of the whole Abbey was started at the King's expense. The Chapter House, built in 1245–55, was where the first meeting of his Great Council was held in 1257. Bastions, gateways, towers and protective walls were erected at the TOWER, making it an invulnerable stronghold. In the barbican, known as the Lion Tower, Henry kept a menagerie of leopards (a present from Frederick II, Holy Roman Emperor), lions, a polar bear and an elephant, the gift of King Louis IX of France.

Henry was the second king to be buried in WESTMINSTER ABBEY. His tomb is before the high altar, from which the body of Edward the Confessor, Saint and King, had been moved to a shrine in the new chapel named after him.

Henry IV (*1367–1413*). Son of JOHN OF GAUNT and grandson of EDWARD III, he was the first king of the House of Lancaster. Having forced his cousin RICHARD II to abdicate, he was chosen King by Parliament in WESTMINSTER HALL in 1399. Twelve days later in the TOWER in the presence of the deposed King, he instituted the Ceremony of the Bath, creating more than 40 new knights, the occasion from which dates the Order of the Bath. During the fortnight before his coronation in WESTMINSTER ABBEY he stayed at the Priory of St John of Jerusalem in Clerkenwell. His coronation is believed to be the first in which the Ampulla (the vessel containing the sacramental anointing oil) was used. In 1405, stricken with what the chroniclers called leprosy, he lived at Rotherhithe for a time. Thereafter his health was never good. His will of 1408 is dated from Greenwich, and he spent the last Christmas of his life, as well as some previous Christmases, at ELTHAM PALACE. While he was praying at St Edward's shrine in WESTMINSTER ABBEY he had a fit, from which he died in the Jerusalem Chamber of the Abbot's house.

Henry V (*1387–1422*). Succeeded his father, HENRY IV, in 1413. His coronation procession took place in an April snowstorm. When he rode into London simply dressed after his victory at Agincourt in 1415 to give thanks at St Paul's and WESTMINSTER ABBEY, Londoners received him with great enthusiasm. He founded two religious houses, the Carthusian monastery in the former garden and park of RICHMOND PALACE, and the Bridgettine monastery at Syon. His body was brought back to England from France where he had died on campaign. His splendid tomb is in his own chantry in the chapel of St Edward the Confessor in WESTMINSTER ABBEY, to which he had been a generous benefactor. His helmet, shield and saddle are in the Abbey Museum.

Henry VI (*1421–71*). Succeeded his father, HENRY V, when only nine months old. He was four when he was 'led upon his feet . . . unto the choir, whence he was borne to the high altar' at St Paul's, and afterwards conveyed 'upon a fair courser . . . through Chepe [Cheapside] and the other streets of the city'. After his coronation in 1429 there was a feast in WESTMINSTER HALL, where the little King was 'served with three courses'. At the age of 15 he started to take part in government at the Great Council at Clerkenwell Priory. In May 1445 his bride, Margaret of Anjou, entered London under an arch on London Bridge symbolising Peace and Plenty. For their honeymoon the King's uncle, Humphrey, Duke of Gloucester, lent them GREENWICH PALACE, which they appropriated after his death two years later. They also kept Court at Shene Palace, later renamed RICHMOND PALACE.

In 1450 a rebellious army led by Jack Cade was entrenched on Blackheath. The King marched with a large force to meet them, and they dispersed; but on their return the King fled, panic-stricken, up the Thames back to London. He was again at Blackheath in 1452, early in the Wars of the Roses, when his antagonist the Duke of York, later EDWARD IV, was encamped at Dartford. Though battle seemed inevitable, truce was negotiated. Defeated and captured by York in 1464 he was imprisoned in the TOWER for six years and there he died, reputedly murdered while at prayer. His corpse was exposed in St Paul's, and afterwards at Blackfriars Monastery. It is uncertain where he is buried. He was the last king of the House of Lancaster.

Henry VII   (*1457–1509*). First monarch of the Tudor dynasty. After the defeat and death of RICHARD III in the final battle of the Wars of the Roses in 1485, Parliament assented to the accession of the Duke of Richmond, a descendant of EDWARD III, as King Henry VII. The King's Bodyguard of the Yeomen of the Guard, the oldest royal bodyguard and military corps in the world, was founded to attend him at his coronation in October that year. His marriage to the Princess Elizabeth of York, daughter of EDWARD IV, reinforced his claim to the throne. She had been born in the PALACE OF WESTMINSTER, and it was in WESTMINSTER ABBEY that they married in 1486.

Henry's favourite residence was Shene, where in 1492 a great tournament, lasting a month, was held on the Green. After a fire in 1499 he rebuilt the palace, renaming it RICHMOND PALACE after his earldom in Yorkshire. In 1487 he rebuilt Castle Baynard and, in 1505, the SAVOY PALACE as a hospital for the poor. The Henry VII chapel in WESTMINSTER ABBEY is his foundation.

Henry VIII   (*1491–1547*). Son of HENRY VII and Elizabeth of York, he was born at GREENWICH PALACE and brought up at Shene Palace, the name of which was later changed to RICHMOND PALACE. Here he married Catharine of Aragon in 1509, and their joint coronation took place on 'Midsomer daie'.

Henry VIII presenting a charter in 1541 to the City Livery Companies, Barbers and Surgeons, who had been amalgamated the year before.

63

By 1532 it was apparent that she could not give him a son. For this reason, and because he had fallen deeply in love with Anne Boleyn, he sought an annulment of his marriage from the Pope, who refused to grant it. Thereupon Henry broke away from the Roman Catholic Church and seized the lands of the monasteries. Because she was pregnant, Henry married Anne Boleyn secretly either at Greenwich or at York House, later to be called WHITEHALL PALACE, in January 1533. In May Anne left Greenwich Palace to be rowed up the Thames to the TOWER, and from there, two days later, she rode in a horse-litter to her coronation. She was Queen but a short time, for in May 1536 she was executed on Tower Green for adultery, a fate suffered for the same crime by Henry's fifth wife, Catherine Howard, six years later. Both these queens were buried in the Chapel of ST PETER AD VINCULA.

The day after Anne Boleyn's execution Henry and Jane Seymour were betrothed at HAMPTON COURT PALACE and there the following year she died, twelve days after giving birth to Henry's longed-for son, EDWARD VI. HAMPTON COURT, with its park, and Bushy Park had been gifts to the King from Cardinal Wolsey, and he had acquired HYDE PARK at the Dissolution of the Monasteries. He used them all as hunting reserves, and ST JAMES'S PARK as a deer-nursery and tilt yard.

The King's fourth wedding was to the German Princess Anne of Cleves. He welcomed her to England at Blackheath and married her at Greenwich – a marriage that was annulled within a few months, to the relief of both. He gave her RICHMOND PALACE, where she lived till her death in 1557; she was buried with considerable pomp in WESTMINSTER ABBEY.

Henry's sixth and last wedding took place at HAMPTON COURT again. He gave Chelsea Manor House with Queen's Park to Catherine Parr on their marriage in the summer of 1543. She was a devoted wife until Henry's death at WHITEHALL PALACE in 1547.

Henry was the first sovereign to use WHITEHALL PALACE as the home of the Court and as his main residence instead of the PALACE OF WESTMINSTER. He largely rebuilt it, and he also built BRIDEWELL, Chelsea Manor House, ST JAMES'S PALACE and Nonsuch Palace. A statue by Francis Bird stands over the gateway of St Bartholomew's Hospital.

Henry VIII's Wine Cellar   *Whitehall, SW1.* A portion of this beneath the Ministry of Defence is the only surviving part of Wolsey's palace. It is a vaulted undercroft supported by four octagonal pillars. The whole crypt, weighing 800 tons, was lowered 18 ft 9 in during the rebuilding of Whitehall in the 1950s, without a brick being disturbed, at a cost of £100,000.

The cellar can be visited on Saturday afternoons from April to September if prior application is made by telephone to 01-928 7999, ext. 2200.

UNDERGROUND *Westminster.*   BUS ROUTES *3, 11, 12, 24, 29, 53, 77, 77A, 88, 109, 159, 170, 184, 196.*

The Horse Guards, showing the troopers on either side of the gateway.

Horse Guards   *Whitehall, SW1*. In 1649 a small guardhouse was built here in the tilt-yard of WHITEHALL PALACE. This was replaced in 1663–5 by a larger building for the horse guards and some of the foot guards. In 1750–8 the present building was constructed to a picturesque Palladian design by William Kent which was executed after his death by John Vardy. Only members of the Royal Family are allowed to drive through the central arch. Hogarth in plate 2 of *The Election* depicted the royal coach emerging with a headless driver as it is impractically low. Until 1872 the building was also the headquarters of the general staff. Subsequently it became the headquarters of London District and the HOUSEHOLD DIVISION. Two mounted troopers of the Household Cavalry are posted outside daily from 1000 to 1600 and are relieved every hour.

Horse Guards Parade   *SW1*. On the site of the tilt-yard of WHITEHALL PALACE. A great tournament was held here in 1540 by Henry VIII and attended by knights from all over Europe. For many years exercises were held here on Elizabeth I's birthday; and from the 17th century reviews, parades and medal presentation ceremonies. The funeral procession of the Duke of Wellington formed up here in 1852. TROOPING THE COLOUR takes place here. On the parade ground there are bronze statues of the Field Marshals Kitchener, Wolseley and Roberts; a Turkish gun 'made by Murad son of Adbdullah, chief gunner in 1524, taken in Egypt by the British Army, 1801'; and the Cadiz Memorial (*see* MEMORIALS).

UNDERGROUND *Charing Cross, Embankment, Westminster*.   BUS ROUTES *1, 3, 6, 9, 11, 12, 24, 29, 53, 77, 77A, 88, 109, 159, 170, 184, 196.*

Mounting Guard on Horse Guards Parade in 1809.

Household Division   Of the seven regiments of Guards, two are Household Cavalry and five are Foot. The reigning sovereign is their Colonel-in-Chief. The regiments concerned are the Life Guards, the Blues and Royals (the latter have been amalgamated since 1969), the Grenadier, Coldstream, Scots, Irish and Welsh Guards. All the regiments, except the Irish and Welsh Guards, which were formed respectively in the reign of Queen Victoria and during the 1st World War, date back to the 17th century. The Major General Commanding London District also commands the Division. While the full dress uniforms of the two mounted regiments are quite distinctive, those of the foot guards can only be recognised by the colour or presence of plumes in the bearskins and the arrangement of jacket buttons. The Household Cavalry, with a strength of about 1,600, includes a mounted regiment of some 300 representing both the Life Guards and the Blues and Royals and two armoured regiments, the roles of which are in accordance with other mechanised cavalry units. While the mounted regiment is quartered in Knightsbridge Barracks, the other two normally alternate between Windsor and the British Army of the Rhine in Germany.

Ceremonial occasions for the Division include TROOPING THE COLOUR on the sovereign's official birthday, CHANGING THE GUARD at BUCKINGHAM PALACE and various guard and escort duties relevant to the mounted or dismounted troops at the HORSE GUARDS, ST JAMES'S PALACE, the TOWER OF LONDON and elsewhere as the occasion demands.

Houses of Parliament   *see* PALACE OF WESTMINSTER

Hyde Park   *W1, W2, SW7*. The largest of the London parks, extending over 340 acres from Bayswater Road in the north to Knightsbridge in the south. Park Lane marks the eastern boundary and in the west it merges with KENSINGTON GARDENS, this western boundary being a line running from Alexandra Gate across the Serpentine bridge and along Buck Hill Walk to Victoria Gate. The park was once one of those properties, Ebury, Neate and Hyde, which comprised the manor of Eia and which were bequeathed to the monks of Westminster soon after the Conquest by Geoffrey de Mandeville. It was then a haunt of deer, boar and wild bulls. In 1536, at the Dissolution of the Monasteries, the manor was appropriated by Henry VIII who sold Ebury and Neate and retained Hyde as a hunting ground. Deer were hunted in the park until 1768. Elizabeth also hunted here and inaugurated military reviews which were to be held here for centuries.

The park was opened to the public at the beginning of the 17th century and it soon became fashionable, particularly on May Day, the great day for visiting it. In about 1642 fortifications were built along the east side to defend the city against Royalist attacks. A large fort stood opposite Mount Street but it was never used; another was built near the present Hyde Park Corner and near where MARBLE ARCH now stands was a strong-point where travellers' credentials were examined. In 1649 Lord Essex's troops camped in the park. Other military camps appeared here in 1665 during the Great Plague, in 1715 during the Jacobite Rebellion and in 1780 at the time of the Gordon Riots.

A military review in Hyde Park in May 1804.

In 1652 the park was sold by order of Parliament. It was divided into three lots and fetched £17,000, but at the Restoration in 1660 Charles II took the park back into royal hands and enclosed it for the first time with a brick wall. In his time 'nothing was so much in fashion during the fine weather as a large enclosure called the Tour, and later the Ring, which was the rendezvous of fashion and beauty. Everyone who had either sparkling eyes or a splendid equipage constantly repaired thither and the King seemed pleased with the place.'

When William III came to live at KENSINGTON PALACE he had 300 lamps hung from the branches of the trees along the *route du roi* (from which Rotten Row takes its name) between the palace and St James's. It was the first road in England to be lit at night. It was hoped that this lighting would deter the highwaymen who were so active in the park of whom one had, in 1687, been hanged for killing a woman who had swallowed her wedding ring to prevent his taking it. The park, however, continued to be plagued by highwaymen: it was here in 1749, when returning from Holland House, that Horace Walpole was stopped by two highwaymen who threatened him with a blunderbuss and took his watch and eight guineas.

The park was also well known as a duelling ground. Lord Mohun, 'one of the arrantest rakes in town', and the Duke of Hamilton fought their duel here in 1712. 'They fought with so violent an animosity that, neglecting the rules of art they seemed to run on one another, as if they'd tried who should kill first, in which they were both so unhappily successful that the Lord Mohun was killed outright and the Duke died in a few minutes.' Here also John Wilkes fought Samuel Martin in 1772, Sheridan fought Captain Matthews over Miss Linley in 1772, Lord Thurlow fought Andrew Stuart in 1770.

A duel in Hyde Park, the scene of many such contests throughout the 18th century.

A van with four horses was driven across the frozen Serpentine for a bet in the winter of 1826.

In 1730 work began for Queen Caroline, a keen landscape gardener, on forming the lake to be known as the Serpentine by damming the Westbourne. When it was completed two yachts were put in the water for the Royal Family's use.

In 1820 George IV's coronation was celebrated in the park by firework displays and balloon ascents, and in 1822 the statue of Achilles by Westmacott was erected to commemorate Wellington's victories. In 1825 Decimus Burton designed lodges for Hyde Park Corner, Grosvenor Gate, Stanhope Gate and Cumberland Gate. In 1826 George Rennie's bridge, which commands such lovely views to WESTMINSTER ABBEY and the PALACE OF WESTMINSTER, was built over the Serpentine dividing it from the Long Water. In 1832 the Ranger's Lodge was built.

In 1845 Albert Gate was erected and in 1847 the Prince of Wales's Gate. It was near the latter gate, between Rotten Row and the Carriage Road, that the Great Exhibition of 1851 was held. The idea of the Exhibition was conceived by Henry Cole, later chairman of the Council of the Society of Arts. A Royal Commission, presided over by Prince Albert, sat in 1850 to work out the details and raise the money. When it was announced that the Exhibition would be held in Hyde Park, *The Times*, horrified, forecast that

A view across the Serpentine at the time of the opening of the Great Exhibition in 1851.

the whole of the park would become 'a bivouac of all vagabonds. Kensington and Belgravia would be uninhabitable and the Season would be ruined'. A competition was held for the design of the building. Over 230 entries were rejected before Joseph Paxton designed his Crystal Palace, based on the conservatory at Chatsworth, in Derbyshire, where he was superintendent of the gardens. Two thousand workmen were employed to construct the monumental building from 4,000 tons of iron and 400 tons of glass, and containing 30 miles of guttering and 200 miles of wooden sash bars. The park's precious trees were incorporated inside the building, but so were sparrows, whose droppings spattered the Persian carpets and other exhibits until the Duke of Wellington thought of introducing sparrowhawks. To test the building's capacity to remain in one piece when crowded with visitors, squads of soldiers were marched in and ordered to stamp and jump on the floor and to roll round shot about, while 300 workmen jumped up and down in the galleries. On 1 May 1851, the Great Exhibition was opened by Queen Victoria, who was so delighted with it that she came almost every other day in the first three months. Exhibits came from all over the world, and when the Exhibition closed on 15 October, it had been visited by over six million people, including one woman of 84 who had walked from Cornwall. The building was taken down in 1852 and re-erected as the Crystal Palace at Sydenham. It was destroyed by fire in 1936.

In 1855 150,000 people gathered in the north-east corner of the park to demonstrate against Lord Robert Grosvenor's Sunday Trading Bill. There was no legal right of assembly there then but when the police arrived to arrest an inflammatory orator he had already gone. After more demonstrations the right of assembly was recognised in 1872; and in this part of the park, known as Speakers' Corner, anyone with a mind so to do may now declaim on any subject he chooses, provided he is not obscene or blasphemous, and does not constitute an incitement to a breach of the peace.

In 1860 flowers were first planted in the park by William Nesfield, the architect and landscape gardener, who was often consulted about improvements in the London parks and in 1861 the Italian Water Garden at Victoria Gate was made. These include fountains, an Italianate summer house and Queen Anne's Alcove, which was built to the design of Christopher Wren and moved here from KENSINGTON GARDENS. Beside the fountains is a large bronze statue of Dr Jenner by W. Calder Marshall. The fountain at Grosvenor Gate, designed by Alexander Munro, was put up in 1863; the *Joy of Life* fountain by T. B. Huxley-Jones which stands on the Park Lane side of the park opposite Mount Street was given by the Constance Fund, an organisation founded in 1944 by Mrs Constance Goetze in memory of her husband. A dogs' cemetery was made at Victoria Gate in 1880 when the Duchess of Cambridge's pet was buried here; the last interment was in 1915. The statue of *Diana* by Feodora Gleichen was erected in 1906; and Sir Henry Tanner's Tea House (later turned into the Serpentine Gallery) was built in 1908. Epstein's bas-relief of *Rima* provoked cries of outrage when it was

A summer's day in Hyde Park in 1858.

unveiled by the Prime Minister in 1925. It represents the goddess in *Green Mansions*, the novel by W. H. Hudson, the naturalist and writer, after whom the bird sanctuary in which it stands is named. The Cavalry Memorial was erected in 1924. The Serpentine Restaurant, designed by Patrick Gwynne, was opened in 1963 and Gwynne's smaller restaurant in the Dell, at the east end of the Serpentine, in 1965. The so-called Standing Stone in the Dell is traditionally said to have been brought here by Charles I from Stonehenge. In fact it is a 7-ton piece of Cornish stone once part of a drinking fountain erected in 1861 and subsequently removed. In the park are four acres of greenhouses where all the bedding plants for the royal parks are raised. The large bronze group of Pan playing his pipes, a man, a woman, their child and a dog running into the park by Edinburgh Gate is by Epstein. More than 9,000 elms in the park have been killed by Dutch elm disease in recent years. The trunks of three of these, between the bird sanctuary and the Serpentine, were sculpted by first-year students of the Chelsea School of Art in 1978. Henry Moore's 19 ft high sculpture *The Arch*, carved in 1979 in Roman travertine, a gift of the Henry Moore Foundation, was unveiled on the east bank of Long Water opposite Watts's *Physical Energy* in September 1980. By the east end of the Serpentine is a small artificial stone fountain (originally marble, but this weathered so badly that it was replaced in 1975) by W. R. Colton (1896). Barbara Hepworth's *Family of Man* sculptures were removed in 1982.

The park is open from 0500 to midnight.

Dandies in Rotten Row in 1819, a caricature satirising the sartorial excesses of the time.

James I, 'the wisest fool in Christendom', portrayed at the age of fifty-five.

James I *(1566–1625)*. Son of Mary, Queen of Scots. On the death of ELIZABETH I in 1603 James VI of Scotland, a great great nephew of HENRY VIII, succeeded to the English throne. He entered the City of London at Aldersgate. Two years after his accession Guy Fawkes and Roman Catholic confederates hatched the Gunpowder Plot with the intention of blowing up the Protestant King and Members of both Houses of Parliament with gunpowder hidden in the cellars of the PALACE OF WESTMINSTER. The conspirators were discovered and taken for interrogation to the TOWER. King James was the last English monarch to use the TOWER as his palace. On his death, after a comparatively peaceful reign interrupted only by the outbreak of war against Spain in 1625, his body was taken to Denmark House (now SOMERSET HOUSE), the mansion belonging to his Queen, Anne of Denmark, to lie in state for a month before an extravagant funeral in WESTMINSTER ABBEY. The Duc de Sully called him 'the wisest fool in Christendom'.

James II *(1633–1701)*. Born at ST JAMES'S PALACE, in 1685 he succeeded his brother CHARLES II, who had no legitimate children. He was thoroughly unpopular because of his autocratic rule and his Roman Catholic sympathies. He discontinued the ceremony of the coronation procession from the TOWER; before proceeding from ST JAMES'S PALACE he attended

73

mass in the CHAPEL ROYAL. He did, however, agree to coronation with Anglican rites. He was deposed in 1688 in favour of his Protestant daughter MARY and her cousin and husband William of Orange (WILLIAM III). When the Dutchman landed with an army, James 'stole away from WHITEHALL [PALACE] by the Privy Stairs'. Thereafter he lived in exile in France.

Jewel Tower *Westminster Abbey precincts, SW1*. A survival of the PALACE OF WESTMINSTER. Built of Kentish ragstone in 1365–6, it was probably designed by Henry Yevele. On three storeys, and surrounded by a moat, it was used to contain the King's valuables including his jewels, clothes, furs and gold vessels. Its use for this purpose continued until the reign of Henry VII. From 1621 to 1864 parliamentary records were kept here; thereafter it was used, until 1938, by the Weights and Measures Office. It now houses a collection of pottery and other objects found during excavations in the area.

It is open from 0930 to 1830 from Monday to Saturday (from 0930 to 1600 from October to March).

For directions *see* PALACE OF WESTMINSTER.

John *(1167–1216)*. Youngest son of HENRY II, he tried to seize the crown when his brother, RICHARD II, was in captivity. Richard forgave him and nominated him his successor. Having acceded in 1159, he became a thoroughly unpopular monarch, rapacious and unreliable. In 1215 the barons raised an armed rebellion and at Runnymede, near Windsor, compelled him to grant Magna Carta, a document protecting the baronial rights against incursion by the king. Little more than a year later he died of dysentery, said to have been brought on by a surfeit of peaches and new beer.

John of Gaunt *(1340–99)*. The fourth son of EDWARD III. Gaunt is a corruption of Ghent, the name of his birthplace. He married his cousin Blanche, and on the death of her father he inherited the earldom of Lancaster, and was created Duke in 1362. EDWARD III, towards the end of his reign, allowed the government to fall almost entirely into the hands of John of Gaunt who became even more powerful when his great-nephew, RICHARD II, came to the throne in 1377. After years of his misrule popular risings broke out, the worst, in the summer of 1381, being the Peasants' Revolt in which Lancaster's magnificent SAVOY PALACE was attacked and rendered uninhabitable by an accidental gunpowder explosion. After Richard II's deposition Henry Bolingbroke, son of John of Gaunt and his first wife, acceded as HENRY IV. With the death of HENRY VI in 1471 the line of Lancastrian kings ended. Fourteen years later another descendant of John of Gaunt started the Tudor dynasty. He was HENRY VII, who claimed Lancastrian descent through his mother.

74

John of Gaunt died at Ely House in Holborn. He and his first Duchess were buried in St Paul's Cathedral, 'where they had a noble monument which was utterly destroyed in the time of the late usurpation'. The Duchy of Lancaster still has property in the Strand and in the City; its office is in Whitehall.

Kensington Gardens   *W8.* The grounds were originally attached to Nottingham House which in 1689 was bought by William III and converted into KENSINGTON PALACE. In 1690 John Evelyn said that 'a straight new way had been made through the park from the palace to the West End.' Part of this survives as Rotten Row (*see* HYDE PARK). Queen Mary took a great interest in the gardens and had those south of the palace laid out by the royal gardeners, Henry Wise and George London, with box and yew hedges in formal Dutch patterns. *An Account of Gardens near London* described the palace grounds as 'not great nor abounding with fine plants. The orange, lemon, myrtle and other trees they had there in summer were all removed to Mr London's and Mr Wise's greenhouse at Brompton Park a little mile from

Kensington Palace in 1819, the former Jacobean mansion as reconstructed by Wren and Hawksmoor.

75

them. But the walks and grass laid very fine.' In 1702–8 an alcove was built for Queen Anne by Sir Christopher Wren at the end of the walk leading directly south from the palace but was moved to its present position near Marlborough Gate in the late 19th century (*see* HYDE PARK). Queen Anne did not like formal Dutch gardens and had most of them uprooted. In about 1705 Wise produced a plan for laying out the garden, showing the Round Pond as an oblong, the Serpentine as a chain of ten ponds, and the Broad Walk.

In 1712 Addison mentions in the *Spectator* that a gravel pit to the north had been made into a sunken garden. In about 1726 Wise and Charles Bridgman produced another scheme for the gardens which was adopted. George II opened the gardens on Saturdays to 'respectably dressed people' when the court was at Richmond. The Broad Walk became as fashionable as the Mall had been a century before. In about 1726–7 a small temple was built, probably by William Kent, in the south-east corner of the gardens. It was later incorporated into Temple Lodge but has now been restored and cleared of encumbrances. The Round Pond was filled with water in 1728.

William IV opened the park to the public all the year round and in 1843 a Flower Walk was made. Kensington Palace Gardens were built on the site of the palace kitchen garden. In 1863 the ALBERT MEMORIAL was begun and completed in 1872. A granite obelisk of 1864 commemorates John Hanning Speke's discovery of the source of the Nile. The statue of Queen Victoria outside her birthplace was erected in 1893 and that of William III in 1907 (*see* STATUES). The sculpture, *Physical Energy*, is by G. F. Watts (1904). The sunken garden to the east of the palace was created in 1909. The statue of Peter Pan by Sir George Frampton dates from 1912 and the Elfin Oak, a tree stump carved with small animals by Ivor Innes, was set up in 1928 in the children's playground at the north end of Broad Walk by Black Lion Gate. The original swings here were a gift from J. M. Barrie. Diseased elms along the Broad Walk were cut down and replaced with oak and copper beech in 1953. The park extends to 275 acres. The bronze does and fawns on the top of the Queen's Gate entrance are by P. Rouillard (1919).

The park is open daily from 0730 to dusk.

Kensington Palace   *W8*. Originally a Jacobean house built for Sir George Coppin, it was later purchased by King William III's Secretary of State, the Earl of Nottingham, and hence became known as Nottingham House. Neither William III nor Queen Mary liked WHITEHALL PALACE where the King's chronic asthma was much exacerbated and the Queen felt excessively confined and able to 'see nothing but water or wall'. So, moving out to HAMPTON COURT and keeping WHITEHALL for state and ceremonial purposes, in 1689 they bought Nottingham House, whose grounds strongly appealed to the King, an enthusiastic landscape gardener. Wren was instructed to reconstruct the house and Hawksmoor was appointed Clerk of the Works. The Queen, impatient to move in, went over frequently 'to

Wren's picture gallery at Kensington Palace was redecorated by Kent in the 1720s.

hasten the workmen', as she put it herself; and, in November, the work having been hurried forward too speedily, 'the additional buildings . . . being newly covered with lead, fell down in a sudden and hurt several people and killed some, the Queen herself there but little before.' By Christmas, however, work had progressed far enough for the Royal Family to move in. Though far from complete, it was certainly quite adequate for Queen Anne, who succeeded her brother-in-law, and for her husband, Prince George of Denmark, who, like William III, was asthmatic. Queen Anne decided to have the gardens altered to conform to the *'English* model'; the Orangery House was built for her in 1704, probably to the designs of Hawksmoor as modified by Vanbrugh. In 1714 Queen Anne died here from an attack of apoplexy brought on by overeating. She left the house 'very much out of repair'; but her successor, George I, liked it because it reminded him of his palace at Herrenhausen in Hanover. He brought over with him a large retinue of German servants and attendants, from mistresses and advisers to trumpeters and plate cleaners; and he appointed William Benson, who had worked for him in Hanover, to replace Wren and to supervise improvements to the house. William Kent also worked here at this time, as did Colen Campbell who was probably responsible for the three state rooms which were constructed in 1718–21. After the death of George I, in his coach on the way to Hanover in 1727, the house became the principal residence of George II and his wife, Caroline. The house was not structurally altered but Queen Caroline spent much of her time rearranging the furniture and pictures and supervising the new layout of the gardens with the help of Charles Bridgman who succeeded Henry Wise as Royal Gardener in 1728. The Broad Walk and the Round Pond were both made at this time (*see* KENSINGTON GARDENS). In 1760 George II died in his water closet and, since his grandson, George III, preferred BUCKINGHAM HOUSE, the house, now more usually known as Kensington Palace, fell into disrepair. After George III's son, the Duke of Kent, was allocated rooms here in 1798, extensive alterations were begun under the direction of James Wyatt. The Duke, however, saw little of them. His debts obliged him to go abroad where he lived with his mistress, Mme St Laurent. In his absence other members of the Royal Family lived here. In 1806 his brother Augustus, Duke of Sussex, moved in and remained for many years, building up a remarkable library of religious books and manuscripts. In 1808–13 Caroline, the eccentric Princess of Wales, had apartments here. Her daughter, Charlotte, was a regular visitor until her father discovered she had been left alone in a room with a Captain Hesse and told to enjoy herself. In 1819 the Duke of Kent, having left Mme St Laurent and married Princess Victoria of Saxe-Coburg-Saalfeld the year before, returned to the palace so that his child could be born in England. This child, the future Queen Victoria, was born in a ground-floor room of his apartments on 24 May 1819. In June Princess Victoria was christened here. The Prince Regent, her uncle, created a scene by disagreeing with the choice of names and reducing her mother to tears. After her father's death, the Princess was brought up in the palace by her mother and governess, Louise Lehzen, under the strict 'Kensington system' advocated by the Duchess's calculating adviser, Sir John Conroy. On 20 June 1837 she was called from her bed by the Archbishop of Canterbury and the Lord Chamberlain to be told she was Queen. The next day she held her accession council here and managed it so well that both the Duke of Wellington and Charles Greville were deeply impressed. David Wilkie painted the scene, none too accurately. That night she slept away from her mother's room for the first time, and within three weeks had moved to BUCKINGHAM PALACE. The Duke and Duchess of Teck lived here in 1867–80, and their daughter, later Queen Mary, was born here in 1867. From 1880 to 1939 Princess Louise, Queen Victoria's sixth child, lived here. In 1889 the State Apartments were opened to the public on the occasion of Queen Victoria's 70th birthday. In 1912 these Apartments were used for the London Museum which in 1914 was moved to LANCASTER HOUSE. The State Apartments were then closed, being reopened in 1923. In 1950 the London Museum was brought back here and remained until 1975 when its exhibits were removed to be shown later in the Museum of London.

Kensington Palace is still lived in by members of the Royal Family. The London residences of the Prince and Princess of Wales, Princess Margaret, the Duke and Duchess of Gloucester and Prince and Princess Michael of Kent are all here, though not accessible to the public. The State Apartments on the eastern side of the Palace, however, can be visited. They are entered from the garden via a doorway dating from 1690–1 showing the royal monogram of William and Mary. They include, as well as formal State Rooms, the closet where Queen Anne and the Duchess of Marlborough had their last meeting, and the rooms used by Queen Victoria before and at the time of her accession to the throne.

The State Apartments are open from 0900 to 1700 from Monday to Saturday; and from 1300 to 1700 on Sundays, but are closed on some national holidays and at Christmas.

UNDERGROUND *Queensway, Bayswater (north side of Gardens), High Street, Kensington (south side of Gardens)* BUS ROUTES *9, 12, 27, 28, 31, 33, 49, 52, 52A, 73, 88.*

Kew Gardens *see* ROYAL BOTANIC GARDENS.

Kew Palace *Kew Gardens, Kew.* A small Jacobean mansion, formerly known as the Dutch House, it is the last survivor of a group of royal residences which once stood in, or near, Kew Green. Situated about a mile from Richmond Lodge, the favourite home of George II, the Dutch House

The Dutch House at Kew with Frederick, Prince of Wales, father of George III, and his sisters in 1733.

The Royal Palace or White House at Kew in 1765, forty years before its demolition.

was leased by Queen Caroline in 1728 for 99 years for 'the rent of £100 and a fat Doe'. Thereafter it was frequently occupied by members of the Royal Family. In 1731 the house adjacent to it, the former White House, was rented by Frederick, Prince of Wales, who, despite his feud with his parents, settled in their immediate vicinity with his family and court. This house, in which George III spent much of his boyhood, stood some 50 yards south of the present Palace. A two-storeyed mansion, it had been built of timber and stone in the second half of the 17th century by Sir Henry Capel and featured, according to John Evelyn, a great hall surmounted with a cupola. 18th-century accounts suggest that, apart from the royal apartments, the rooms of the White House were small, dark and draughty, in spite of Prince Frederick's enlargements. The Prince died in 1751 and his widow, Augusta, Dowager Princess of Wales, continued to occupy and improve the property until her death in 1771, after which George III and Queen Charlotte took possession of it. As the White House, however, was not large enough for the rapidly growing Royal Family, the Dutch House was used as an annexe – at first for the new Prince of Wales and Prince Frederick and later for some of the younger princes.

In 1802 George III caused the White House to be demolished, and most of its furniture and fittings were taken to the Dutch House into which the King moved while awaiting the completion of a new and grandiose palace only 200 yards away. This eccentric edifice, designed by James Wyatt in the Gothic style, was known as the Castellated Palace. Costly and impractical, it was never finished, and the Dutch House remained in royal occupation until Queen Charlotte's death in 1818, after which the Prince Regent ordered its destruction, considering it 'unworthy of Repair, but Execution of the Order was afterwards suspended.' Thereafter the reprieved mansion began to be known as the 'Old Palace' to distinguish it from the Castellated Palace, which was finally demolished in 1827–8. Of the White House, for 72 years a royal residence, only the mid-18th-century kitchen wing survives; a late 17th-century sundial, originally one of a pair at HAMPTON COURT, which was erected by William IV in 1832, marks its site.

The Dutch House was built over the Tudor vaults of an earlier house by Samuel Fortrey, a prosperous London merchant of Dutch parentage, for himself and his wife, Catherine, in 1631. The date, together with their initials, SFC, are commemorated above the main entrance. All that survives of the previous building is a vaulted brick basement containing a well which, as late as 1806, was the only immediately available source of water in the Palace; the reset and much restored linenfold panelling in the library anteroom and, on the 2nd floor, a large Tudor fireplace. The Palace, three-storeyed with attics, is only 70 ft long by 50 ft wide and is built of red brick laid in 'Flemish bond' which gives a rich and varied appearance. The main south front, which faces the site of the former White House, consists of a central block of three bays containing the entrance, and two side wings of shallow projection.

In the garden the older children of George III were instructed in 'practical gardening and agriculture'. A doorway in the garden wall gave access to the river bank. The present garden behind Kew Palace is named the Queen's Garden after Queen Elizabeth II, who opened it to the public in May 1969. It is laid out in the style of a 17th-century garden with herbal plants of the period, much grey stone, and features such as a 'mount' with a rotunda on top.

The Palace is open daily from 1100 to 1730 from April to September.

UNDERGROUND *Kew Gardens* BRITISH RAIL *Kew Bridge* BUS ROUTES *27, 65.* RIVER BOATS *from Westminster Pier in summer.*

King Edward VII's Hospital for Officers *Beaumont House, Beaumont Street, W1.* In 1899 Miss Agnes Keyser and her sister Fanny, at the suggestion of the Prince of Wales, whose friendship they enjoyed, started the hospital in their own house, 17 Grosvenor Crescent, to nurse sick and wounded officers from the South African War. At the end of the Boer War King Edward, as he had then become, insisted that the hospital should be kept open on the ground that there was a great need in times of peace for a place to which sick officers, serving in so many climates all over the world, might gain admission. In 1903 he gave the hospital his name and became its first patron. In 1904 the hospital was moved to 9 Grosvenor Gardens, and in 1948, after several more moves, to Beaumont House, where in 1960 they opened a wing for 'patients of the educated middle class of moderate means but not necessarily with service connections'.

81

The Grand Hall of Lancaster House, St James's, in the middle of the 19th century, showing the spectacular staircase and the exuberant Louis XV style of decoration.

Lancaster House   *Stable Yard, St James's Palace, SW1.* In 1807 Frederick, Duke of York, second son of George III, moved to the 17th-century Godolphin House in Stable Yard and renamed it York House. Ten years later, on the death of Princess Charlotte, he became heir to the throne. Robert Smirke was engaged to rebuild York House to be worthy of his new position but the Duke's brother, George IV, hated Smirke's plans so much that he was replaced as architect by Benjamin Dean Wyatt. Building began in 1825. The house was still unfinished when the Duke died, much in debt, at the Duchess of Rutland's house in Arlington Street. The government paid off the mortgages on it and sold a lease for £72,000 to one of his many creditors, the Marquess of Stafford. (The money was used to buy Victoria Park.) In 1833 the Marquess was created 1st Duke of Sutherland but died later that year. Stafford House, as it was then known, was roofed but still unfinished. The 2nd Duke asked Wyatt to plan the interior decorations and Smirke to carry them out. Charles Barry was also consulted. In 1841 Smirke added another storey for servants.

   The completed mansion was a solid rectangle of Bath stone, three storeys high with a two-storey portico on the front. The interior was decorated in the exuberant French style of Louis XV. The family's rooms and the library were on the ground floor. The staircase was the most spectacular part of the house, decorated with imitation marbles and copies (by Lorenzi) of Veronese's paintings. On the first floor were the state rooms – the State Drawing Room, the Music Room which served also as a State Dining Room, and the Great Gallery which held the Duke's magnificent art collection. Among the paintings were works by Raphael, Tintoretto, Titian, Velasquez, Rubens, Van Dyck, Watteau, Murillo and others.

The 2nd Duke's wife, Harriet, was a close friend of Queen Victoria and her Mistress of the Robes in 1837–61. The Queen was often a guest at the house and once said, 'I have come from my house to your palace.' In 1848 Chopin played here for the Queen, Prince Albert and the Duke of Wellington. Lord Shaftesbury, the great social reformer, and William Garrison, the American abolitionist of slavery, were also entertained here. But the greatest excitement was caused by the stay in the house in 1864 of the Italian patriot Garibaldi. His visit to England provoked frenzies of popular acclaim and while he was at Stafford House crowds gathered daily in the courtyard hoping to see him. The Duke's servants gathered the soapsuds from Garibaldi's washbasin and sold bottlesful to willing buyers in the crowd. In 1882, the Italian community of London erected a medallion and plaque in the house to commemorate this visit; the room where they are to be found is now known as the Garibaldi room.

The Liberal tradition of the house continued: at the time of the 4th Duchess, it became the London headquarters of 'The Souls', an aristocratic intellectual group who were concerned with the serious social problems of the day.

In 1912 the 4th Duke of Sutherland sold the house to Sir William Lever, later 1st Viscount Leverhulme. He renamed it Lancaster House after his native county. In 1913 he gave the remainder of the lease to the nation so the house could be used for Government hospitality and as a home for the London Museum, which remained here until 1946. It is now, as the Museum of London, housed in its own building in the City. In 1953, Sir Winston Churchill gave a splendid banquet here for Queen Elizabeth on the occasion of her Coronation. Lancaster House is now used for Government receptions and conferences. It is sometimes open on weekend afternoons in the summer, but not when it is required for a Government function.

For directions *see* ST JAMES'S PALACE.

Leicester House *Leicester Square.* Built in the 1630s by Robert Sidney, 2nd Earl of Leicester, on land which a century earlier had come into the hands of Henry VIII. It was a fairly plain house externally, but extremely large and expensively furnished. For a generation it remained one of the biggest houses in London, celebrated for its entertainments: in 1672 John Evelyn dined here with the wife of the 2nd Earl's grandson, the English ambassador in Paris, and was beguiled by Richardson, 'the famous Fire-Eater, who before us devour'd Brimston on glowing coales, chewing and swallowing them downe'. In 1717 the Prince of Wales, who became George II in 1727, moved here from his apartments in ST JAMES'S PALACE from which he had been evicted after a quarrel with his father. He agreed to pay a rent of £500 and, in addition, took over the neighbouring Savile House with which Leicester House was then linked by a covered passage. For ten years Leicester House was frequented by George I's opponents until the old King died and his son was proclaimed his successor outside the gates. Soon afterwards the new King moved out of the house which, in 1742, the 7th Earl agreed to let to Frederick, Prince of Wales, father of the future George III. Prince Frederick died here in 1751, after being hit on the throat by a cricket ball. His widow remained in the house until 1764 when she moved to CARLTON HOUSE; her son, Prince Henry, Duke of Cumberland, continued to live there until 1767.

The house was eventually demolished in 1791–2. Leicester Place was laid out across the site of the forecourt and Lisle Street extended eastwards over the site of the house.

Maids of Honour Row *The Green, Richmond, Surrey.* George I's son, Frederick George, Prince of Wales (later George II) acquired the Duke of Ormonde's house in the OLD DEER PARK so that he and his wife, Princess Caroline of Anspach, could hold their own court. In 1724 the *British Journal* announced, 'His Royal Highness hath given directions for erecting a new building near his Seat at Richmond to serve as Lodgings for the Maids of Honour attending the Princess of Wales.' The building was, in fact, a terrace of four houses of three storeys and a basement, set off by forecourts with wrought-iron gateways. These delightful houses adjoin the gateway to the palace overlooking Richmond Green.

The Maids of Honour cannot have occupied all the houses for long, for in about 1744 John James Heidegger, the Swiss theatre manager, lived at No. 4 and is said to have commissioned the scene painter Antonio Jolli to decorate the entrance hall. The panels show views of Switzerland, Italy and China and emblems of the arts and the seasons.

Marble Arch *W1.* Designed by John Nash, who based it on the Arch of Constantine in Rome, and constructed at a cost of £10,000, it was erected in 1827 in front of BUCKINGHAM PALACE. The reliefs on the north side were by R. Westmacott, those on the south by Baily. A statue of George IV by Chantrey was intended to be set on the top but stands instead in Trafalgar Square.

It was moved to its present site at the north-east corner of HYDE PARK in 1851 and islanded in 1908. Only senior members of the Royal Family and the KING'S TROOP ROYAL HORSE ARTILLERY may pass through it.

Marble Arch was removed from Buckingham Palace to its present site in 1851.

Margaret, Princess *(b. 1930)*. Born at Glamis Castle, the younger daughter of the Duke and Duchess of York. Their London house was 145 Piccadilly until the Princess's father's accession as KING GEORGE VI, when they moved to BUCKINGHAM PALACE. After the King's death she and the QUEEN MOTHER went to live at MARLBOROUGH HOUSE until her marriage in 1960 to Antony Armstrong-Jones. The marriage took place in WESTMINSTER ABBEY, and thereafter she and her husband lived in apartments in KENSINGTON PALACE, where she still lives. On the eve of the birth of their first child, Princess Margaret's husband was created the Earl of Snowdon. Their son, Viscount Linley, was born in 1961 and their daughter, Lady Sarah Armstrong-Jones, in 1964. Princess Margaret's marriage was dissolved in 1978.

Marlborough House *Pall Mall, SW1*. Built for Sarah, Duchess of Marlborough, who obtained a 50-year lease of land adjoining ST JAMES'S PALACE from her friend, Queen Anne. The Duchess invited Wren to design her new house; Vanbrugh had been the Duke's choice for Blenheim Palace. She later recalled that she made Wren promise two things: 'First that he would make the contracts reasonable and not as Crown work . . . the other . . . that he must make my house strong plain and convenient and that he must give me his word that this building should not have the least resemblance of anything in that called Blenheim which I have never liked. . . .'

The red bricks were brought as ballast from Holland in ships that had carried troops and supplies to the Duke's armies. The Duchess herself laid the foundation stone in 1709 and the house was finished in 1711. The actual design was probably drawn by Christopher Wren the Younger, under the supervision of his father. The Duchess dismissed Wren before completion, feeling that the contractors took advantage of him. She supervised the completion of the unpretentious house herself.

In 1722 the Duke died at Windsor Lodge but his body was brought here to lie in state before burial in WESTMINSTER ABBEY. A series of historical paintings of his battles lines the walls of the central *salon* and the staircases. His widowed Duchess divided her time between her houses at London, Windsor, St Albans and Wimbledon. In 1733 she tried to improve access to the house by making a new drive from the front entrance to Pall Mall; she had built the gateway when Sir Robert Walpole bought the leases of the obstructing houses to spite her. The blocked-up arch can still be seen. The Duchess died at Marlborough House in 1744.

In the early 1770s Sir William Chambers added a third storey and put in marble fireplaces. The house remained in the Marlborough family until 1817 when it reverted to the Crown and preparations were made for Princess Charlotte, the heir to the throne, and her husband, Prince Leopold of Saxe-Coburg-Saalfeld, to move in; but she died in childbirth at Claremont Park. Prince Leopold came here alone and lived in it until he accepted the invitation to become the first King of the Belgians in 1831. In 1837–49 the Dowager Queen Adelaide lived here. Between her death and the coming of age of Edward, Prince of Wales, it provided accommodation for the Vernon and Turner collections of pictures, the Government School of Design and the Department of Practical Art. For several years the Duke of Wellington's funeral carriage, a product of the School of Design, was exhibited in a shed in the forecourt. It was later moved to St Paul's Cathedral and is now on display at Stratfield Saye, the Iron Duke's house near Reading.

In 1861–3 Sir James Pennethorne removed Chambers's attic storey and replaced it with two of his own. The carriage porch was added, a range of rooms to the north, and stables. The work was for the new occupant, Edward, Prince of Wales. The small rooms were enlarged by combining two or even three together. In his time visitors to the house were admitted to the entrance hall by a Scots gillie in Highland dress. In the hall they were met by two scarlet-coated and powdered footmen, their hats and coats being passed to a hall porter in a short red coat with a broad band of leather across his shoulders. A page in a dark blue coat and black trousers would then escort them to a walnut-panelled ante-room on the first floor next door to which the Prince would be waiting to receive them in a cluttered sitting-room. As they passed upstairs they were conscious of the flittings of many maids, all in neat uniform, whose business it was to maintain the character of the Prince's residence as 'the best kept house in London'. It was also, of

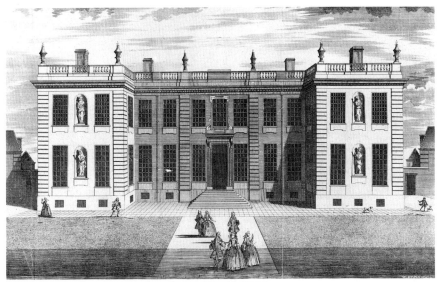

Marlborough House as seen from the Mall in the 1750s

course, the centre of fashionable society. In 1865 the future George V was born here and in 1903–10 lived here as Prince of Wales. From 1910 to 1925 it was the home of the widowed Queen Alexandra. In the garden are gravestones to her dogs Muff, Tiny and Joss and one to Benny the Bunny. Her own Queen Alexandra Memorial is in Marlborough Road (*see* MEMORIALS). In 1936, on the death of King George V, his widow, Queen Mary, moved here. She died here in 1953. There is a memorial plaque to her, also in Marlborough Road.

In 1959 the house was donated to the Government for use as a Commonwealth Centre, and was opened as such in 1962. It also houses the Commonwealth Foundation. The principal room is the saloon which is two storeys high. On its wall are paintings of the Battle of Blenheim by Louis Laguerre. On the ceiling are Gentileschi's *Arts and Sciences* painted in 1636 for the QUEEN'S HOUSE at Greenwich but removed by the Duchess of Marlborough by permission of Queen Anne. Beyond is the main conference room with two smaller ones on either side. On the staircases to the first floor are more paintings by Laguerre of the Battles of Ramillies and Malplaquet. There is also Edward VII's smoking-room lined appropriately with bogus books.

The assembly and conference rooms and other former state apartments are occasionally open to the public when the house is not in use for Commonwealth conferences and meetings. For information telephone the Administration Officer: 01-930 9249.

UNDERGROUND *Green Park*   BUS ROUTES *9, 14, 19, 22, 25, 38, 55.*

Mary Tudor with her husband King Philip II of Spain, whom she married in 1554.

Mary I, Tudor (*1516–58*). Daughter of HENRY VIII and Catharine of Aragon, she was born at GREENWICH PALACE. On the death of her brother EDWARD VI, the Duke of Northumberland and the Council had the Protestant LADY JANE GREY proclaimed Queen, but the whole populace supported Mary, who disbanded her army at Wanstead where she was met by her sister ELIZABETH. They rode into London and at Aldgate the Queen was received by the Lord Mayor. From thence she went to the TOWER. She lived at RICHMOND PALACE until her coronation. Her sister and the Princess Anne of Cleves attended her at the coronation banquet in WESTMINSTER HALL. After her marriage in 1554 at Winchester to Prince Philip of Spain (soon to become King Philip II) she spent a fortnight at RICHMOND PALACE with her husband, after which there were more festivities at Whitehall and then the royal couple retired to HAMPTON COURT. Later that year a service of thanksgiving for the Queen's pregnancy was held at St Paul's and it was at HAMPTON COURT that she awaited in vain the birth of an heir to the throne. When it became apparent that the supposed pregnancy was a delusion, Philip returned to Spain. The Queen took leave of him at Greenwich. In that year, 1555, began the religious persecution for which her reign is notorious and which earned her the not entirely just sobriquet 'Bloody Mary'. Two hundred Protestant martyrs were burned at the stake at Smithfield. Philip returned to England only once more. In March 1557 he rejoined her at Greenwich and on 4 July he left England for ever. Within a year Mary died at ST JAMES'S PALACE where she lay in state for three days, dressed not in the customary robes of state but as a member of a religious order. She was buried in Henry VII's Chapel, Westminster Abbey, with full Roman Catholic rites.

MEMORIALS (*See also* STATUES; ALBERT MEMORIAL; QUEEN VICTORIA MEMORIAL)

Queen Alexandra *Marlborough Gate, SW1*. One of Sir Alfred Gilbert's last works, this bronze was unveiled in 1932 by the Queen's son, George V. Behind the memorial, which includes a number of bronze allegorical figures on a red granite plinth, is a bronze screen with lamps in the top corners, and below is a fountain.

Cadiz Memorial *Horse Guards Parade, SW1*. A French mortar mounted on a cast-iron Chinese dragon. The inscription reads, 'To commemorate the raising of the siege of Cadiz in consequence of the glorious victory gained by the Duke of Wellington over the French near Salamanca, 22 July 1812. This mortar cast for the destruction of the great fort, with powers surpassing all others, and abandoned by the besiegers on their retreat, was presented as a token of respect and gratitude by the Spanish nation to HRH Prince Regent.' Known to his contemporaries as the Regent's Bomb (then pronounced bum), it became a favourite subject for caricaturists and is depicted on numerous irreverent prints, often in conjunction with the Regent's then mistress, Lady Hertford.

Eleanor Cross *Charing Cross Station Yard, SW1*. A very high stone and granite memorial designed by E. M. Barry and executed by Thomas Earp in 1863. On the death of Queen Eleanor, the wife of Edward I, her body was

The Cadiz Memorial, a captured French mortar satirically known as the 'Regent's Bomb', then pronounced 'bum', in Horse Guards Parade in 1816.

One of the crosses marking the resting places of the funeral cortège of Queen Eleanor was erected in Cheapside, shown here as it appeared in 1638.

brought to London in 1290 to be buried in WESTMINSTER ABBEY. The king ordered 20 crosses to be erected to mark the resting places of the cortège, the last one at Charing Cross. The site of the original one, now lost, was in what is now Trafalgar Square, then called Charing.

Philip, Prince, Duke of Edinburgh   (*b. 1921*). Son of Prince Andrew of Greece and Denmark and Princess Andrew, who was the great granddaughter of QUEEN VICTORIA. On his naturalisation as a British subject, Prince Philip adopted the surname Mountbatten. In 1947 he was created Duke of Edinburgh shortly before his marriage in WESTMINSTER ABBEY to the Princess Elizabeth, later QUEEN ELIZABETH II. Their London home is BUCKINGHAM PALACE.

Prince Henry's Room   *17 Fleet Street, EC4*. The house containing Prince Henry's Room was built in the early 17th century, but the site itself has a longer history. In the 12th century it formed part of the land owned by the Order of the Knights Templar. In 1312 their order was dissolved and a few years later the buildings were taken over by the Knights Hospitallers of the Order of St John of Jerusalem. They in turn leased their property, the main part to lawyers and the buildings which faced on to Fleet Street, including No. 17, to various other tenants. By the beginning of the 16th century the eastern half of No. 17 was an inn called The Hand, the rooms over the gate being known as the Prince's Arms. In 1592 the owner of The Hand was Zachary Bennett whose son, John, decided to rebuild the premises in 1610. The rebuilding was carried out in 1610–11 by William Blake who took over the inn from John Bennett and thereafter called it The Prince's Arms. The main room above the gateway, which can still be seen, was beautifully constructed with oak panelling all around and on the ceiling were the three feathers of the Prince of Wales together with the letters 'P.H.'. It seems likely that this was done because Prince Henry, son of James I, became Prince of Wales in 1610.

After 30 years the name of the inn seems to have been changed to The Fountain and then, in 1795, Mrs Salmon's Waxworks were moved here from the other side of the street. Some time during the 19th century the front was crudely covered over with paint and boards. In 1898 the London County Council bought the premises which were then restored.

Prince Henry's Room is open from 1345 to 1700 from Monday to Friday and from 1400 to 1600 on Saturday.

UNDERGROUND *Aldwych, Temple* BUS ROUTES *4, 6, 9, 11, 15, 15A, 171, 513.*

The house containing Prince Henry's Room as it appeared in 1807, when the building housed Mrs Salmon's Waxworks.

The marble memorial to Queen Victoria, which was unveiled in front of Buckingham Palace in 1911 by her grandson, George V.

Queen Victoria Memorial *and* **Gardens**   *Opposite Buckingham Palace, SW1.* Conceived in 1901 by the Queen Victoria Memorial Committee as part of a 'great architectural and scenic change' near BUCKINGHAM PALACE, the sculpture forms the nucleus of Aston Webb's design for the transformation of the Mall. Standing 82 ft high, the white marble memorial group was unveiled in 1911 by George V who knighted its creator, Thomas Brock, on the spot. A 13 ft high seated figure of Queen Victoria faces eastwards down the Mall. It was made from one block of marble. The Queen is surrounded by what Osbert Sitwell called 'tons of allegorical females in white wedding cake marble, with whole litters of their cretinous children'. Behind, marble groups representing Charity (west), Truth (south) and Justice (north) occupy the other three sides of the column that rises to a gold-leafed figure of Victory with figures of Courage and Constancy at her feet. This is set in the middle of a circular ponded podium approached by two flights of steps to the east and west flanked by figures of Progress and Peace (east) and Manufacture (west). To the north are figures representing Painting and Architecture, and to the south War and Shipbuilding.

A secondary creation was the Memorial Gardens around it designed by Aston Webb. These are enclosed by a low stone balustrade which links the three main ornamental exit gates: on the north side the entrance to GREEN PARK, the gift of Canada, the pillars therefore topped by wheat and fruit and a seal; on the east side the entrance to Constitution Hill, the gift of West and

South Africa (West Africa is represented by a leopard and an eagle, South Africa by an ostrich and monkey); on the south side the entrance to Birdcage Walk, the gift of Australia, hence a kangaroo and ram. The gates on the east and south sites are by Alfred Drury. There are two less elaborate subsidiary gateways: at the junction of Birdcage Walk and Buckingham Gate (two columns topped by urns given by the Malay States); and at the Constitution Hill exit (the gift of Newfoundland). The intended plain grass counterpoint to the memorial was changed at the request of Edward VII and spectacular flower beds have been the tradition since.

For directions *see* BUCKINGHAM PALACE.

Queen's Bodyguard of the Yeomen of the Guard   Founded in 1485 for the coronation of Henry VII. It is the oldest royal bodyguard and the oldest military corps in the world. Its distinctive Tudor uniform of knee-length tunics, white ruffs and round black hats is distinguished from that of the Yeomen Warders of the TOWER OF LONDON (*see* BEEFEATERS) by a cross belt originally designed for supporting an arquebus. There are six officers and some 80 men.

Queen's Chapel   *Marlborough Gate, SW1*. First classical church in England, designed by Inigo Jones for the Infanta of Spain who was intended to marry Charles I. Building began in 1623 but when the wedding negotiations stopped so did the construction work. It was completed for Henrietta Maria in 1626–7 and refurnished for Charles II's Catholic wife Catherine of Braganza, in about 1662–80. In 1761 George III married Charlotte of Mecklenburg-Strelitz here. As well as Roman Catholic services, Dutch Reformed services for William and Mary, German Lutheran for the Hanoverians and Danish for Queen Alexandra have been held here. From the 18th century until 1901 it was known as the German Chapel Royal. Open for Sunday morning services except in August and September.

UNDERGROUND *Piccadilly Circus, Charing Cross*   BUS ROUTES *1, 3, 6, 9, 11, 12, 13, 15, 15A, 24, 29, 53, 77, 77A, 88, 109, 159, 170, 176, 184, 196.*

Queen's Chapel of the Savoy   *see* SAVOY CHAPEL.

Queen's Gallery   *Buckingham Palace Road, SW1*. Opened in 1962 in BUCKINGHAM PALACE in what had formerly been a conservatory and was consecrated as a chapel by William Howley, Archbishop of Canterbury, in 1843. There is still a small private chapel in the building, which is screened from public view. The gallery holds public exhibitions of art treasures from the royal collection. It is open from 1100 to 1700 from Tuesday to Saturday and from 1400 to 1700 on Sunday and also on Bank Holiday Mondays.

For directions *see* BUCKINGHAM PALACE.

Greenwich in the early 17th century, showing on the left the Queen's House, and on the right Greenwich Palace, on whose site was built the Royal Naval Hospital.

Queen's House   *Greenwich, SE10.* The surrounding GREENWICH PARK and GREENWICH PALACE were settled on Anne of Denmark by James I in 1605. In 1616 Inigo Jones was commissioned to design a house for her, but it had not progressed far by 1619 when she died. The unfinished building was given to Prince Charles. His Queen, Henrietta Maria, asked Inigo Jones to complete the house in 1629–40. He used the Palladian style and described the exterior as 'sollid, proporsionable according to the rulles, masculine and unaffected'. In the interior, however, he allowed himself 'licentious imaginacey'. The building, which pleased the Queen so much it was named the 'House of Delights', was H-shaped and built on either side of the muddy Deptford to Woolwich road which passed through a bridge connecting the two sides of the house. Its main room was the entrance hall, a perfect 40 ft cube with a gallery at first-floor level. The painted ceiling was by Gentileschi. On the east side a graceful iron staircase, the 'Tulip Staircase', led up to the gallery, the Queen's bedroom and her drawing-room which was to have had panels painted by Rubens and Jacob Jordaens. Across the bridge was the loggia, 'the frontispiece in the midst', which looked out over GREENWICH PARK. In 1642 Henrietta Maria left for Holland to raise funds for arms and men on the pretext of taking the ten-year-old Princess Mary to Prince William, her betrothed. On 3 November the house was searched for arms by Parliamentary forces. Nothing was found but the house was taken from royal keeping. When most Crown lands were disposed of, Greenwich was retained and the Queen's House was occupied by Bulstrode Whitelock. Paintings by Rubens, Raphael and Van Dyck from Charles I's collection, much of which had been kept here, were, however, sold. The house was used for the lying-in-state of Commonwealth generals. At the restoration of 1660 Henrietta Maria returned. In 1662, John Webb, pupil of Inigo Jones, added two first-floor rooms over the highway for her. In 1670 the house was given to Charles II's Queen, Catherine of Braganza; and in 1685 to James II's Queen, Mary of Modena, who rarely used it. William and Mary did not make use of the house either, preferring KENSINGTON PALACE and HAMPTON COURT. In 1690–7 it was occupied by the Earl of Dorset, the first Ranger of GREENWICH PARK, whose appointment included its use. In 1697 Dorset was succeeded by the Earl of Romney who diverted the Woolwich to Deptford road to its present course between the old palace and the Queen's House.

In the 1690s the Royal Naval Hospital was designed by Wren, using the Queen's House as a central point at Queen Mary's insistence (see ROYAL NAVAL COLLEGE). In 1708 it was bought by Prince George of Denmark who probably intended to give it to the Hospital for use as the Governor's residence. The Hospital paid for its repairs but the Prince died before formal arrangements were completed. At about this time Queen Anne gave her favourite, the Duchess of Marlborough, permission to remove the Gentileschi paintings from the entrance hall and take them to MARLBOROUGH HOUSE. From 1710 to 1729 the house was used by the Hospital governors, but it proved very expensive to maintain. On 18 September 1714 George I landed at Greenwich and held his first official reception in the house the next day. Queen Caroline owned the house in 1730–7 and commissioned the painting of the Queen's Bedroom, probably from James Thornhill. In 1743–80 Lady Catherine Pelham, Ranger of the Park, occupied the house. In 1795, Princess Caroline of Brunswick, who had come to marry the Prince of Wales, was received here by his mistress, Lady Jersey. In 1805 Princess Caroline was appointed Ranger and granted the house. It was sold to the Royal Naval Asylum the following year, for a school for sailors' orphans. The colonnades were added in 1809 to commemorate the Battle of Trafalgar. In the same year the wings were added to accommodate the school's 950 pupils. When the school moved to Suffolk in 1933 the house was left in a damaged condition. Partitions had been built, doorways knocked through walls, and floors, fireplaces, bathrooms and staircases put in. It was restored in 1934–6 by the Office of Works, and opened in 1937 as the central portion of the National Maritime Museum, housing the Elizabethan and Stuart exhibits.

BRITISH RAIL *Greenwich, Maze Hill* BUS ROUTES *1, 108B, 177, 180, 185, 188.*

Ranger's House, Greenwich. The home of the Duchess of Brunswick, mother of Caroline, Princess of Wales, in the early 19th century, it now houses a collection of 17th-century portraits.

Queen's Walk   *SW1*. A path laid out in 1730, along the eastern boundary of GREEN PARK, for the private use of Queen Caroline, wife of George II, and other members of the Royal Family.

Ranger's House   *Greenwich, SE10*. An early 18th-century house occupied in 1748–72 by Philip, 4th Earl of Chesterfield, author of the celebrated letters. In 1807–14 the Duchess of Brunswick, mother of Caroline, Princess of Wales, lived here so as to be near her daughter who was then living at Montague House nearby. In 1815 it became the official residence of the Ranger of GREENWICH PARK. In 1888–92 Field-Marshal Viscount Wolseley was the occupant.

The house was bought in 1902 by the London County Council and turned into refreshment rooms. It now houses the Suffolk Collection of Jacobean and Stuart portraits.

The house is open daily 1000 to 1700 Feb–Oct and 1000 to 1600 Nov–Jan. It is closed on Good Friday, Christmas Eve and Christmas Day.

BRITISH RAIL *Blackheath, Greenwich (then 15 mins' walk)* BUS ROUTES *53, 54, 75. Green Line 402.*

River Launches*, to Greenwich from Westminster and Charing Cross Piers, then 15 mins' walk.*

plete restoration and total redevelopment were urged by different parties. In 1946 the Gorell Commission wisely recommended that, since 'the Nash Terraces are of national interest and importance . . . they should be preserved as far as that is practicable and without strict regard to the economies of "prudent" estate management.' Twelve years later, the Crown Estate Commissioners with Sir Malcolm Trustram Eve as their Chairman, and the gifted and imaginative Louis de Soissons as their architect, began the slow rehabilitation of the Park, which was at last, triumphantly, completed in the late 1970s.

The total area of Regent's Park bounded by the Outer Circle is 487 acres. The bronze, *Conversations with Magic Stones*, is by Barbara Hepworth (1977); the *Triton Fountain* is by William Macmillan (1939, with additional work, 1950); the *Dolphin Fountain* in the Broad Walk by Alexander Munro (this was originally erected in HYDE PARK in 1862 and moved here in the 1960s); the *Boy with a Frog Fountain* in Queen Mary's Garden by Sir William Reid Dick (1936); the *Matilda* fountain by Gloucester Gate with the bronze figure of a girl shading her eyes with her hand and standing on a pile of Cornish rocks is by Joseph Durham (1878); and the bronze of a boy with an arrow straddling a turkey, *The Lost Bow*, is by A. H. Hodge (1939) who also made the bronze of a boy with a goose, *The Mighty Hunter* (1939), in Queen Mary's Garden.

The park is open daily from 0500 to dusk; Queen Mary's Rose Garden from 0700 to dusk.

The bear pit in the menagerie, which was laid out by Decimus Burton in Regent's Park in 1827.

Richard I, 'Cœur de Lion' *(1157–99)*. Son of HENRY II and his Queen, Eleanor of Aquitaine, he succeeded his father in 1189. His coronation at WESTMINSTER ABBEY was a magnificent and impressive ceremony, a ritual on which all subsequent coronations have been based. He spent little time in England – indeed he was never here for a year together. He sold lands, privileges and peerages to raise money for the third Crusade, and said he would even sell London if he could find a purchaser. He died of an arrow shot from a crossbow when he was besieging a castle in France.

Richard II *(1367–1400)*. Son of the Black Prince, who died in 1376. He was invested as heir to the throne at Havering by his grandfather, EDWARD III. When he acceded in 1377 at the age of ten, in his coronation procession from the TOWER to WESTMINSTER ABBEY, dressed in white robes, he looked 'as beautiful as an angel'. In protest against three years of misgovernment by his uncle, JOHN OF GAUNT, during the boy-king's minority, the men of Essex and Kent marched upon London in 1380. Richard, appearing on a bastion of the TOWER overlooking Tower Hill, told the angry mob that they would be pardoned if they returned home peaceably. Many of the rebels stormed into the Tower, but the King's mother, Joan, the Fair Maid of Kent, escaped and was rowed up the Thames to safety in Castle Baynard. The King met the

Richard II (left), the son of the Black Prince, acceded to the throne at the age of ten, in 1377. A century later, Richard III usurped the throne and was crowned in 1483.

rebels at Mile End and dispersed most of them with promises of pardon and emancipation from villeinage. He met them again the next day at Smithfield where the rebel leader, Wat Tyler, was knocked off his horse by the infuriated Lord Mayor and stabbed to death. His head was exposed on London Bridge.

Richard and his first Queen, Anne of Bohemia, were married in 1382 in St Stephen's Chapel in the PALACE OF WESTMINSTER, but their favourite home was Shene Palace (later renamed RICHMOND PALACE) where Queen Anne died of plague in 1394. Such was the eagerness of the people to see the arrival in London of the King's second bride, Isabella of France, in 1395 that nine people were killed in the crush on London Bridge. Perhaps under the influence of his French Queen, Richard's rule became increasingly auto-cratic and even tyrannical, until in 1399 his cousin Henry, Duke of Lancaster and Earl of Richmond, forced his abdication and confined him in the TOWER. His body lay in state for one night in ST JOHN'S CHAPEL in the Tower on its way from Pontefract Castle, where he had been murdered, to WESTMINSTER ABBEY where he shares a tomb with Anne of Bohemia. There is a contempor-ary portrait by André Beauneuve in the Abbey.

Richard III   *(1452–85).* Younger brother of EDWARD IV, he became Protec-tor of England on his brother's death, since Edward's son, EDWARD V was only 13 years old. The Protector usurped the throne and was duly crowned at WESTMINSTER ABBEY in July 1483. It was shortly after this that the boy-king and his brother disappeared, believed to have been murdered in the TOWER. Richard was killed in 1485 in the Battle of Bosworth Field, which terminated the Wars of the Roses. He was the last of the Plantagenets.

Richmond Palace   The old palace of Shene was first used extensively by Edward III who enlarged the old manor house, adding magnificent cham-bers and kitchens. In 1377 he died here, deserted by even his servants who, led by his mistress, Alice Perrers, had snatched the rings off his fingers. It was the favourite summer residence of Richard II and Anne of Bohemia. Each day they fed 10,000 guests. In 1394 Anne died of plague at the palace and her broken-hearted husband ordered it to be destroyed. But some of it was left for soldiers and servants to live in. Henry V, while still a prince, had it repaired and enlarged. Henry VI and Margaret of Anjou often held court at Shene. So did Edward IV and Elizabeth Woodville and in their time many jousts and tourneys were held on the Green.

Henry VII preferred Shene to all other royal residences. His two sons, Arthur and Henry, were brought up here. In 1499 the palace was destroyed by fire, but by 1510, it had been rebuilt as a grander palace still and renamed Richmond after the King's earldom of Richmond, in Yorkshire. In 1509 Henry VII died here and is said to have left hoards of gold hidden all over the palace. Catharine of Aragon had lived here, after Prince Arthur's death in

1502, until her marriage to Henry VIII in 1509. In 1510 Catharine came here for the birth of her child – a much wanted son, but he died the following year after catching a chill whilst being christened. In 1540 Anne of Cleves was given the palace on her divorce. Elizabeth often stayed here as a princess and even Henry himself paid cordial visits. Edward VI used it often and entertained both his sisters here. In 1554 Mary and Philip of Spain spent their honeymoon at the palace.

Elizabeth did not use Richmond much in the early days of her reign but later spent the summer here. In 1603 the ailing Queen came to the palace on the advice of her astrologer, but died within a few weeks of a distemper. James I neglected it and in 1610 gave it to Prince Henry who built a gallery for his pictures and sculptures. After Prince Henry's death in 1612 Prince Charles was given the manor and often came here to hunt. In 1625 he gave it to Henrietta Maria on their marriage but later it was transferred to their son Charles. After the King's execution in 1649 most of the palace was destroyed. At the Restoration, Charles II repaired part of it for his mother, but she found it too bleak to live in. James II asked Wren to restore it, but nothing came of the plans and by the 18th century the palace was 'decayed and parcelled out in tenements'. All that is left is the gateway on the Green which bears the weatherbeaten arms of Henry VII and behind it, in Old Palace Yard, the restored buildings of the Wardrobe.

The Thames at Richmond in the early 17th century, showing Morris dancers performing on the towpath with the Palace in the background.

Richmond Park   *Richmond, Surrey and SW15.* This park of 2,470 acres, 2½ miles across, was first enclosed in 1637 by Charles I to enlarge the grounds of RICHMOND PALACE. In 1649 the park was given to the City of London by the Commonwealth Government in return for support in the Civil War. The Corporation gave it back to Charles II in 1660. Ladderstile Gate commemorates the method of entry used by John Lewis who defended and finally won pedestrian public rights of way against the Crown in the reign of George II.

The two Pen Ponds, reserved for anglers, were formed in the 18th century and abound in many species of fish including pike, bream, carp, roach and eel. Adam's Pond is for model boats. The herds number over 350 fallow deer and 250 red deer. Haunches of venison by Royal Warrant are still made available to certain officers of the Crown and Government and the Archbishops of Canterbury and York. Hares, rabbits and other wildlife are plentiful.

Sports facilities include five cricket pitches, two golf courses and 24 football grounds. The Isabella Plantation contains gardens of rhododendrons and other plants. The oaks in the park are very old and with those of Epping Forest represent the survivors of the medieval forests which surrounded London.

The Park is open daily from 1000 to half an hour before dusk.

A proposed design of 1867 for the Royal Albert Hall.

Royal Albert Hall   *Kensington Gore, SW7.* In 1851 Prince Albert suggested that, with the profits of the Great Exhibition, a site in South Kensington should be bought for museums, schools, colleges and a central hall containing libraries, a lecture theatre and exhibition rooms. Gore House was accordingly purchased for that purpose by the commissioners in 1852. The next year Prince Albert asked Gottfried Semper, architect of the Dresden Opera House, to draw up plans for a hall but these were not used. In 1858 Henry Cole, Chairman of the Society of Arts, had plans made by Captain Francis Fowke of the Royal Engineers for a massive concert hall to hold 15,000 but these, also, were not used and the project was temporarily shelved. After Prince Albert's death in 1861 a public fund was opened to finance the ALBERT MEMORIAL and a hall. Seven architects drew up plans for the hall, among them Sir George Gilbert Scott, whose designs were chosen. As barely enough money was raised to cover the cost of the memorial and the hall the scheme was again dropped. In 1863 Cole revived the idea, proposing to finance the building by selling the 999-year leasehold of seats. Over 1,300 seats were sold at £100 each, entitling the owner to free admittance at every performance in the hall, an arrangement only partly modified today (with the agreement of the seat owners) to about 80 occasions each year. In 1865 new designs by Captain Fowke, influenced by Semper's opera house, were approved by the Prince of Wales. The Great Exhibition commissioners gave £50,000 and promised the site at a peppercorn rent of 1s a year which is still paid annually on 25 March. Fowke died in December 1865 and Colonel H. Y. Darracott Scott took over. In 1868 Queen Victoria laid the foundation stone (now behind two seats in block K at the rear of the stalls) and then unexpectedly announced that 'Royal Albert' was to be added to the existing title 'Hall of Arts and Sciences'. Two years later the hall was declared open by the Prince of Wales in place of his mother who was overcome by emotion. The notorious echo was first discovered when the Bishop of London prayed during the ceremony and the 'Amen' reverberated round the building. It has been said that the only place where a British composer can be sure of hearing his work twice is at the Albert Hall. Sir Thomas Beecham said it could be used for a hundred things but music wasn't one of them. The hall is oval – with exterior measurements of 272 ft by 238 ft – and has a capacity of over 8,000 but safety regulations reduce this figure to about 7,000. Its glass and iron dome is 135 ft high internally. The high frieze around the outside wall is by Armitage, Pickersgill, Marks and Poynter and illustrates 'The Triumph of Arts and Letters'. The 150 ton organ by Willis (reconstructed by Harrison and Harrison) has nearly 9,000 pipes and was the largest ever when built. A steam engine worked the bellows. Bruckner played it at the inaugural concert.

In 1877 the Wagner Festival was held, with six concerts conducted by Wagner himself. In the 1880s a dance floor was installed and exhibitions and assaults-at-arms were occasionally held. In 1886 the first of a series of concerts given by Dame Adelina Patti took place. In the 1890s charity balls, bazaars and festivals were held. On one occasion the owners of seats J894 and J895, the Misses Mirchouse, insisted on having a trapdoor cut in the dance floor so they could reach their seats and enjoy the dancing around them. In 1900 Madam Albani gave her farewell concert. In 1906 a record audience of 9,000 heard the first gramophone concert. In 1911 the Shakespeare Ball, which was held just before the coronation of George V, was attended by 80 visiting royals. Another grand ball was held three years later to celebrate 100 years of peace between England and the USA. In 1919 the first boxing contest was held in the hall. The prize was a gold trophy presented by George V. In 1923 the first performance was given of Long-fellow's *Hiawatha*, set to music by Coleridge-Taylor; and from 1930 to 1940 *Hiawatha* was performed annually. In 1941 the 47th Season of Sir Henry Wood's Promenade Concerts moved here after the bombing of the Queen's Hall, and the 'Proms' have since been held here annually. In 1953 the Coronation Ball was held here as it had been in 1937. In 1968, with a government interest-free loan of £40,000, the acoustics were improved by hanging saucer-like shapes from the roof. In 1970–1 the hall was cleaned and restored for its centenary. The Corps of Honorary Stewards comprises about 70 volunteer ushers who receive a pair of tickets in return for each attendance. All tickets are printed on site.

UNDERGROUND *South Kensington* BUS ROUTES *9, 33, 52, 52A, 73.*

Visitors to the Royal Botanic Gardens making their way towards the Palm House, ascribed to Decimus Burton and built in 1844–8.

Royal Botanic Gardens   *Kew.* These unique gardens, extending to 300 acres, combine a scientific centre with an historic pleasure garden dating from the 18th century, possibly earlier. The diarist, Sir John Evelyn, mentions a visit in 1678, to Sir Henry Capel in Kew, 'whose orangerie and myrtetum [myrtle grove] are most beautiful and perfectly well kept.' In 1731, Frederick, Prince of Wales, leased The White House, also known as KEW PALACE, together with its grounds from the Capel family, and this site now forms the eastern part of the present gardens. The Prince instituted a pleasure garden and, after his death, his widow, Augusta, Dowager Princess of Wales, continued to improve it. In 1759 she created a botanic garden of nine acres under the guidance of Lord Bute and the head gardener, William Aiton. The western part was attached to the now vanished Richmond Lodge, the favourite residence of George II. The grounds had been laid out by his wife, Queen Caroline of Anspach, but they were extensively altered and improved, around 1770, by Lancelot 'Capability' Brown after the property had passed to George III in whose reign the two sites were united. Under the unofficial directorship of Sir Joseph Banks the Botanic Garden became famous and, in 1841, was handed over to the nation as the result of a Royal Commission.

A view across th...
to the left and a...

A third Muse...
Kew, close to...
botanical subj...
the building...
opened on 9 J...

Close to the...
site, it is 225 f...
was about 37...
British Colum...
landmark is th...
and erected in...
gettes. Not fai...
size, of a famo...
Chokushi-Mon,...
Association af...
Shepherds Bu...

Just within t...
plain stone b...
windows with...
Nash to flank...
re-erected (sli...
remains *in sit*...

To the desig...
the Gardens is...
1899, this grea...
with much orn...

Today, as well as being a public park, the Royal Botanic Gardens are primarily a scientific institution organised in several divisions principally concerned with the accurate identification of plants, living and dried, from worldwide sources. It acts as a centre for the distribution of economic and decorative plant material, and as a quarantine station, and is also increasingly involved in the conservation of endangered plant species.

Housed in a large block of buildings just outside the main gate, and not open to the public, is the Herbarium, consisting of a collection of between four and five million dried and pressed plants.

Also within the Royal Botanic Gardens stand a number of other buildings, many of them legacies of Royal Kew. In about 1756 Sir William Chambers was employed to instruct the Prince of Wales (soon to be George III) in architectural draughtsmanship, and shortly afterwards he was commissioned to design a series of garden buildings at Kew; several classical temples were built to his design of which three survive: those of Arethusa, Bellona and Æolus. The Temple of War or Bellona stands 100 yards southwest of the Victoria Gate. Built in 1760, it has a projecting portico of four Doric columns, above which there is a frieze carved with alternating helmets and daggers, vases and *paterae*. Inside, the oval dome is painted blue and has in its centre a gilded wooded 'glory' or sun. On a hillock about 70 yards west of the Cumberland Gate stands the 'ring-temple' of Æolus which once contained a large semi-circular niche that could be pivoted to shield the

A late 18th-century view of the Alhambra, and the Great Pagoda designed by Chambers, whose interest in chinoiserie was inspired by a visit to the East in his youth.

111

occupants
renovated
Temple of
designed b
built for th
Gate, and

The imp
House, wa
long, singl
round-head
design, also
youth. This
Although f
which was
the presen
'folly' in the
this structu
even in arc
ment brick.

A later b
William's T
of Bath sto

In the s
stands the
around 177
thatched co
was retaine
memorate I

Cambrid
houses the
Augusta, D
sixth son,
1837 the Du
tially durir
Princess M
Cambridge
VII. The bu
18th-centur

Opposite
Georgian b
It was opei
Hooker, th
second Mu
was opened

to Decimus Burton but built in conjunction with Richard Turner, a civil engineer, in 1844–8. This original piece of architecture is composed of curved sheets of glass; one big curve in the wings up to the clerestory, another from there to the central dome. Among the 3,000 species here is a giant Chilean wine palm, the second oldest specimen at Kew. Connected to the Palm House by a tunnel is the Campanile. Built in brick, this water tower stands 107 ft high and was erected in the 1840s.

The main entrance, at the north-west end of Kew Green, consists of a semicircular drive bordered by Portland stone piers with wrought-iron infilling, and ornamental iron gates bearing the arms and cypher of Queen Victoria, designed by Decimus Burton, and erected in 1848.

The Chinese Guardian Lions by the Pond, a pair of stone lions probably made in the 18th century, though possibly dating from the Ming period, resemble examples in the gardens of the Imperial Palace, Peking. François Joseph Bosio's *Hercules Fighting Achelous* in the Pond was first exhibited in plaster at the Paris salon in 1814 and later in bronze. Acquired by George IV in 1826, it originally stood on the East Terrace at Windsor Castle. It was given by Elizabeth II in 1963.

The gardens are open daily from 1000 to dusk (in summer to 2000).

UNDERGROUND *Kew Gardens* BRITISH RAIL *Kew Bridge* BUS ROUTES *27, 65, 90B (to Kew Green).* **River boats** *from Westminster Pier (summer).*

Royal Hospital Chelsea *see* CHELSEA HOSPITAL.

Inside the Great Palm House at Kew in 1852.

114

Queen Victoria progressing to the Guildhall in 1838 in the Gold State Coach.

Royal Mews   *Buckingham Palace Road, SW1.* The Riding House was built to the designs of Sir William Chambers in 1763–6 and was ornamented with its acanthus frieze and pediment at the beginning of the 19th century. The spirited group on the pediment, *Hercules Capturing the Thracian Horses*, is by William Theed, the Elder. The Mews themselves were built in 1824–5. Here may be seen the carriage horses and carriages including the Gold State Coach which was made for George III in 1762 and has been used at CORONATIONS ever since. It was designed by Sir William Chambers and painted by Cipriani with a series of emblematical subjects. It cost £7,661 16s 5d. The Irish Coach, made in Dublin in 1852, was bought by Queen Victoria for the STATE OPENING OF PARLIAMENT. The Glass State Coach was bought in 1910 by George V for royal weddings. The Royal Mews come under the jurisdiction of the Master of the Horse and are administered by the Crown Equerry who is responsible for the Queen's 30 horses (10 greys and 20 bays), her five coachmen, 15 grooms (who act as postilions on ceremonial occasions) and her 70 carriages, from state coaches to phaetons, all in working order. He also has charge of her 20-odd cars, including the £60,000 three-ton Phantom Six Rolls Royce which was presented to her in 1978 by the Society of Motor Manufacturers as a Jubilee present.

Open to the public on Wednesdays and Thursdays (1400 to 1600) except when there is a carriage procession for such an event as the STATE OPENING OF PARLIAMENT, and when a Bank Holiday falls on an open day.

For directions *see* BUCKINGHAM PALACE.

The new Mint on Tower Hill built in the neo-classical style, shortly after its completion in 1812.

Royal Mint   *Tower Hill, EC3.* According to Herodotus there was a Mint in Lydia in about the 8th century BC. Coins were of gold and uninscribed. The art of coining passed to this country by way of the Romans. Native coins inscribed as in the Roman fashion have been identified bearing names of ancient British chiefs, but their use died out as they were superseded by Roman coinage. The right of coinage has always been a royal prerogative, exercised with varying degrees of honesty and efficiency, by successive monarchs; from the Anglo-Saxon period kings were in the habit of creating their own mints and of issuing coins bearing their own effigy and place of origin. The addition of the name of the moneyer gave proof of the coin's integrity. Severe punishment was meted out for offences against coinage, including cutting off the right hand and emasculation.

Evidence suggests the presence of a Mint in London from the 9th century onwards, and by the next century London had become the most important centre for the coining of money in England, although at that time it is likely that there were still several Mints, consisting of single craftsmen, each with his furnace and coining dies in individual workshops. During the 13th century all these small units were gradually gathered into one enclosure, and the King appointed a porter 'to keep the gate for all incomings and outgoings and to summon all men required when there was work to do'. By 1300, an area within the TOWER OF LONDON had been set aside 'for the workshops in the barbecan for the needs of the moneyers', and at about this time a 400 ft-long building was erected for them. 'The Mint' was well

116

established in the area between the inner and outer walls of the Tower by the beginning of the Tudor era; successive edicts had given it control over all designs and dies, and all coinage was eventually carried out in the Tower Mint.

Under King Henry III a Comptroller had been appointed, and a gold coin, valued at 20 silver pence, was minted, the first gold coin used in England. Soon afterwards, circular silver half-pennies and farthings came into use, replacing the haphazard fragments of the old square penny which had been used until then as small change. The groat (a four-penny piece) and the half-groat followed; and then a gold florin in the reign of Edward III, though this soon gave way to the gold noble. The gold and silver bullion came from mines in Wales and Devonshire. New coins introduced under Henry VII were the gold sovereign – the first £1 coin, and so called because of the representation on its face of the monarch on his throne; also the silver shilling, and, in King Henry VIII's reign, the half-crown, sixpence and three-penny piece.

The reign of Henry VII also saw the first employment – continued from then on – of an engraver to design the dies for coins. The Crown employed all the officials and workmen for a time, paying them a salary direct; but, finding this too large a drain on the Exchequer, the old system was revived. This consisted of employing only a Warden, whose duty was to supervise the activities of the Master of the Mint. The Master paid himself and his workmen by means of a fee taken from each pound of gold and silver coined. After 1666, however, the Master was again paid a salary and taxes on the import of wines, spirits and beer were used to meet the expenses of the Mint.

Ninety-seven chests of silver, carried on twenty carts, were delivered to the Tower for the Mint in 1554, as part of the marriage contract between Queen Mary and King Philip of Spain; and the following year the first contract for a foreign government was undertaken – the minting of Spanish coins.

Following the Restoration, small steel rolling-mills, driven by horse and water power, were established in the Tower. The old hammered coins were deemed so much inferior to the new milled ones that they were all called in, under a Coinage Act of 1696. They were melted in furnaces near Whitehall, and turned into ingots which were sent to the Tower to be made into new milled coinage. But the Mint found it impossible to deal with all the work involved, and extra local Mints were temporarily opened in Bristol, Exeter, York, Norwich and Chester.

The employment of an artist engraver to design the coinage and the royal effigy, led to improvements in appearance and portraiture. The model for Britannia on the Charles II coinage was said to have been Frances Stewart, afterwards Duchess of Richmond, mistress of the King. The new gold 20s pieces, struck at this time, were known as 'guineas', because the gold from

The interior of the Mint in 1809, a year before the introduction of steam engines.

which some of them were made was imported from Guinea. Some years later the guinea was increased in value to 21 shillings.

Sir Isaac Newton was Master of the Mint from 1699–1727, a post which he held with success and distinction. The office of Master was eventually abolished in 1870 and the Chancellor of the Exchequer is now (*ex officio*) Master of the Mint.

By this time, the Mint was once more becoming unable to cope with the pressure of work, and a Privy Council committee recommended that a new Mint should be built outside the Tower. A site on Little Tower Hill was chosen and a new building was designed and executed in the neo-classical style, with a portico of six Tuscan columns. The architect was James Johnson who was succeeded after his death by Sir Robert Smirke. New machines, powered by steam engines, were installed, and the first coins were minted there in 1810. By August 1812, the move out of the Tower of London was complete. From that date, the output of coins has continually increased; about 25 million a year were produced in the mid-19th century. By the time of the 1st World War the figure had risen to 250 million a year and by the 1960s to over 1,000 million, of which over half went overseas. The great increase in the demand for internal circulating coins and from commerce, and latterly for the whole process of decimalisation, resulted in the transfer of the Mint to large new buildings at Llantrisant in South Wales where coins were first minted in 1968. Since 1975 no coins have been minted in the Tower Hill buildings and the shop and exhibitions there were closed in 1980 because of the imminent redevelopment of the site.

After the Prince Regent's accession in 1820, two of his brothers were provided with houses within the palace precincts, the Duke of York with York House, later known as LANCASTER HOUSE and the Duke of Clarence, later William IV, with CLARENCE HOUSE. The King himself had a new palace built on the site of his parents' house. Thereafter the State Apartments were no longer lived in; although foreign ambassadors are still accredited in traditional style to the Court of St James's, they are received at BUCKINGHAM PALACE. Certain functions continued to be held at St James's, however. Queen Victoria, her eldest daughter, Princess Victoria, and her grandson, the future George V, were all married here. The accession of a new sovereign is still proclaimed at St James's and privy councillors still assemble here for the Accession Council as they did on 8 February 1952 in the entrée room to hear Elizabeth II make her first speech as Queen.

Next to the levée room is the throne room which has an overmantel of carved fruit and flowers by Grinling Gibbons as beautiful as any of his works. Other state rooms, none of which is open to the public, contain some fine doorcases by William Kent and are splendidly decorated in white, crimson and gold. The tapestry room contains tapestries woven for Charles II and a Tudor fireplace with the initials H and A. Like the armoury, which also contains an original fireplace, it was redecorated by William Morris's firm in the 1860s, a remarkably early period for the official acceptance of so revolutionary a style. The rest of the palace provides offices for the Lord Chamberlain's department and residences for various officers of the royal household.

The palace is not open to the public.

A variety of weapons decorate the walls of the Guard Chamber at St James's Palace.

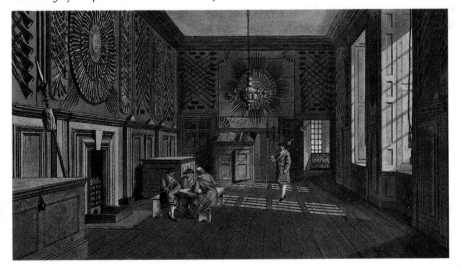

A mid-18th-century view of St James's Palace as laid out by Charles II, seen from Buckingham House, which later became Buckingham Palace.

St James's Park   *SW1.* Takes its name from the hospital for leper women which was rebuilt as ST JAMES'S PALACE. The oldest of London's royal parks, it extends to about 90 acres with the Mall as the northern boundary and Birdcage Walk as the southern. The QUEEN VICTORIA MEMORIAL is at its western end and Horse Guards Road forms its eastern boundary. It was originally a marshy field attached to the hospital where the lepers fed their hogs. Henry VIII had the field drained and had a bowling alley and tilt-yard made here and used the land as a nursery for his deer. Later he made it part of a chase which extended up to Islington, Marylebone and Hampstead. The trees were gradually cut down during the reigns of Edward VI and Mary I. Elizabeth I hunted here. James I had formal gardens laid out with a menagerie (containing, amongst other strange beasts, two crocodiles) a physic garden and an aviary. Charles I was escorted across the park to his execution on 30 January 1649, his dog, Rogue, running after him. 'The Park had several companies of foot drawn up,' Sir Thomas Herbert remembered. 'And a guard of halberdiers in company went, some before, and some followed; the drums beat, and the noise was so great as one could hardly hear what another spoke.'

During the Commonwealth the park was much neglected and most of the remaining trees were cut down by the citizens for fuel. Charles II extended it by 36 acres and laid it out afresh, advised, so it has been said, by André Le Nôtre, the great landscape gardener whose work at Versailles he so much admired. He planted it with fruit trees, stocked it with deer and built an avenue, lined with trees and covered with powdered cockleshells where he

124

could play pall-mall. He also converted several small ponds into a long strip of water known as the Canal, leaving untouched the romantic pond known as Rosamond's Pond which was mentioned by both Congreve in *The Way of the World* and by Pope in *The Rape of the Lock*. (It was filled in in 1770.) The Canal became one of Charles II's favourite spots. He could often be seen, accompanied by his mistresses, walking his dogs around it, feeding the ducks and sometimes swimming in it. John Evelyn visited the park at this time and found it 'stored with numerous flocks of severall sorts of ordinary and extraordinary wild fowle, breeding about the Decoy, which for being neere so great a city and among such a concourse of soldiers and people, is a singular and diverting thing. There were also deere of several countries – white, spotted like leopards, antelopes, an elk, red deere, roebucks, stags, etc.' There were also two pelicans, a present from the Russian ambassador, and a crane with a wooden leg. Pepys, too, came to see the birds and was amazed by the 'variety of fowle' to be seen there. One winter's day in 1662, he recorded, 'Over to the Parke, where I first in my life, it being a great frost, did see people sliding with their skeates, which is a very pretty art.' A fortnight later he accompanied the Duke of York into the park 'where though the ice was broken and dangerous, yet he would go slide upon his skeates.' 'I did not like it,' Pepys added, 'but he slides very well.' The readiness with which the royal family appeared among the people

St James's Park, a notorious haunt of prostitutes in the early 18th century, had become a fashionable promenade by the 1750s.

occasionally led to disorders. In 1677 one Deborah Lyddal was committed to Bethlehem Hospital for 'she doth frequently intrude herself into St James's Park where she hath committed several disorders and particularly took a stone offering to throw it at the Queen.' A Richard Harris was similarly confined for 'throwing an orange at the King'.

Already the park was becoming a less pleasant place than it had been in earlier years; and after the death of Charles II in 1685 it ceased to be the haunt of the sovereign, although William III built himself a bird-watching house on an island in the lake – a salient point at the east end still known as Duck Island – and could occasionally be seen here smoking his Dutch pipe. In Queen Anne's reign the park became notorious for prostitutes and for the depredations of those ruffianly aristocrats known as Mohocks; and in 1736 a writer in the *New Critical Review* complained of the stagnant water in the lake and the trees and shrubs all wanting attention. After the appointment of Lord Pomfret as Ranger in 1751 the condition of the park began to improve. The 1755 guidebook *London in Miniature* writes of it in complimentary vein: 'In this park are stags and fallow deer that are so tame as to take gently out of your hand and [at] each end of the Mall there are stands of cows, from whence the company at small expence, may be supplied with warm milk.' A French visitor of 1765 elaborated, 'The cows are driven about noon and evening to the gate which leads from the Park to the quarter of Whitehall.

Crowds strolling in St James's Park in the 1790s with Buckingham House in the background.

Children feeding ducks by the lake in St James's Park in 1842, with Buckingham Palace in the background.

Tied in a file to posts at the extremity of the grass plot, they will swill passengers with their milk, which is being drawn from their udders on the spot [and which] is served with all the cleanliness peculiar to the English, in little mugs at the rate of 1d per mug.'

'If a man be splenetic' wrote Goldsmith at about this time, 'he may every day meet companions in the seats in St James's Park, with whose groans he may mix his own, and pathetically talk of the weather.' If, however, St James's park was not as rowdy as it had been in the earlier years of the century, and if fewer duels were fought here than in other parks (it was illegal to draw a sword within its boundaries), it remained a recognised haunt of whores. The gates were locked at night but 6,500 people were authorised to possess keys to them and thousands of others had keys unofficially. James Boswell was a frequent visitor here, sometimes in the afternoons when he liked to watch the soldiers on parade, but more often after dark when the gates were unlocked by girls who came in to stroll up and down the paths, and he was likely to be accosted, as he was one evening in 1762 'by several ladies of the town'.

In 1814 St James's, like the other parks, was the scene of a splendid gala, organised by the Regent and his favourite architect, John Nash, to celebrate the anniversary of the Battle of the Nile and the centenary of the accession to the English throne of the House of Hanover. A seven-storey Chinese

The Chinese bridge and Pagoda, built for the Peace Celebrations of 1814.

pagoda was built and, across the Canal, a picturesque yellow bridge ornamented with black lines and a bright blue roof. It was a 'trumpery' affair, in the opinion of Canova who, when asked what had struck him most forcibly during his visit to England, had replied that this bridge should have been the production of the Government whilst Waterloo Bridge was the work of a private company. The 'trumpery' bridge, however, remained until 1825. The pagoda caught fire during the celebratory fireworks display, killing a lamplighter and injuring five other workmen.

After the accession of George IV further improvements were made to the park. It was lighted by gas in 1822 and in 1826–7 the canal was remodelled into its present graceful curvilinear shape. Trees were planted and new walks laid out. Improvements to the park were continued intermittently throughout the 19th century. In 1840–1 a lodge for the Ornithological Society was built on an island at the east end of the lake to the designs of J. B. Watson. It contained a council room, keepers' apartments and steam hatching apparatus. (This has recently been demolished.) In 1855 the lake was dredged, concreted and made a uniform 4 ft deep. In 1857 an iron suspension bridge, designed by James Meadows Rendel, and decorated by Sir Matthew Digby Wyatt, was built across the lake. (Although this was the only remaining early suspension bridge in London, it, too, was demolished and replaced by the present concrete bridge, designed by Eric Bedford, in 1956–7.) The Lake House north of Duck Island was built in 1922, demolished in 1968 and replaced in the 1970s by the present tent-like structure which has a hand-painted ceramic tile mural by Barbara Jones depicting the history of the park. In 1873 an ornithologist listed 28 species of birds in the park. Today there are over 42,including ducks, geese, gulls and pelicans. The Guards' Memorial is at the east end. The view across the lake to the spires, pinnacles and domes of Whitehall has been described as 'the most astonishing and romantic roofscape in London'.

St John's Chapel   *Tower of London, Tower Hill, EC3.* A classic example of early Norman architecture, the Chapel of St John on the second floor of the White Tower is the best preserved and one of the most beautiful Romanesque chapels in the country. Built of Caen stone in about 1080, the chamber, overlooked by clerestory windows, measures about 56 ft by 31 ft. The only perfect barrel-vault in England spans the nave and apse. The triforium, which is supported by twelve massive round pillars, was once reserved for the ladies of the court. The carved capitals of the columns relieve the otherwise stark austerity of the chapel. It was while praying here that Archbishop Sudbury, Treasurer Hales, John Legge, a collector of taxes, and John of Gaunt's physician were discovered by the mob during the Peasants' Revolt of 1381 and dragged from the altar, down the steps and out of the gates on to Tower Hill where all four were beheaded.

In the reign of Charles II two skeletons were found under the staircase leading to the chapel. These were reburied in WESTMINSTER ABBEY. Exhumation in 1933 suggested that they were those of the young Edward V and his brother, the Duke of York, whom Richard III may have had murdered.

The Order of the Knights of the Bath has long been associated with the chapel. Having spent the eve of his coronation in the TOWER, Henry IV initiated the Order's ceremonies: 46 of his followers were selected as members. As a symbol of their spiritual cleansing they first had to step into baths in the hall adjoining the Chapel. While they were in the bath the King made a cross on each man's back and knighted him. After a token rest, representing ease after labour, the new knights spent the night in prayer in the chapel. At the end of their vigil they offered up a prayer to God and a penny to the King on the altar. (*See also* TOWER OF LONDON.)

St Peter ad Vincula   *Tower Green, EC3.* Founded in the 12th century for the use of TOWER prisoners and aptly dedicated to St Peter in Chains. The present building is mostly 16th century and is full of royal and noble bones. Anne Boleyn was buried in a common oak chest here in 1536. Other persons buried here include Thomas Cromwell, Earl of Essex, 1540; Margaret, Countess of Salisbury, 1541; Catherine Howard, 1542; Thomas, Lord Seymour, 1549; Protector Somerset, 1552; the Duke of Northumberland, Bishop Fisher and Sir Thomas More, 1535; Lady Jane Grey and her husband, Lord Guildford Dudley, 1554; Robert Devereux, Earl of Essex, 1601; the Duke of Monmouth, 1685; and the Jacobite lords of the 1745 Rebellion. (*See also* TOWER OF LONDON.)

The Savoy Chapel which was rebuilt in 1510, as it appeared in 1819.

Savoy Chapel   *Savoy Street, WC2.* In the SAVOY PALACE owned by John of Gaunt there was a chapel dedicated to St John the Baptist but it was destroyed with the rest of the building in the Peasants' Revolt of 1381. In 1510 when the SAVOY was rebuilt as a hospital for the poor, a new chapel was dedicated to St John the Baptist. It had a 75 ft-high belfry. At the southern end was an antechapel, above which were two rooms whose windows overlooked the chancel, for the use of women who wanted to hear mass and for the election of the masters of the hospital. The main window had a stained glass of the *Last Judgment* by Barnard Flower. On the walls were paintings of Henry VI, John the Baptist and other saints. The wooden ceiling was divided into 138 panels decorated with religious and heraldic bosses. A gallery was added in 1518.

In 1642–3 Thomas Fuller, author of the *Church History of Britain* and *Worthies of England*, was lecturer and packed the church. He returned at the Restoration but died a year later. Pepys heard some of the sermons but thought them poor and dry. Some time before the 18th century the window of the *Last Judgment* was removed and the embrasure bricked up. The chapel was extensively repaired in 1723. In 1754–6 illegal marriages were performed here by the incumbent, John Wilkinson, who advertised, 'There are five private ways by land to this chapel and two by water'. He was arrested, tried and transported.

The ceiling was whitewashed in about 1787 and in 1820–1 the south wall and tower were rebuilt by Robert Smirke. After a fire at the south end in 1843, restoration work was carried out by Sydney Smirke. In 1859–60 the gallery was removed and a south-east door made. In 1864 another fire left only the exterior walls standing, but the chapel was rebuilt as before by Smirke in 1864–5.

Thomas Willement designed the ceiling and the windows. In 1877 the vestry was rebuilt and a new eastern entrance made. In the 1880s the chapel became as fashionable as St George's, Hanover Square, for upper-class weddings. In 1890 it became the first place of worship to be lit by electricity. In 1909–33 Hugh Boswell Chapman was the incumbent; and, since he was vice-president of the Divorce Reform Union, both innocent and guilty parties in divorce cases could be remarried here. In 1937 the Savoy became the Chapel of the Royal Victorian Order. It was refitted in 1939 and given the title of the King's Chapel of the Savoy. Further alterations were carried out by A. B. Knapp-Fisher in 1957–8.

The chapel is open from 1130 to 1530 from Tuesday to Friday.

UNDERGROUND *Embankment* BUS ROUTES *1, 4, 5, 6, 9, 11, 13, 15, 15A, 68, 77, 77A, 170, 188, 196, 199, 501, 502, 513.*

Savoy Palace *Strand.* In the early 13th century the land on which the palace was built belonged to Brian de l'Isle, one of King John's counsellors, who died in 1233, and the land passed to his heir. In 1246 Henry III granted it, for an annual rental of three barbed arrows, to his wife's uncle Peter, the future Count of Savoy, who bequeathed it in 1268 to the monastery of St Bernard, Montjoux, Savoie. In 1270, Queen Eleanor bought it for 300 marks for her second son, Edmund, Earl of Lancaster. In 1293 Edward I gave his brother permission 'to strengthen and fortify his mansion called the Sauvoye with a wall of stone and mortar'. Between about 1345 and 1370 this mansion was rebuilt by Henry, 1st Duke of Lancaster, for £35,000, the proceeds of his French campaign. The house was said to be without equal in England.

Little is known of the building, but there were stables, chapel, cloisters, river gate, a vegetable garden and fish pond in addition to the Great Hall. The Duke added more land to the west which completed the boundaries of the future Savoy precinct – the Strand to the north, the Thames to the south, Ivy Bridge to the west and the Temple to the east. In 1361 the palace was inherited by John of Gaunt through his wife, Blanche, Henry of Lancaster's daughter. In 1377 the palace was attacked by a mob because of Gaunt's support for Wycliffe but little damage was done. It was again attacked by Wat Tyler's followers in 1381. His gold and silver plate, furnishings and hangings were thrown on to a bonfire and his precious stones crushed and thrown into the river, as the assailants refused to steal from so hated a figure. One man who tried to pillage was also thrown on to the fire. The explosion of a box of gunpowder, consigned to the flames in the belief that it contained gold, brought down the Great Hall. Afterwards the Palace was no longer usable, though many of the buildings were still standing. Between 1404 and 1405 a new stone wall was built along the Strand frontage.

In 1505 Henry VII ordered the palace to be rebuilt as a hospital for the poor with 100 beds and he endowed it with land. Dormitories were built in the shape of a church in 1510–15. There were also three chapels including SAVOY CHAPEL and many outbuildings. In 1553 the hospital was suppressed by Edward VI and its land given to the City. It was subsequently refounded in 1556 by Queen Mary.

In 1559 Thomas Thurland was appointed Master. In 1570 a Bill of Complaint stated that Thurland's relations were maintained by the hospital, that he rarely went to church, that he had sexual relations with the hospital staff and that he owed the institution £2,500. However, he was not replaced and the hospital never recovered from his misrule. In the 16th and 17th centuries, houses in the precinct were occupied by noblemen and high-ranking clergy. The hospital itself continued to be misused. Stow wrote that vagabonds lay idly in the fields during the day, spending the night in the hospital. During the second half of the 17th century tradesmen occupied the former houses of the nobility.

In 1670 a fire destroyed the west end of the precinct. In 1675 the hospital was taken over for wounded servicemen; and in 1679 the Great Dormitory and the Sisters' dwellings were requisitioned as a barracks for foot guards. In 1685 the French Protestant chapel was rebuilt by Wren. In 1687 a Jesuit school was founded for 400 boys. The children, irrespective of their religion, were taught free of charge but had to pay for their books and writing materials. On the abdication of James II the following year the school was closed. In 1694 German Lutherans were given the former Sisters' Hall as a

The Savoy Palace as it would have appeared c. 1550, then largely a hospital.

King Henry VII, who in 1505 had the Savoy Palace rebuilt as a hospital, and his wife, Elizabeth of York.

church. Princess Caroline, the future wife of George II, built them a schoolhouse. A Calvinist congregation moved to the Savoy about the same time. In 1695 a military prison was built here by Wren. In 1697 the right of sanctuary for criminals was abolished. In 1702 the hospital was formally dissolved, and in the 1730s the French Protestants moved to Soho. The Lutheran Church was rebuilt in 1766–7, by Sir William Chambers, on the site of the former French chapel. In 1772 a long dispute over the ownership of the precinct was settled: the Crown took possession of the centre part and the Duchy of Lancaster took the outer ring and the SAVOY CHAPEL. By now most of the buildings were in ruins. In 1775 Chambers made plans for building a barracks for 3,000 officers and men but they were never carried out. In 1776 the old barracks were burned down.

In 1816–20 the site was cleared to make way for the approach road to Waterloo Bridge. By 1823 Savoy Street, Lancaster Place and two wharves were completed. In 1864–70 Victoria Embankment and Embankment Gardens were made. Savoy Street and Savoy Hill extended to the embankment. The Lutheran church and minister's house were demolished and rebuilt at the corner of Howland and Cleveland Streets. The only relic of the hospital is now the SAVOY CHAPEL. Most of the rest of the site is covered by the Savoy Hotel, the Savoy Theatre, the Victoria Embankment, Embankment Gardens and the west wing of SOMERSET HOUSE.

The terrace of Somerset House in the late 18th century with Westminster Bridge and St Paul's in the background.

Somerset House *Strand, WC2.* Site of the first Renaissance palace in England built in 1547–50 for Lord Protector Somerset. Pennant said the architect was John of Padua, others Sir John Thynne. To clear a site for it, the inns of the Bishops of Chester and Worcester were demolished, as were Strand Inn, an Inn of Chancery, and the Church of the Nativity of Our Lady of the Innocents. The Priory Church of St John Clerkenwell and St Paul's Charnel House and Cloister were pulled down to provide stone. Attempts were made to take stone also from St Margaret's, Westminster, but the parishioners drove the Duke's men off. The entrance gate was carved by Nicholas Cave, Henry VIII's master mason at Nonsuch. In 1552 Somerset was executed, and the house was later given to Princess Elizabeth in exchange for Durham House. She used it occasionally and rode out from here to welcome her sister Mary to London as Queen. Soon after the house was searched and anti-Catholic literature was found. Elizabeth's tutor and governess were taken to the TOWER but later released. In 1558, on her accession, part of the house was given back to the Protector's son, Edward Seymour. The rest was kept as a meeting-place for the Council, and for grace and favour residences and apartments for foreign ambassadors. The Queen herself stayed here from time to time before starting on long journeys.

134

In 1603 the house was given to Anne of Denmark. During her residence it was the scene of many spectacular masques organised by Ben Jonson and Inigo Jones. (Jones had apartments here.) In 1604 the peace conference between England, Spain and the Spanish Netherlands was held here. A painting of this occasion hangs in the National Gallery. In 1604 John Gerard, the herbalist, was granted a lease on a 2-acre site to the east of the house on condition that he supplied the Queen with plants, herbs, flowers and fruit. In 1605 he parted with it to Robert Cecil, Earl of Salisbury. In 1606 the house was renamed Denmark House in honour of Anne's brother, Christian IV of Denmark, who was staying with her. In 1619 Anne's embalmed body lay in state for two months while the Countesses of Arundel, Nottingham and Northumberland argued over who was to be the chief mourner. Soon after the funeral the house was given to Prince Charles but he preferred to live at ST JAMES'S PALACE and so the late Queen's household stayed on. In 1623 a Catholic chapel was built in anticipation of the Spanish Infanta's marriage to Prince Charles. After the death of James I at Theobalds in 1625, his body was brought to Denmark House to lie in state for a month. £50,000 was spent on the funeral, the greatest ever known in England. 8,000 mourners followed the coffin to the Abbey. In 1625 the house was given to Henrietta Maria. To

Spanish and English statesmen in attendance at the Peace Conference held at Somerset House in 1604.

135

compensate for sending her French attendants home, Charles built her a large new chapel designed by Inigo Jones in 1630–5. The consecration ceremonies lasted for three days. In 1645 Henrietta Maria left for the Netherlands, and the house was taken over by Members of Parliament and the Army and was once more known as Somerset House. The chapel was wrecked. Inigo Jones died there in 1652, and in September 1658 Cromwell lay in state. 'This folly and profusion so far provoked the people that they threw dirt in the night on his escutcheon that was placed over the great gate of Somerset House'. His body was badly embalmed and had to be buried quietly. The official funeral was held a fortnight later. After Richard Cromwell's abdication Parliament decided to sell Somerset House to pay the Army but there were no bidders. In February 1660 the garrison mutinied and surrendered to General Monk.

At the Restoration the house was put in order for Henrietta Maria who went to France the following year to attend her daughter's wedding. While she was away a gallery along the water front was built, probably to the designs of John Webb. After Henrietta Maria's departure from England in 1665 Catherine of Braganza often retired here. On Charles II's death in 1685 she lived here permanently, amusing herself with cards and music. With her encouragement Italian opera was performed for the first time in England. It was mentioned in an advertisement in 1676 that Somerset House was the first English building to have parquet flooring. In 1693 Catherine left to become Regent of Portugal. Successive Queen Consorts took little interest in the house and it was mostly let out as grace and favour residences until 1775. Queen Charlotte considered living there but chose BUCKINGHAM HOUSE instead. The house was then demolished and its site was allocated for government offices, the first large block ever built. William Robinson was asked to draw up designs. Meanwhile Sir William Chambers, the Surveyor General, went to Paris to study new buildings, presumably intending to get the commission for himself. Fortunately for him, Robinson died in 1775 and he was appointed architect. The imposing building he designed is built round a large courtyard with a free-standing north wing. The unembanked river used to lap against the south terrace.

In 1788 the statue of George III was erected in the courtyard (see STATUES). The ornamented Keystones are by Joseph Nollekens, Agostino Carlini, Joseph Ceracchi, John Bacon the Elder, and Nathaniel Smith. In 1796 when Chambers died, the building was still not complete. It was not until 1835 that the east wing was added by Robert Smirke, and the west wing by James Pennethorne.

The Royal Academy was here during 1771–1836, the Royal Society in 1780–1857 and the Society of Antiquaries in 1781–1873. These were allotted the north wing. The Navy had the west wing and part of the river wing, with the Stamp Office occupying the rest. In the remaining parts were many smaller offices, for example the Hackney Coach and Barge Master.

The Exhibition Room at Somerset House, home of the Royal Academy between 1791 and 1836.

In 1836–1973 the offices of the General Register of Births, Deaths and Marriages were there and the Inland Revenue Office occupied most of the building.

The Courtauld Institute of Art, with its fine collection of paintings, its libraries and academic establishment, is expected to move into the renovated Somerset House in 1987 but at present the building is not open to the public.

State Opening of Parliament A ceremonial which has changed little since the 16th century. The monarch rides in the Irish State Coach (*see* ROYAL MEWS) from BUCKINGHAM PALACE to the PALACE OF WESTMINSTER through the Mall and Whitehall. At WESTMINSTER the monarch and accompanying members of the Royal Family are greeted by a salute of guns fired by the King's Troop of the Royal Horse Artillery. The royal party enters the Houses of Parliament by Victoria Tower, and the sovereign enters the Robing Room before proceeding to the House of Lords whose members are present. When the Commons have been summoned by the official known as the Gentleman Usher of the Black Rod, the monarch reads the speech which is, in fact, a summary of the Government's intentions.

STATUES (also busts and medallions) *All the statues listed may be seen out of doors and all, unless otherwise stated, are full length.*

Prince Albert *Steps of Albert Hall, SW7.* A 42 ft-high memorial by Joseph Durham (1863). It was originally intended to commemorate the Great Exhibition. The Prince is surrounded by 'Europe', 'Asia', 'Africa' and 'America'. The statue was paid for from a public fund and was first put up in the gardens of the Royal Horticultural Society. It was moved to its present site in 1899.

Prince Albert *Holborn Circus, EC1.* Equestrian bronze by Charles Bacon erected in 1874. The Prince is in field-marshal's uniform. On either side of the oblong plinth are bronze plaques of Britannia and of Prince Albert; and at either end are bronze figures of Commerce and Peace. Presented to the City of London by Charles Oppenheim, it cost £2,000.

Queen Alexandra *London Hospital, Mile End Road, E1.* Bronze by George Edward Wade (1908). The Queen is depicted wearing coronation robes and with crown and sceptre. According to the inscription she 'introduced to England the Finsen Light cure for lupus and presented the first lamp to this hospital'.

King Alfred *Trinity Church Square, SE1.* 14th-century stone figure removed from the site of WESTMINSTER HALL in 1822 and placed here in 1824. The identification with King Alfred is uncertain.

Queen Anne *Market Hall, Kingston-on-Thames, Surrey.* Gilt-leaden statue by Francis Bird (1706).

Queen Anne *In front of St Paul's Cathedral, EC4.* Marble statue by Richard Belt, 1886, a bad copy of the one by Francis Bird which was erected in 1712 to commemorate the completion of the cathedral and which deteriorated badly over the years. Around the Queen are statues of women who depict England, France, Ireland and North America. Lampoonists made the most of the statue's position and the Queen's love of brandy:

> Brandy Nan, Brandy Nan, you're left in the lurch,
> Your face to the gin shop, your back to the church.

Bird's original sculpture was rescued from a stonemason's yard by Augustus Hare, the writer of guides to London and Rome, and can still be seen in St Leonard's-on-Sea.

Queen Boudicca *Victoria Embankment, SW1.* Bronze group of the Queen and her daughters in a chariot. Made in the 1850s by Thomas Thornycroft though not unveiled until 1902. Prince Albert lent horses as models.

Field-Marshal HRH George, Duke of Cambridge *Whitehall, SW1.* Equestrian bronze of Queen Victoria's cousin who was Commander-in-Chief for many years. By Adrian Jones (1907).

King Charles I *Banqueting House, Whitehall, SW1.* Lead bust by an unknown sculptor over the entrance, placed here in 1950.

Le Sueur's bronze statue of Charles I in Trafalgar Square.

King Charles I   *St Margaret Westminster, SW1.* Lead bust by an unknown sculptor over the east door, placed here in 1949.

King Charles I   *Trafalgar Square, SW1.* Bronze equestrian statue by Hubert Le Sueur (1633) ordered by Lord Weston, High Treasurer, but not erected immediately. In 1649 John Rivett, a brazier, was ordered to destroy it, but buried it in his garden and made a fortune by selling souvenirs allegedly from the metal. In 1660 he refused to give it up to Lord Weston's son and by purchase or gift it came into the hands of Charles II. It was erected on its present site in 1765–7. The pedestal is said to have been designed by Wren and carved by Grinling Gibbons. The Royal Stuart Society lays a wreath here on the anniversary of the King's death, 30 January.

King Charles II   *Soho Square, W1.* Stone statue by Caius Gabriel Cibber. For a time it was in private ownership, the last owner being the librettist W. S. Gilbert, whose widow returned it to Soho Square where it was erected in 1938.

King Charles II   *South Court, Chelsea Hospital, Royal Hospital Road, SW3.* Bronze by Grinling Gibbons (1676) of the King in Roman costume presented to Charles by Tobias Rustat, a member of the Court. It was not erected here until 1692. On Oak Apple Day (29 May) it is wreathed in oak leaves to celebrate King Charles's birthday and to commemorate his escape from the Battle of Worcester when he took refuge in the Boscobel Oak (*see* CEREMONIES).

Queen Charlotte (of Mecklenburg-Strelitz) *Trinity House, Trinity Square, EC3.* Coade Stone medallion by M. J. Baker (1776).

Queen Charlotte (of Mecklenburg-Strelitz) *Somerset House, Strand, WC2.* Stone medallion on the façade. By Joseph Wilton (1780).

Queen Charlotte (of Mecklenburg-Strelitz) *Queen Square, WC1.* A lead statue by an unknown sculptor, believed to represent the consort of George III (*c.* 1780).

King Edward I *National Westminster Bank, 114 High Holborn, WC1.* Elevated stone by Richard Garbe (1902).

King Edward VI *North wing of St Thomas's Hospital, SE1.* Two statues of Henry VIII's only son, who refounded St Thomas's Hospital after its closure during the Dissolution. The bronze by Peter Scheemakers was cast in 1737 and the earlier one in stone was sculpted by Thomas Cartwright in 1681.

King Edward VII *Caxton Hall, SW1.* Terracotta statue on the façade. Queen Victoria stands by him.

King Edward VII *Edward VII Memorial Park, Shadwell, E1.* Bronze medallion by Sir Bertram Mackennal (1922) on the memorial pillar.

King Edward VII *55 Knightsbridge, SW7.* Small stone bust, almost obscured under a second-floor window (1902).

King Edward VII *Mile End Road, E1.* Opposite the London Hospital stands a column supporting a winged angel and bearing a bronze medallion of the King. The column is flanked by fountains and sculptures of Justice and Liberty. The memorial, the work of W. S. Frith, was the gift of the Jews of East London (1911).

King Edward VII *National Westminster Bank, 114 High Holborn, WC1.* Elevated stone by Richard Garbe (1902).

King Edward VII *Temple Bar Memorial, Fleet Street, EC4.* Marble by Sir Joseph Edgar Boehm (1918). Edward faces Queen Victoria.

King Edward VII *Tooting Broadway, SW17.* Bronze statue by L. F. Roselieb (1911).

King Edward VII *University College School, Frognal, NW3.* Stone statue, in a niche above the school doorway (1907).

King Edward VII *Waterloo Place, SW1.* Bronze equestrian statue by Sir Bertram Mackennal (1922).

Queen Elizabeth I *St Dunstan in the West, Fleet Street, EC4.* Stone by William Kerwin (1586) over the vestry porch. The statue originally stood on LUDGATE and was moved to St Dunstan's after the gate's demolition.

King George I *St George's Church, Bloomsbury, WC1.* Figure, placed at the top of the church steeple, representing the King in a toga. William Hicks, brewer, gave the statue for the steeple, built in 1730 by Nicholas Hawksmoor. Horace Walpole satirised the arrangement:

When Henry VIII left the Pope in the lurch,
The Protestants made him head of the church,
But George's good subjects, the Bloomsbury people
Instead of the Church, made him head of the steeple.

King George II   *Golden Square, W1.* This Portland stone figure is attributed to John Van Nost and is supposed to represent George II, the monarch at the time of its erection in the Square in March 1753. It was said to have come from the Duke of Chandos's seat at Canons and to have been bought at the auction there in 1748 by an anonymous bidder, who presented it to the public. Certainly there were several allegorical figures by Van Nost on the roof of Canons before its demolition and this 'George II' may, perhaps, be one of these. Dickens described it in *Nicholas Nickleby* as 'a mournful statue of Portland stone, the guardian genius of a little wilderness of shrubs'.

King George II   *Greenwich Hospital, SE10.* Marble, by J. M. Rysbrack. The marble was found in a French ship, captured in the Mediterranean, and the statue was presented by Sir John Jennings, Prefect of Greenwich Hospital. It was placed on the river side of the hospital in 1735.

King George III   *Cockspur Street, SW1.* Bronze equestrian figure of the King, by Matthew Cotes Wyatt (1836). In 1820 a subscription for the statue was started. On the eve of its unveiling an unspecified 'calamity' causing 'loss and distress' to the artist occurred. After three months it was restored and unveiled, prompting the verse:

Here stands a statue at which critics rail
To point a moral and to point a Tail.

The horse's tail is extended horizontally.

King George III   *Somerset House, Strand, WC2.* Baroque fountain in bronze, including a figure of the King, by John Bacon the Elder (1788). Neptune is represented in the foreground. When Queen Charlotte asked Bacon why he had created such a frightful figure, he replied, 'Art cannot always effect what is ever within reach of Nature, the union of beauty and majesty.'

King George III   *Somerset House, Strand, WC2.* Stone medallion on the façade by Joseph Wilton (1780).

King George III   *Trinity House, EC1.* Medallions on Coade Stone of the King and his wife, by M. J. Baker (1796).

King George IV   *Somerset House, Strand, WC2.* Stone medallion on the façade by Joseph Wilton (1780, when its subject was Prince of Wales).

King George IV   *Trafalgar Square, SW1.* Bronze equestrian statue by Chantrey (1834). Ordered by George IV in 1829 for the top of MARBLE ARCH which then stood in front of BUCKINGHAM PALACE. The King died before the statue was finished and it was finally erected 'temporarily' in Trafalgar Square.

King George V *Old Palace Yard, SW1.* Stone statue by Sir William Reid Dick of the bareheaded King in Garter robes, holding the Sword of State. The plinth was designed by Sir Giles Gilbert Scott. King George VI unveiled the statue in 1947.

King George VI *Carlton House Terrace, SW1.* Stone statue of the King in the uniform of Admiral of the Fleet and Garter robes, by William Macmillan (1955).

King Henry VIII *St Bartholomew's Hospital, EC1.* Stone, by Francis Bird (1702). Henry VIII founded the hospital. The figure stands over the gateway.

King James II *Trafalgar Square, SW1.* Bronze by Grinling Gibbons (and/or his pupils) of the King in Roman dress. It is a companion piece to the statue of Charles II at the ROYAL HOSPITAL, CHELSEA. It stands on the grass in front of the National Gallery, its fourth resting place, having previously stood in two places just off Whitehall and in ST JAMES'S PARK. It was commissioned by Tobias Rustat, Page of the Backstairs, 'a very simple, ignorant but honestly loyal creature'.

Edward Augustus, Duke of Kent *Park Crescent, W1.* Bronze of Queen Victoria's father by S. S. Gahagen (1827). Erected by the charities he had supported.

Queen Mary *Marlborough House, The Mall, SW1.* Bronze medallion by Sir William Reid Dick (1967).

Mary, Queen of Scots *143–144 Fleet Street, EC4.* Stone, placed here in a first floor niche by Sir John Tollemache Sinclair, an admirer (*c.* 1880).

King Richard I *Old Palace Yard, SW1.* Equestrian bronze figure by Carlo Marochetti (1861), a cast of the plaster figure made for the Royal Academy.

Queen Victoria *Broad Walk, Regent's Park, NW1.* Stone bust by unknown artist (1869) on the Parsee Fountain in REGENT'S PARK.

Queen Victoria *Caxton Hall, SW1.* Terracotta, by an unknown artist (1902). A figure of Edward VII stands next to her.

Queen Victoria *Kensington Gardens.* Marble seated statue of the newly crowned Queen by Princess Louise, her daughter (1893). In the Broad Walk near the Round Pond.

Queen Victoria *121 Mount Street, W1.* White marble bust, standing in a niche over the shop entrance. A bust of the Duke of Westminster, who presented both pieces, stands round the corner. They commemorate the Queen's Jubilee (1887).

Queen Victoria *New Bridge Street, EC4.* Bronze figure with sceptre and orb by C. B. Birch (1896).

Queen Victoria *Temple Gardens, Victoria Embankment, EC4.* Marble medallion in the railings of the Gardens by C. H. Mabey (1902) commemorating the Queen's last visit to the City in 1900.

Queen Victoria *Warwick Gardens, W14.* Bronze medallion by F. L. Florence (1904) on a red granite column, formerly on the corner of Kensington High Street and Church Street and moved here in 1934.

The statue of William IV, on its original site in King William Street.

King William III *Bank of England, EC2.* Stone figure by Sir Henry Cheere (1735) in the Princes Street entrance.

King William III *St James's Square, SW1.* Bronze equestrian statue commissioned, probably by CHRIST'S HOSPITAL, from John Bacon the Elder, and executed to his designs by his son, John Bacon the Younger. It was placed in its present position in the square in 1808. The King is portrayed as a Roman General, as he is in Rysbrack's statue of him in Queen Square, Bristol, which seems to have been the principal influence of Bacon's work. Under the horse's hooves is the molehill (in bronze) which caused the King's fatal accident while he was riding at HAMPTON COURT.

King William III *Kensington Palace, W8.* Bronze by Heinrich Baucke (1907). Presented by Kaiser Wilhelm II to his uncle, Edward VII, 'for the British nation'.

King William IV *William Walk, Greenwich, SE10.* Foggit Tor granite by Samuel Nixon, removed to GREENWICH PARK in 1938 from King William Street where it had been erected in 1844.

Stephen *(1097?–1154)*. Grandson of WILLIAM I, the Conqueror. He invaded England, seized the royal treasure, and occupied London. On the death of his uncle, HENRY I, whose only legitimate son had been drowned on his way from Normandy to England, Henry's only daughter, Matilda (widow of the Holy Roman Emperor – hence her title Empress Matilda) also laid claim to the throne. There followed intermittent warfare, a period known as the Anarchy, lasting from 1139–53. The Empress's cause was lost by 1148 when she returned to Normandy. King Stephen was crowned at WESTMINSTER ABBEY on 22 December 1135. He was the first monarch to use the TOWER as a royal residence. He died at Faversham, Kent.

Swans on the Thames   Legend has it that the first swans came to England as a gift to Richard I from Queen Beatrice of Cyprus, and the species known as *Cygnus olor* still haunts the river. Paul Hentzner, who visited England during the reign of Elizabeth I, noted in his journal that many companies of swans frequented the Thames. 'They live', he wrote, 'in great security, nobody daring to molest, much less kill, any of them, under penalty of a large fine'. That was because the swan was, and still is, regarded as a royal bird. The swan was sacred to Apollo and Venus in ancient Greece. Swans have thus survived through the centuries under strong legal protection, and the owning of swans on an English river has always been a privilege. In 1483 anyone who did not own a freehold valued at an annual income of at least 5 marks could not own any swans. In 1496 it was ordained that anyone stealing a swan's egg should be imprisoned for one year and be fined at the monarch's will, and the stealing or snaring of swans was even more severely punished. At the same time it was ordered that on every river in the kingdom all the swans were to be counted, examined and recorded each year. Henry VIII decreed that no one who owned swans could appoint a swanherd without a licence from the royal swanherd, and he instituted the marking of cygnets with nicks on their beaks with the proviso that any bird not so marked became Crown property. Queen Elizabeth supported these injunctions and the *Order of Swannes* of 1570 also laid down that those who erased or counterfeited any owner's marks should be imprisoned for a year.

For some time only those of royal or noble blood were allowed to keep swans, but later the City Livery Companies, among others, were given the concession to do so as a royal gesture towards the encouragement of trade. Eton College was also accorded the privilege. For centuries the Thames swans were regarded, not only as decorative in a majestic way, but as a delicacy at royal feasts, while swan feathers were used for palace upholstery. Their economic value has declined, and it is their decorative effect that is now most valued.

Today on the Thames all the swans belong either to the sovereign or to the Dyers' and the Vintners' Companies. The Queen still employs her Keeper of

Swanherds marking the beaks of swans in 1874, during the annual ceremony known as Swan Upping.

the Swans, a title which has descended from that of the Middle Ages: 'Keeper of the Swans in the Thames from the town of Graveshende to Cicester'. That official still presides over the ceremony of Swan Upping or Swan Hopping, when, assisted by the swanherds of the Dyers' and Vintners', he rounds up the new cygnets each year in late July or early August to mark their beaks – one nick for the Dyers, two for the Vintners', and none for the Queen. A small fleet of boats with banners flying and bearing the Royal Swan Keeper, his assistants and the swanherds of the two City Companies, travels up river to 'up' the birds, sometimes in lively scrimmages, the men all in colourful garments of red, green, blue, white and gold. The voyage concludes with a traditional banquet at a riverside inn when the main course is a dish of swan meat. In 1980 the length of the journey, which once began at Southwark Bridge, was curtailed. It now starts at Sudbury and ends at Pangbourne. In the early 1950s there were almost 1,000 swans on the Thames; but owing to lead poisoning, probably from anglers' weights, the numbers have fallen drastically.

The Tower of London, c. 1500, with London Bridge in the background.

Tower Armouries   *Tower of London, EC3.* While armour has always been kept in the TOWER, the present collection took shape in the reign of Henry VIII, who was personally interested. Later, Charles II had the King's armour concentrated here; but before this the armouries had for some time been a showplace to which the royal nucleus of armour gave a special character, closely associating it with the history of England. The displays consist essentially of armour and weapons of offence. The former covers the development of body armour to the full armour of the 15th century and its later virtual disappearance as a result of the development of gunpowder. The latter are divided into four categories which consist of swords and daggers, weapons relying on percussion, like the club and mace, staff weapons, such as the lance and pike and all forms of projectile, ranging from javelins, slings and bows to firearms.

In the White Tower are found the Sporting Gallery, with weapons used for sport throughout the ages; the Tournament Gallery, displaying jousting

146

and tournament equipment; the Medieval Gallery, which has arms and armour from the Viking period to the end of the 15th century; the 16th-century Gallery, containing the personal armour of Henry VIII and prominent Elizabethans; the 17th-century Gallery, with its Stuart royal armours; and the mortar and cannon rooms, containing a variety of the earlier heavy firearms. The late 17th-century red brick building, known as the New Armouries, provides additional display and contains oriental arms and armour and firearms of foreign countries.

Tower of London   *Tower Hill, EC3.* The most perfect medieval fortress in Britain, begun by William I and added to by successive monarchs until Edward I completed the outer wall, enclosing an area of 18 acres. It has been a palace, prison and place of execution and has housed the royal armouries, the mint, the royal observatory, the royal menagerie, the public records, and still guards the Crown Jewels (*see below*).

Soon after the Battle of Hastings in 1066 William I ordered a temporary fort to be built on a strategic site outside the city wall to awe the people into submission. He later required a stone tower and this was probably designed by Gundulf, a tearful, emotional monk from the Abbey of Bec in Normandy who became Bishop of Rochester and was much respected as a designer of both churches and fortresses. Caen limestone, Kentish ragstone and local mudstone were used in the building.

The walls range from 15 ft thick at the bottom to 11 ft at the top. They are 90 ft high and although the building looks square, in fact the sides vary between 107 ft and 118 ft long. The only entrance to the keep was on the south side, about 15 ft above ground, with a flight of steps which would be removed in times of danger. Inside there were four floors. The ground floor was originally intended as a store but was later used as dungeons. Here is the Little Ease, a dark unventilated cell 4 ft square, where the prisoner could neither stand nor lie down. The first floor was used as the soldiers' and servants' quarters; the second floor contained the banqueting hall, st john's chapel and sleeping accommodation for the nobility; and on the third floor were the royal bedrooms and the council chamber. The only staircase was in the north-east corner. It spiralled in a clockwise direction so defenders could have the advantage of holding their swords in their right hand. From every apartment the garrison could keep watch on the city and surrounding countryside. There were three large fireplaces, two on the first floor and one in the banqueting hall. Water was supplied by three wells. The top three floors each had two garderobes, or latrines, with seats and chutes. When the keep was completed is uncertain – it is not mentioned in the *Domesday* survey carried out in 1086. Some authorities maintain that it was finished in the reign of William Rufus (1087–1100); others in that of Henry I (1100–35). It is more certain that the Chapel of st peter ad vincula was built in Henry I's reign for the use of the Tower's garrison, servants and prisoners.

During Henry II's reign (1154–89) a kitchen, bakery and gaol were built. In 1189 Richard I appointed William of Longchamp, a Norman of humble birth, Chancellor of England, Bishop of Ely and Constable of the Tower in his absence abroad. Longchamp spent enormous sums on fortifying the Tower. A wall was thrown round the keep; the Bell Tower and perhaps the Wardrobe Tower were built, and a ditch was dug on the west and north sides. Longchamp also spent £100 on mangonels, machines for hurling large stones, when he heard that Prince John was plotting to seize the throne. In 1191 Longchamp was besieged in the Tower by the Council, who were jealous of his power, and by John's supporters. After three days he surrendered and was exiled to France, and John took over the kingdom.

During John's reign (1199–1216) the Tower was further strengthened: the Bell Tower seems to have been finished and the northern ditch deepened. In 1215 the Barons seized the Tower in their attempts to force John to accept the Magna Carta. After he had signed it, however, they did not trust him to keep his word and continued to occupy the Tower. When John did break faith they offered the throne to the French Dauphin. Louis arrived in 1216 and held court in the Tower for a year.

During Henry III's reign (1216–72) there was a great spate of building: repairs were carried out on what are referred to as the King's Houses, the first mention of the royal palace south of the White Tower. A new kitchen and great hall were also built at this time; work began on building or rebuilding the inner wall; and a new moat was dug under the expert advice of a Fleming. In 1235 the Holy Roman Emperor gave Henry three leopards, an allusion to the leopards on the Plantagenet coat of arms. Thus the royal menagerie was begun. The animals were open to public viewing and the expression 'going to see the lions' probably dates from this time. On the occasion of Henry's marriage to Eleanor of Provence in 1236 the coronation procession set out from the Tower for the first time.

At the coronation of Edward I the procession set off from the Tower through streets hung with tapestries. The conduits ran with wine and the King flung coins to the crowd. Feasting continued for a fortnight. Between 1275 and 1285 the western inner wall was built between the Bell and Devereux Towers. This included the construction of what later became known as the Beauchamp Tower probably because Thomas, Earl of Warwick, of the Beauchamp family, was held here for a time in the reign of Richard II. The Outer Wall was also built including the Byward and Lion Towers and Traitors' Gate.

In 1278 600 Jews were imprisoned in the sub-crypt of st john's chapel, accused of clipping coins. The next year 267 of them were hanged and the rest banished. In 1300 the royal mint was moved here from Westminster; and in 1303 it was decided that the Crown Jewels should also be kept in the Tower after various valuables had disappeared mysteriously at Westminster. The Abbot of Westminster, 48 monks and 32 other suspects were brought here as prisoners. Miles Podlicote, Keeper of the Royal Palace, was hanged for the theft, but the true culprits were never found. In 1308 several suspects were arrested and tortured, accused of offences ranging from blasphemy to perversion.

During the troubled reign of Edward II the defences were strengthened: two new portcullises and a gate were installed, and five springalds for throwing missiles were set up. Edward's Queen, Isabella, gave birth to Princess Joan in the Tower in 1322. The royal apartments were in such bad repair by this time that the Constable was dismissed for endangering the health of the mother and child. That same year Roger Mortimer, a rebellious Welsh baron, was imprisoned here. He escaped in 1324, aided by his paramour, the Queen. Two years later he and the Queen, at the head of an invading army, seized the Tower, released the prisoners, and gave the keys to the citizens of London. After Edward II was murdered at Berkeley Castle in 1327, Mortimer and Isabella governed, while Edward III, still a minor at the time, was kept a virtual prisoner in the Tower. Before he was 18, however, the new King, with the support of the Barons, had Mortimer arrested and executed, and had his mother banished to Castle Rising in Norfolk.

In 1377 the ten-year-old Richard II rode from the Tower to his coronation clad in white robes, looking 'as beautiful as an angel'. The procession took three hours to reach Westminster, pageants being performed along the way. The conduits and fountains once more flowed with wine. During the Peasants' Revolt in 1381, Richard left the Tower to speak to a rabble gathered at Mile End. While the King was making promises of pardons and emancipation some of the more violent rebels, led by Wat Tyler, managed to break through the open gate to the Tower. Once inside they ransacked the kitchens, bedchambers and armoury. They broke down the door to the Queen Mother's private apartments, seized and mockingly kissed her, and destroyed her furniture and wall hangings. The Queen herself, aided by her pages, escaped, but the King's ministers did not. Four of them were dragged from the altar to Tower Hill and beheaded.

Five years later Tower Hill was the scene of the first of many official executions when Richard II's tutor, Sir Simon de Burley, was beheaded. Richard had displayed great courage and an aptitude for statesmanship in the early years of his reign, but after the death of his wife and most of his close friends his strength and powers of judgement began to fail. In 1399, at the age of 32, he was forced to abdicate in favour of his cousin, Henry Bolingbroke, and was kept prisoner in the Tower.

The young Prince James of Scotland was also imprisoned here in 1406, having been captured when on his way to France to be educated. His father died when he heard the news and the Prince became King. He lived in the Tower for two years and was then moved to Nottingham where he was kept for 16 years before his ransom was paid.

Henry V's coronation procession set off from the Tower in 1413. Even though it was April there was a snowstorm, which was taken as a sign that the King 'had put off the Winter of his Youth'. Soon afterwards the persecution of the Lollards began and many were imprisoned, including Sir John Oldcastle, Shakespeare's Falstaff who had been the King's closest friend while he was still a prince. Oldcastle, under sentence of death, escaped in 1414, probably with the King's help. He was subsequently recaptured and found guilty of heresy and treachery; after being hanged in St Giles's Fields, his body was burned. Captives brought here after the Battle of Agincourt in 1415 included Charles, Duke of Orléans, the French King's nephew.

In 1446, John Holland, Duke of Exeter, held the post of Constable of the Tower and introduced the rack, thenceforth known as the Duke of Exeter's daughter. Edward IV was received ceremoniously at the Tower gates in 1461, having defeated Henry VI at the Battle of Towton, and was escorted to the royal palace. Three months later his coronation took place. In 1464, however, Henry was captured at Clitheroe, Lancashire. He was brought to London and made to sit on a sickly horse with his legs tied to the stirrups. A straw hat was put on his head and a placard on his back, and he was led into the Tower. He was imprisoned in the Wakefield Tower and had with him a

The Tower Liberties in 1597, when they were restricted to an area within the walls and the land on Tower Hill.

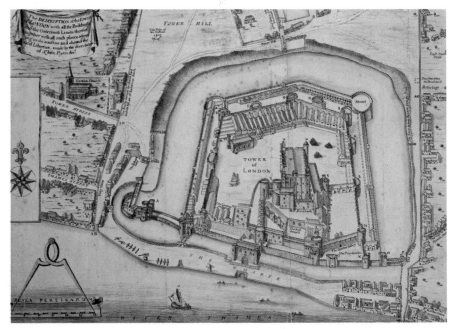

Bible, breviary, a pet dog and a pet sparrow. He told the chaplain, 'I do not mind, so long as I can have the Sacrament. I am not worried about the loss of my earthly kingdom.' After six years of imprisonment he was rescued from his prison by Warwick, the King Maker, supported by the Archbishop of York and Bishop Wainfleet, and proclaimed King at Westminster. Recaptured at the Battle of Tewkesbury, he was returned to the Tower; and in May 1471 is believed to have been murdered at his prayers in the Wakefield Tower. Edward IV announced that he had died of pure displeasure and melancholy. Every year, on the anniversary of his death, the institutions which he founded remember him, Eton College by laying lilies at the place of his death, and King's College Cambridge white roses.

During Edward's reign the Tower became the centre of a gay and relatively informal court. Though every royal activity was precisely ordered there were many games, picnics and competitions on the Tower lawns. The handsome and sensual king was popular with the citizens of London in the early years of his reign but later his increasing debaucheries turned them against him. In 1478 his brother, the Duke of Clarence, was arrested for plotting against him. He was found guilty and died, under mysterious circumstances, in the Tower. Upon Edward's death in 1483, Richard of Gloucester took charge of the boy king Edward V and brought him to London, appointing himself Protector. According to Sir Thomas More, the Protector had Lord Hastings immediately executed for defending Queen Elizabeth Woodville and Jane Shore, the late King's mistress, against Richard's accusation of sorcery. The Queen, who had taken sanctuary with her children at Westminster, was persuaded to part with her younger son to keep his brother company in the Tower. Richard, declaring the children illegitimate, left the Tower by river for his own coronation at Westminster. The next month the two princes were found dead in the Garden Tower, thereafter known as the Bloody Tower. It is thought they were smothered by two men named Green and Forest on the orders of Sir James Tyrrell, Master of the Horse. Their bodies were said to have first been buried in the Wakefield Tower and later reburied by a priest in consecrated ground.

In 1485, Henry, Earl of Richmond, ascended to the throne after the Battle of Bosworth Field. At his coronation Henry VII was attended by the newly formed YEOMEN OF THE GUARD. Soon afterwards, to show the unity of the factions which had fought each other during the Wars of the Roses, representatives from York and Lancaster rode, two on a horse, through the City in procession from the Tower. As a pledge to the country that the rivalry between the two families was truly over, Henry married Elizabeth of York, daughter of Edward IV, in 1486. In 1501 Catharine of Aragon stayed at the Tower before her marriage to Prince Arthur, Henry VII's elder son, and was entertained with feasts and tournaments. Two years later Prince Arthur's mother, Queen Elizabeth of York, gave birth to a daughter and died nine days later. She lay in state for three days in ST JOHN'S CHAPEL before her

151

funeral procession set out for WESTMINSTER ABBEY. 'The body was put in a carriage covered with black velvet with a cross of white cloth of gold . . . and an image exactly representing the Queen was placed in a chair above in her rich robes of state . . . and at every end of the chair knelt a gentlewoman usher by the coffin which was in this manner drawn by six horses trapped in black velvet.'

In 1509 the joint coronation procession of Henry VIII and Catharine of Aragon was an occasion of great splendour. Following precedent, Henry created 24 new Knights of the Bath. The streets were decorated with tapestries, the goldsmiths' houses in Cheapside were hung with cloth of gold, and pageants were performed along the route. Soon afterwards Empson and Dudley, Henry VII's despised tax collectors, were sent to the Tower and the following year executed on Tower Hill. The chapel of ST PETER AD VINCULA was destroyed by fire in 1512, and rebuilt three years later. During Henry's reign part of the royal palace was also rebuilt and the half-timbered houses which still survive on Tower Green were constructed. These included the Lieutenant's Lodgings, which have been known since about 1880 as the Queen's House.

The palace was redecorated for the coronation of Henry VIII's second wife, Anne Boleyn, in 1533 and for a fortnight there were great festivities. On the day of the coronation she set out in a litter decked in damask, accompanied by the nobles of the land. She wore a robe of crimson brocade covered with precious stones, pearls and diamonds round her neck, and a coronet of rubies. However, she was coldly received by the people, who were still loyal to Henry's first wife, Catharine.

Although a great number of prisoners had been detained in the Tower since its construction five centuries earlier, it was not until the Reformation brought Henry VIII's victims to the Tower that harsh treatment of prisoners became almost normal policy. Two of the first victims were Thomas More and John Fisher, who were imprisoned in the Bell Tower for refusing to take the Oath of Supremacy. More was at first allowed writing materials, but later these were taken away from him. By 1535 John Fisher was so weak he had to be carried to the scaffold. After praying, he said that he forgave both the executioner and the King. A fortnight later More was told he was to be executed that day, but the traitor's fate of being drawn and quartered was commuted to beheading. On this he commented, 'God forbid the king shall use any more such mercy on any of my friends.' More asked for help to mount the scaffold, 'I pray you, Mr Lieutenant, to see me safe up and for my coming down let me make shift for myself.' He prayed and at the last moment moved his beard from the block, saying, 'Pity that should be cut that has not committed treason.'

The next year Anne Boleyn was brought to the Tower accused of adultery with her brother, Lord Rochford, one of the court musicians, Mark Smeaton, and three courtiers. All were found guilty and were executed. Anne herself was tried in the Great Hall of the palace by 26 peers presided over by her uncle, the Duke of Norfolk. He wept as he pronounced the sentence of death. Anne asked to be executed with a sword instead of an axe and an executioner expert in the art was brought over from France. Three years to the day after her coronation she was led to the scaffold on Tower Green. She said, 'I am not here to preach to you but to die. Pray for the King, for he is a good man and has treated me as good could be. I do not accuse anyone of causing my death, neither the judges nor anyone else for I am condemned by the law of the land and die willingly.' She knelt to pray and was blindfolded. The executioner crept up to her, snatched out the sword from under a pile of straw and cut off her head. Her body was thrown into an old arrow chest and buried in ST PETER AD VINCULA.

In 1542 the King's fifth wife, Catherine Howard, was also brought to the Tower, accused of infidelity. As she passed under London Bridge she saw the heads of her lovers, Culpepper and Dereham, on the spikes. On 12 February she was told she was to die the next day and coolly asked for the block to be brought to her so that she could practise putting her head on it. On the scaffold she said, 'If I had married the man I loved instead of being dazzled with ambition all would have been well. I die a Queen but I would rather have died the wife of Culpepper.' Afterwards her body – like those of her predecessor, Anne Boleyn, and of all the other five people known to have been executed on Tower Green – was buried in the Chapel of ST PETER AD VINCULA. In 1547 the Duke of Norfolk and his son, the Earl of Surrey, were accused of treason and imprisoned. Surrey was beheaded on Tower Hill in January. But on the eve of the day set for his father's execution the King died and Norfolk remained a prisoner throughout the reign of Henry's son, Edward VI.

Edward was nine years old at the time of his father's death and, according to custom, was taken to live in the royal apartments of the Tower until the day of his coronation. His uncle, the Duke of Somerset, became Lord Protector. The Duke of Somerset, however, did not live long to enjoy his new position of power. In 1551 he was imprisoned for plotting to overthrow John Dudley, Duke of Northumberland, his successor as Lord Protector. The next year he was beheaded on Tower Hill surrounded by a thousand soldiers to prevent a rescue attempt. In 1553, after six years of rule, young Edward VI became seriously ill. The Duke of Northumberland, determined to retain his power, arranged for his son, Lord Guildford Dudley, to marry the King's cousin Lady Jane Grey. He then persuaded the dying King to nominate Lady Jane as his successor in place of his elder half-sister, Princess Mary, daughter of Henry VIII by his first wife, Catharine of Aragon. Most Londoners, however, supported the claims of Princess Mary, and eventually the Tower was deserted except for the Northumberland family. Shortly after Lady Jane's arrival at the Tower, the Duke was arrested and imprisoned; he was later executed on Tower Hill.

Mary entered London in triumph accompanied by her sister, Elizabeth. She arrived at the Tower to take part in the festivities that preceded her coronation. The usual pageants were performed on the route and a Dutch acrobat bravely balanced on the top of the spire of St Paul's. In November Lady Jane Grey and her husband, Lord Guildford Dudley, were tried at Guildhall and found guilty of treason; but they were allowed to live separately in comparative comfort in the Tower.

In January 1554, however, Mary announced that she would marry Philip of Spain. Rebellions broke out all over the country, one in Leicester led by the Duke of Suffolk, another in Devon, and a third in Kent, led by Thomas Wyatt. Wyatt reached London and created a great deal of panic before he was arrested and brought to the Tower. Under torture he incriminated Princess Elizabeth and orders for her arrest were made. On 12 February Lady Jane Grey and Guildford Dudley were executed, as they were now too dangerous to keep alive. Dudley asked to say farewell to Jane but she refused him, saying their separation would be temporary. He was taken out to Tower Hill early in the morning, and from the window Jane saw his headless body being brought back in a cart. She herself was executed in the relative privacy of Tower Green. She wore a simple black gown and carried a prayer book in which she had written. 'As the preacher sayeth, there is a time to be born and a time to die.' She spoke briefly, admitting she had been the unwilling tool of others, but accepted the justice of her sentence.

On 18 March Princess Elizabeth was brought through the Traitors' Gate and conducted to the Bell Tower. Mass was celebrated in her cell every day, but she refused to be converted to Roman Catholicism. The close confinement affected her health and she was allowed to walk in the Lieutenant's garden and on the part of the ramparts between the Bell and Beauchamp Towers, which is still known as Princess Elizabeth's Walk. At the end of the month, when order had been restored, Mary was betrothed by proxy in ST JOHN'S CHAPEL to Philip of Spain. On 19 May Princess Elizabeth was released, as no further evidence of her complicity in the plots could be discovered. Mary and Philip rode from Whitehall to the Tower in August 1555, to dispel the rumour that Mary had died of dropsy.

When Mary did die in 1558 the new Queen, Elizabeth, rode from Hatfield to the Tower. When she arrived she patted the earth and said, 'Some have fallen from being princes of this land to be prisoners in this place. I am raised from being prisoner in this place to be the prince of the land.' She stayed for a week while she appointed her ministers; and returned in January 1559, three days before her coronation. The day before her coronation she rode from the Tower to Whitehall seated in a golden chariot, wearing a blue velvet robe covered in precious stones. The streets were decorated with triumphal archways, and tableaux were performed at the street corners.

From 1565 to 1567 Lady Lennox was imprisoned for arranging the marriage of her son, Lord Darnley, to Mary Queen of Scots without

Elizabeth's consent. She was released just after Darnley's murder, but again imprisoned between 1574 and 1577 for allowing her younger son to marry without the Queen's consent. In prison she wove some lace from the grey hairs on her head and sent it to Mary Queen of Scots as a token of her sympathy. Until Mary's execution in the great hall of Fotheringay Castle in 1587 there were almost as many of her supporters being held in the Tower as there were Jesuit prisoners. In 1585 John Ballard, a Jesuit priest, and Anthony Babington conceived a plan for a general uprising of Catholics, the murder of Queen Elizabeth, and the accession of Mary to the English throne. They were discovered, tried, and condemned to traitors' deaths. The 12 other conspirators were also executed. Mary's own complicity was discovered and this hastened her own execution. In 1592 Sir Walter Ralegh was briefly imprisoned for seducing Elizabeth Throgmorton, one of the Queen's ladies-in-waiting. Robert Devereux, Earl of Essex, was imprisoned after his ineffectual rebellion in 1601. He was tried at Westminster and executed six days later on Tower Green rather than on Tower Hill, a privilege granted him by the Queen. His body was buried in the chapel of ST PETER AD VINCULA.

King James I, son of Mary Queen of Scots, who succeeded to the throne at the death of Queen Elizabeth, was the last monarch to occupy the Tower as a palace. He was very interested in the royal menagerie, an interest which mainly took the form of staging trial-of-strength spectacles. To observe the

Robert Devereux, Earl of Essex (left), held in the Tower before his execution, and Sir Walter Ralegh, a prisoner for many years.

lions fighting the mastiffs, James had a viewing gallery built above the Lion Tower. Animal fights were staged regularly until 1609 when one of the Tower bears killed a small child. The King, hoping for a grand battle, ordered the culprit to be forced into the lions' den, but the lions only cowered in the corners; the bear was finally given to the dogs to be baited to death. At this time the inventory of the zoo was recorded as 11 lions, two leopards, three eagles, two owls, two mountain cats, and a jackal.

In 1603 Sir Walter Ralegh was imprisoned again, this time for plotting to place on the throne Arabella Stuart. He was found guilty and sentenced to death but was reprieved on the eve of his execution. He lived in the Tower fairly comfortably during his long imprisonment. He was allotted the upper floors of the Bloody Tower, and his wife and son lived with him. He was often visited by Henry, Prince of Wales, who encouraged him to write his *History of the World* and to carry out scientific experiments in a makeshift laboratory.

In 1605 Guy Fawkes and some of his accomplices were arrested after being caught in their attempt to blow up the Houses of Parliament and were taken to the Lieutenant's Lodgings to be interrogated. The King himself wrote out the questions he wanted answered, but they refused to say anything. They were taken to the dungeons and the next year Fawkes, Winter, Rookwood and Keyes were executed in Palace Yard, Westminster.

In 1617 King James granted permission for Sir Walter Ralegh to leave the Tower to conduct an expedition to South America where he believed they would find rich deposits of gold. The expedition, however, was a disaster and when they returned to England the next year Ralegh was again arrested and taken to the Tower. No new trial was held as he had already been sentenced to death for treason years before. He was executed in Palace Yard, Westminster.

In 1629 nine Members of Parliament, including Sir John Eliot, were imprisoned for their harsh attacks on the King's favourite, the Duke of Buckingham. The conditions under which Eliot was kept were so squalid that he contracted tuberculosis and died three years later. Eliot's son asked permission of King Charles to remove his father's body for burial in the Cornish churchyard where his ancestors lay, but this was denied.

The split between the King and Parliament was becoming deeper. In 1641 Thomas Wentworth, Earl of Strafford, the King's principal adviser, and Archbishop Laud were impeached by Parliament and sent to the Tower. Strafford was found guilty of high treason and, with regret, Charles was forced to sign his death warrant. On the way to his execution Strafford saw Archbishop Laud standing at the window and received his blessing. Laud was afterwards executed on Tower Hill. In the face of a civil war Charles determined to retain control of the Tower. He dismissed the Constable and appointed in his place Colonel Thomas Lunsford, a desperately patriotic man who could be depended upon to defend the Tower to the death. He was

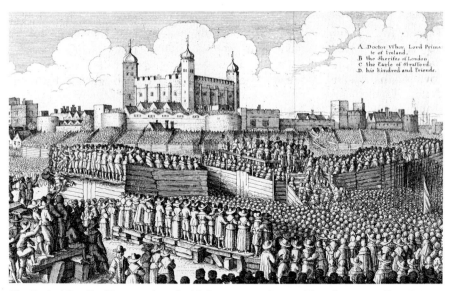

The Earl of Strafford's execution, for high treason, witnessed by a large crowd on Tower Hill in 1641.

condemned by the House of Commons as a dangerous man, and among the citizens of London was rumoured to be a cannibal. At length Charles agreed to remove him, and replaced him with Sir John Byron.

On 10 January 1642, after a disastrous attempt to arrest five of his leading opponents in Parliament, Charles fled London, leaving Byron to defend the Tower. Philip Skippon, commander of the Trained Bands, was ordered by the Commons to blockade the Tower and the Constable was eventually forced to surrender control of it. At Stow-on-the-Wold, on 26 March 1646, the commander of the King's last army surrendered to Cromwell's men and Parliament's control over London and the Tower was confirmed. Early the next year Charles was delivered back from Scotland by his enemies and arrested. In 1649 he was tried by a parliamentary high court, found guilty of treason, and executed at Whitehall. After the war the buildings were neglected and in 1672–4 the Jewel House and Coldharbour Gate were demolished. Most of the Crown Jewels were seized.

With the restoration of the monarchy in 1660 several of the regicides were imprisoned before being executed. Charles II returned from exile on the Continent and spent the eve of his coronation in the Tower in April 1661. Pepys found it 'impossible to relate the glory' of the following day. A new collection of Crown Jewels was made for the occasion, but the monks of Westminster produced the ampulla, the anointing spoon and Queen Elizabeth's salt cellar which they had hidden during the Commonwealth. An attempt was made to steal these jewels by Colonel Blood, an Irishman.

Special stands were erected for witnessing the beheading of the Jacobite rebel Lords, Balmarino and Kilmarnock, on Tower Hill in 1746.

Blood disguised himself as a clergyman to gain the confidence of the Jewel House Keeper, and the unsuspecting man invited Blood and his supposedly wealthy nephew to supper, hoping that the nephew would take a fancy to his daughter. During the evening the Keeper sold a pair of pistols they affected to admire, thus leaving himself unarmed. The next morning Blood arrived with some friends to view the jewels. Once inside the Jewel House they gagged and bound the Keeper. However, they were disturbed. One of Blood's accomplices stuffed the orb down his breeches and ran off but was caught on Tower Wharf. Another grabbed the sceptre and escaped from the Tower but was caught when he was knocked off his horse by a barber's pole. Blood flattened the crown with a mallet and placed it in a bag, but he too was caught by one of the Tower's garrison. He refused to speak to anyone but the King and was taken to Whitehall. Charles was much taken with his charm and impudence and not only pardoned him but gave him estates in Ireland and a pension of £500 a year. His accomplices were also released. The Keeper's daughter married Captain Beckman who had captured Blood.

At the coronation of James II the ceremony of the procession from the Tower was abandoned. In 1685 James, Duke of Monmouth, was imprisoned after the Battle of Sedgemoor. He was executed on Tower Hill on 15 July. The axe was blunt and after the first blow he got up and rebuked the executioner, John Ketch. After two more attempts Ketch had to resort to a knife. Between

1688 and 1692 the Grand Storehouse was built, possibly to the designs of Wren who also probably supervised the alterations to the windows of the White Tower.

By 1822 the royal menagerie had dwindled to 'a grizzly bear, an elephant and one or two birds'. However, in that year Alfred Copps was appointed as the Royal Keeper. He had an excellent knowledge of animal behaviour and in a short time assembled 59 different species. Unfortunately, in 1835 one of his lions attacked some members of the garrison, and the animals were moved to the Zoological Gardens. Only the ravens still remain at the Tower.

The moat was drained in the 1840s when Waterloo Barracks were built on the site of the old armouries. On 24 January 1885 Fenians planted a bomb on the second floor of the White Tower. The explosion occurred almost simultaneously with others in the Houses of Parliament and WESTMINSTER HALL. Fire broke out but the Tower's fire brigade soon brought the flames under control and no one was killed, though several people were seriously injured.

During the 1st World War Sir Roger Casement was imprisoned in St Thomas' Tower. He was found guilty of planning the Easter Rising with German help, and was hanged at Pentonville. Eleven spies were shot in the outer ward by the Martin Tower. In the 2nd World War Rudolf Hess was imprisoned in the Lieutenant's House for four days. Two bombs fell near the

The view of Tower Hill showing the repaired White Tower as it appeared in 1841.

White Tower, killing five people and exposing an underground tunnel thought to have been built in Charles II's reign.

The ancient Ceremony of the Keys still takes place at the Tower every night at ten o'clock when the Chief Yeoman Warder, in long red cloak and Tudor bonnet, carrying a lantern, marches out toward the Byward Tower with the keys of the fortress in his hand, and calls out: 'An escort for the Keys.' Four armed soldiers of the garrison fall into step beside him, and march through the gates of the Byward Tower and over the causeway to the entrance gate beyond the Middle Tower. The gate is locked; the escort marches back in the darkness toward the towers of the outer ward; the gates of the Byward Tower are locked. As the Chief Yeoman Warder and his escort approach the Bloody Tower, the sentry on guard comes forward with the challenge:

'Halt, who goes there?'

The Chief Yeoman Warder replies, 'The Keys.'

'Whose Keys?'

'Queen Elizabeth's keys.'

The sentry presents arms, the Chief Yeoman Warder removes his bonnet and calls out, 'God preserve Queen Elizabeth!'

The whole guard replies, 'Amen!'

Crown Jewels   The regalia, the ornaments of the sovereigns of England, date for the most part from the 17th century. After the execution of Charles I in 1649 the Parliamentary party ordered the destruction of the existing crowns and sceptres, and a new set was made for the coronation of Charles II in 1661. As well as these, a few individual pieces which appear to go back to the Middle Ages, or before, are preserved and displayed in the Tower.

One of the most important pledges William the Conqueror made to the citizens of London was to preserve the constitution of the saint-king Edward the Confessor. It is probable that by the end of the 13th century certain ancient robes and ornaments, taken from Edward's body when Henry III transferred it to a new shrine, were actually placed upon the king at his coronation. Even when the actual crown was destroyed by the Parliamentary Commissioners the name and tradition survived, and the name of St Edward's Crown is still given to the coronation crown of the kings of England.

The Ampulla and Spoon, the oldest objects among the regalia, are not actually royal ornaments, and this is probably why they survived the Commonwealth when all things 'royal' were destroyed. They are, however, connected with the most solemn moment of the coronation ceremony, when the holy oil is poured from the beak of the golden eagle into the spoon and is applied by the officiating bishop to the new sovereign's head, breast and palms. The Spoon probably dates from the late 12th century, and the Ampulla was probably first used at the coronation of Henry IV in 1399.

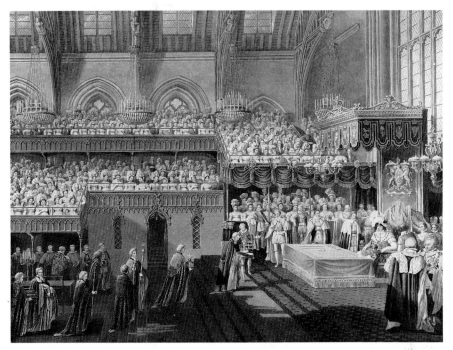

The coronation regalia being paraded through Westminster Hall before the coronation of George IV in 1821.

St Edward's Crown, the name given to the crown made for Charles II, is still used for the coronation ceremony. It is likely that it was made from one of the old crowns broken up during the Commonwealth. Because of its great weight – nearly 5 lb – it is worn only for the ceremony of coronation, and is afterwards changed for the lighter Crown of State.

This crown was made for the coronation of Queen Victoria and was used by her and by Edward VII. It has been used at every coronation since then and is worn when the sovereign appears in state, as at the STATE OPENING OF PARLIAMENT. The frame, remade for the coronation of George VI, is of fine gold, and thickly set with over 3,000 precious stones, mainly diamonds and pearls. The largest is the irregular ruby given to the Black Prince in the 14th century.

As well as being anointed and crowned, the monarch is invested with sword and spurs, the attributes of knighthood. The Golden Spurs, made for the coronation of Charles II, are not actually buckled on, but applied for a moment to the monarch's heels and then placed upon the altar. The Sword, however, is still girt about the monarch, then offered on the altar by the monarch. It is then 'redeemed' for a fee and carried before the Sovereign for the rest of the ceremony.

A new State Crown was made for the coronation of Queen Victoria in 1838, to replace the far heavier St Edward's Crown used since the time of Charles II.

The Jewelled Sword now used was originally made for the coronation of George IV, and has been so used since the coronation of Edward VII. Clusters of precious stones are set into the hilt and scabbard, making up a pattern that incorporates the national emblems of England, Scotland and Ireland.

The Bracelets, also made for the coronation of Charles II, were not worn but carried at later coronations, their place being now taken by the stole that forms part of the Coronation Robes. They are decorated with the fleur-de-lis, a reminder that, until the early 19th century, the royal title was 'King of England, Scotland, France and Ireland'. The new Bracelets were presented by the Commonwealth countries and were first used for the coronation of Queen Elizabeth in 1953.

The officiating bishop emphasises the symbolism of the Orb, a globe of the world dominated by the emblem of Christianity, when he presents it to the Sovereign, who then gives it back so as to leave his or her hands free for the Ring and the two Sceptres.

The 'ring of kingly dignity' is a sapphire with the Cross of St George set on it in rubies. The ring made for William IV was not used by Queen Victoria, who had a smaller one made for her, but has been used by all her successors.

The Sceptre with the Cross, symbolic of the king's role as ruler of his people, is described, at its delivery, as the 'Ensign of Kingly Power and Justice'. The sovereign's paternal function as guardian and guide is symbolized by the Rod with the Dove, the dove suggesting divine inspiration. In the present century the great diamond, weighing 530 carats, has been added to the Sceptre with the Cross; it was the largest of the four 'Stars of Africa' presented by the Union of South Africa to Edward VII. The second of these stones is in the State Crown and the other two, previously in the Crown of Queen Mary, are now in the Crown of the Queen Consort.

St Edward's Staff is another sceptre, traditionally carried in the coronation procession but not used in the actual ceremony. It is longer than the others, and its golden shaft ends in a steel ferrule. The original Staff was probably used as a walking stick.

The Great Sword of State, representing the king's own personal sword, is of the late 17th century, decorated with a lion and unicorn supporting the Royal Arms. During the coronation ceremony this sword is actually delivered to the Sovereign; but there are three others carried before him in token of his power. The custom of bearing these swords, named the Swords of Justice, can be traced as far back as 1189, when Richard I was crowned. The three swords stood for Mercy, Justice and the championship of the Church.

A Victorian Beefeater showing children how traitors were beheaded in the Tower.

The oldest crown preserved at the TOWER is one worn by Mary of Modena, the second wife of James II, at her coronation in 1685. It has a cap of purple velvet and ermine, surrounded by a gold band set with diamonds and pearls. Another small crown is also known as Mary of Modena's, but was most probably made for the coronation of Queen Anne in 1702. The Prince of Wales's crown was probably made for Frederick Louis, son of George II. Queen Victoria had a small diamond crown made, and is shown wearing it in her statue at Windsor. It was preserved for a long time at BUCKINGHAM PALACE, but is now exhibited at the TOWER. Conspicuous in the crown made for the coronation of George VI and Queen Elizabeth in 1937 is the famous Indian diamond known as the Koh-i-Noor. It has been worn by all the queens of England since Queen Victoria, and is traditionally supposed to bring good luck to the woman who wears it but ill-luck to the man.

When a king and queen are crowned together, the queen's coronation ornaments are normally those of a consort, but in 1689 Mary II was invested as a Queen Regnant. Daughter of the deposed James II, she was heiress to the throne in her own right, but her husband, William of Orange, insisted that he be crowned on terms of absolute equality with her as King William III.

Most of the silver-gilt plate preserved among the Crown Jewels was made at the Restoration. One piece, however, the great cylindrical 'salt', bears a hallmark for the year 1572–3. It is set with rubies, sapphires, emeralds and amethysts and was popularly supposed to be a model of the White Tower, although it bears no real resemblance to it. It was a Restoration gift to Charles II from the city of Exeter. The city of Plymouth presented a silver-gilt wine fountain. The font and basin, first used for the christening of James, known later as the Old Pretender, was made in 1600. They were subsequently used for the christenings of George IV, William IV, and the other children of George III. The great alms dish used at the ceremony of the Royal Maundy (*see* CEREMONIES) is another piece of Restoration plate, though it has subsequently been inscribed with the arms of William and Mary. Of the 13 Royal Maces still in existence, ten are at the TOWER, two at the House of Lords and one at the House of Commons. Most of these are composites, made from parts of other maces, probably numbering 30 in all, which were made during the period 1660 to 1695.

The TOWER, which includes the TOWER ARMOURIES, the Crown Jewels and ST JOHN'S CHAPEL, is open from 0930 to 1700 from Monday to Saturday from March to October and from 0930 to 1600 from Monday to Saturday from November to February. From March to October the Tower is also open on Sundays, from 1400 to 1700. Services are held on Sundays in ST PETER AD VINCULA at 0915 and 1100.

UNDERGROUND *Tower Hill* BUS ROUTES *15, 42, 47A, 56, 78; with short walk from Aldgate 5, 10, 15A, 22A, 25, 40, 44, 67, 225, 253.*

Horse Guards Parade, the scene of Trooping the Colour, in 1753, shortly after the completion of William Kent's new building.

Trooping the Colour A ceremony which takes place annually on the monarch's official birthday. First performed in 1755, and regularly since 1805, it is commemorative of the ancient military practice of parading flags and banners in front of troops so that they were made familiar with the colours – later emblems of regimental honour – around which they were to rally in the chaos of battle. The ceremony takes place on HORSE GUARDS PARADE; and the colours trooped are those of a battalion of one of the five regiments of Foot Guards (*see* HOUSEHOLD DIVISION). The Monarch takes the salute wearing the uniform of whichever Guards regiment is trooping. Queen Elizabeth II wears a specially designed tricorn hat and for the past 18 years has ridden side-saddle. But, it was announced in December 1986, in future she will inspect the parade from her coach. The ceremony takes place at 1100 on the Saturday nearest to 11 June.

Victoria, Queen *(1819–1901)*. Daughter of the Duke of Kent, GEORGE III's third son, she was born, baptised and brought up at KENSINGTON PALACE. It was there, on the death of her uncle WILLIAM IV, that she was roused from bed at 6 o'clock in the morning to be told by the Archbishop of Canterbury and the Lord Chamberlain that she was Queen. Within three weeks she had moved into BUCKINGHAM PALACE, the first sovereign to live there. She and PRINCE ALBERT of Saxe-Coburg-Gotha were married in the CHAPEL ROYAL, ST JAMES'S PALACE, in 1840. In the same year, and again in 1842 and 1849, attempts were made on her life in Constitution Hill. Her Golden Jubilee in 1887 was celebrated with a procession through London and a service of

thanksgiving in WESTMINSTER ABBEY. To mark her Diamond Jubilee she presented the ROYAL BOTANIC GARDENS at Kew to the nation. A quarter of a million pounds had been spent on decking the streets of London for the procession for the short service of thanksgiving on the steps of St Paul's. The Queen died at Osborne, her home on the Isle of Wight.

Victoria and Albert Museum   *Cromwell Road, SW7*. A museum of fine and applied art of all countries, styles and periods. Its origins lie with the Museum of Manufactures, which had opened at MARLBOROUGH HOUSE in September 1852 (and became known as the Museum of Ornamental Art in 1853) and with the School of Design, a forerunner of the Royal College of Art, which had collected at SOMERSET HOUSE a number of plaster casts, models, engravings and examples of contemporary manufacture for study by its students. In 1857 both the School and the Museum were removed to South Kensington where, with the help of funds voted by Parliament, and with the active encouragement of Prince Albert, the Royal Commissioners for the Great Exhibition of 1851 had bought over 80 acres of land to further the aims of the Exhibition and to extend 'the influence of Science and Art upon Productive Industry' by building various museums, concert halls, colleges, schools and premises for learned societies.

Queen Victoria and various members of her family in a painting commemorating her Golden Jubilee in 1877.

Its first director was Sir Henry Cole, whose declared policy was 'to assemble a splendid collection of objects representing the application of Fine Art to manufactures'. With this end in view he had already arranged for the purchase of the Bandinel Collection of Pottery and Porcelain, part of the Bernal Collection of glass, plate and china, enamels, armour, medals, jewellery, ivories and furniture, as well as objects from the Paris Exhibition of 1856.

Picture galleries and display areas, as well as refreshment rooms, lecture rooms, courts, quadrangles and staircases, were subsequently added, and the Museum's acquisitions continued to grow with increasing disregard to its original purpose. 'Future purchases should be confined to objects wherein Fine Art is supplied to some purpose of utility,' the Museum was instructed in 1863, 'and works of Fine Art not so only be permitted as exceptions and so far as they may tend directly to improve Art applied to objects of utility'. But, as Sir Roy Strong, the Museum's director, has since observed, the advice was 'totally ignored . . . the pull between a practical museum of the arts of manufacture and design, with its aim to educate the masses, as against a museum of masterpieces, the resort of antiquarians and connoisseurs, has never been resolved to this day. . . . Any visitor to the Victoria and Albert Museum today is likely to be bemused as to what exactly is the central thread that animates these discrepant if marvellous collections. The answer is that there is none. For over a century the Museum has proved an extremely capacious handbag.' Into this handbag were deposited, amongst numerous other items, the Tapestry Cartoons of Raphael which had been purchased for the Royal Collection by King Charles I when he was Prince of Wales in 1623 and which, lent by Queen Victoria, are still lent by the Queen today; fine collections of British watercolours and 18th-century French paintings; numerous canvases by William Dyce and John Constable; and the contents of the India Museum, transferred from the India Office. In 1884 the National Art Library was opened in the Museum.

By then it had been realised that the various structures in which all these treasures were congested were quite inadequate for their purpose. And at last, in 1890, the Chancellor of the Exchequer authorised a competition for a new design. Eight architects, each to be paid 300 guineas, were invited to enter the competition which was won, on the recommendation of Alfred Waterhouse (whose Natural History Museum had already appeared nearby), by Aston Webb. It was not until 1899, however, that the foundation stone was laid by the Queen who, in this last important public engagement of her reign, directed that the Museum should be given its present name; and it was not until 1909 that the new building, which had cost over £600,000 including its fittings and furniture, was officially opened by King Edward VII. The terracotta brick is surmounted by a central tower 185 ft high, shaped at the top like an imperial crown. Above the ornate main entrance are statues of Queen Victoria and Prince Albert by Alfred Drury and, on either side of them, statues by W. Goscombe John of Edward VII and Queen Alexandra who, to the disgust of *The Gentlewoman*, was carved 'wielding an enormous fan! Could bathos descend lower!' Around the building are other sculptures representing British artists; these were made by students of the Royal College of Art.

Under the Museum's aegis have now come Ham House, Osterley Park and the Wellington Museum. The Museum's collection of dolls, toys and games may be seen at the Bethnal Green Museum; and its theatrical collections have been amalgamated with those of the British Theatre Museum and the Museum of Performing Arts to create the Theatre Museum.

UNDERGROUND *South Kensington*   BUS ROUTES *14, 30, 45, 49, 74, 264.*

Westminster Abbey   *SW1.* Legend has it that the first church on Thorney Island in the Thames was built by King Sebert, of the East Saxons, in the 7th century on the instructions of St Peter who materialised at its consecration by Melitus, first Bishop of London. The designs of salmon in the Chapter

Westminster Abbey and St Margaret's Church in 1753.

House floor are said to relate to the tradition that St Peter rewarded the ferryman who transported him across the river with the promise of plentiful catches. No mention of such a church is made by Bede, however, in his *Ecclesiastical History* although Thorney was undoubtedly a suitable place for such a foundation, since it had fresh-water springs and the food resources of the River Thames at hand.

A Charter purporting to be of King Offa of Mercia in 785, now in the Abbey Muniments, granted land 'to St Peter and the needy people of God in Thorney in the terrible place which is called Westminster'. St Dunstan is also said to have obtained a charter from King Edgar in the 10th century and to have restored the Benedictine Abbey to which he brought monks. Undoubtedly a substantial foundation existed here when, in 1042, Edward the Confessor became king.

He had vowed to make a pilgrimage to the tomb of the Apostle Peter in Rome but his Great Council dissuaded him for political reasons, and the Pope, Leo IX, was prepared to release the King from his vow if he would found or restore a monastery to St Peter. Edward moved his palace to Westminster and began building a church on a site east of the previous building. He also planned a new monastery for a greatly increased number of monks. Nothing now remains above ground of Edward's solid cruciform structure which was built to an advanced Continental design, although traces of it were discovered in the 19th century in the nave and sanctuary of the present Abbey. The church is depicted in the Bayeux Tapestry as having a central tower and transepts, covered with a lead roof. On 28 December

1065 the church was consecrated and eight days later Edward died and was buried before the high altar.

William I was crowned in the Abbey on Christmas Day 1066 and the Saxons, gathered around the doors, shouted in acclamation. The Normans, believing the noise to signify an uprising, attacked the crowds and several nearby houses were set on fire. This coronation was the first in a long line: all kings thereafter with the exception of Edward V and Edward VIII, have been crowned in the Abbey (*see* CORONATIONS). In 1139, Edward the Confessor was canonised and successive kings, anxious to be associated with the Saint, showered the Abbey with gifts, endowments and privileges. Henry III added a Lady Chapel in 1220 and in 1245 began rebuilding the Abbey. To demonstrate his veneration for the Saint he was determined that it would be the most sumptuous building possible. The old church was pulled down as far west as the nave, the new building being started from the east, as was the custom with medieval builders. The work was supervised in turn by three master masons: Henry de Reyns to 1253, Master John of Gloucester to 1260 and Master Robert of Beverley to 1284. Mystery surrounds the identity of Henry de Reyns. It is probable that the King found him at Rheims which he visited in 1243 but whether he was an Englishman who had gone to France to work, or a Frenchman, is uncertain. Many details about the early building are obscure but it was certainly influenced greatly by the buildings the King himself had seen at Rheims and by those at Amiens and the Sainte-Chapelle in Paris. 'The Abbey,' comments Pevsner, 'is the most French of all English Gothic churches.' The nave is 103 ft high, far higher than that of any other English church. The plan of the apse, with its radiating chapels, derives from Amiens, as do the recessed portals of the north transept, resembling those of Amiens's west front. The form of the apsidal chapels with tall windows and wall arcades, comes from Rheims, although the gallery in the ambulatory is entirely English. The flying buttresses, rose windows in the transepts, bar-tracery of the other windows and iron tie-bars connecting the columns are all French. Indeed, the whole design of the church is based on the French system of geometrical proportion. There are many English features incorporated into this Continental plan, however: notably single rather than double aisles, a long nave and widely projecting transepts, the elaborate moulding of the main arches, lavish use of polished Purbeck marble, the method of filling the stone vaults and the overall sculptured decoration.

The work proceeded rapidly, at the King's own expense, and by 1254 the transepts, north front, rose windows, parts of the cloisters and the Chapter House had been finished. By 1269, the choir and one bay of the nave were completed and the body of St Edward was moved to a special shrine in the chapel bearing his name. The Roman pavement before the high altar was also laid in this year by Abbot Ware. In 1272 Henry III died and, no longer ruler of Anjou, was buried before the high altar in the Abbey at the spot made available by the removal of the Confessor's body to its new site. His heart, however, was transported to Fontevrault Abbey in France to join his dead Angevin ancestors.

Little further building was undertaken until the middle of the following century. In 1303 while Henry's successor, Edward I, was fighting in Scotland, the Treasury, kept in the crypt of the Chapter House, was robbed, despite the thickness of its walls and its supposed impregnability. Richard de Podlicote, Keeper of the PALACE OF WESTMINSTER, was executed for his part in the theft, although it is generally believed that the ecclesiastics themselves must have been implicated.

Abbot Nicholas Littlington began the continuation of the nave in 1376, using money given by Simon Langham, a former Abbot and efficient administrator who had succeeded in putting the financial affairs of the Abbey in order. Littlington also rebuilt the Abbot's house which included a fine parlour, the Jerusalem Chamber. Richard II gave £1,685 towards the cost of building and under the direction of the master mason, Henry de Yevele, the original plan of Henry de Reyns was continued after 100 years

Henry VII's Chapel in Westminster Abbey which was completed in 1519, as depicted by Canaletto in 1750.

with only very minor alterations of architectural design, giving the Abbey a unity of style rare in English cathedrals. Henry IV had a fit when praying one day in the Abbey before the Confessor's shrine and was carried into the Jerusalem Chamber where he died on 20 March 1413, thus fulfilling the prophesy that he would die in Jerusalem. Under Henry V, the Abbey received regular royal financing once more, to the generous extent of 1,000 marks (£666 13 4d) annually. When Henry died in 1422, a new chantry chapel was built under the direction of John Thirske over the King's grave at the entrance to Edward the Confessor's Shrine. Prior Thomas Millyng gained royal support from Edward IV after his recovery of the throne in 1461, for having offered sanctuary to his queen, Elizabeth Woodville, in the preceding year. She built the chapel of St Erasmus adjoining the Lady Chapel and Millyng was made a bishop.

Henry VII, the fourth great royal benefactor of the Abbey, conceived the idea of building a new chapel where the body of his predecessor, Henry VI, would lie. Henry VI had been buried at Windsor and miracles were recorded as happening at his tomb, so that Henry VII wished to have him canonised. The Pope agreed to this but demanded an enormous sum of money before the canonisation process could be completed. This caused the parsimonious Henry VII to modify his building plans and he decided to erect a chapel in honour of the Virgin Mary instead. So, in 1503, the foundation stone of this 'orbis miraculum' was laid, the building eventually being completed in 1519. The master mason was probably Robert Vertue and the skill of his builders was praised many years later by Washington Irving: 'Stone seems, by the winning labour of the chisel, to have been robbed of its weight and density, suspended aloft, as if by magic and the fretted roof achieved with the wonderful minuteness and airy security of a cobweb.' The fan-vaulting is, undoubtedly, one of the greatest achievements of Tudor building. When he died in 1509, Henry was buried in the chapel beside his queen, a magnificent monument by Torrigiano subsequently being erected over their tomb. The chapel is estimated to have cost Henry £14,000. By 1532, when he died, the chantry chapel of Abbot Islip, who had supervised Henry VII's building, had been completed as had the nave of the Abbey itself. The great building begun by Henry III in 1245 had at last been finished.

The monastery was dissolved in 1540 but its royal associations saved it from the destruction of statuary which occurred elsewhere. Part of the Abbey revenues were transferred to St Paul's Cathedral, the origin of the expression: 'Robbing Peter to pay Paul'. The Abbey became the cathedral of the new diocese of Westminster and Edward VI appointed a Dean and Chapter to replace Bishop Thomas Thirlby, accused of embezzling Abbey revenues. Mary restored the monks but they were turned out again under Elizabeth who reinstalled the Dean. During the Civil War, Cromwell's army camped in the church and 'broke down the rails before the Table and burnt them in the very place in the heat of July but wretchedly profaned the very

Table itself by setting about it with their tobacco and all before them.' Cromwell, Bradshaw and Ireton were all buried in the Abbey but, at the Restoration, their bodies were disinterred, hanged at Tyburn, beheaded and then buried at the foot of the gallows.

From 1698 to 1723 Sir Christopher Wren was Surveyor. He undertook restoration work and designed the West Towers. His designs were subsequently modified by Nicholas Hawksmoor and completed in 1745. From the early 18th century onwards, the Abbey became increasingly crowded with monuments of all kinds to all sorts of men and women. So prolific are they that they obscure the lines of the actual building. In 1849, Sir George Gilbert Scott was appointed Surveyor and carried out the restoration of the Chapter House 1866. Further restorations were carried out in the north transept by John Oldrid Scott from 1878 and his successor as Surveyor, J. L. Pearson.

Tombs and Monuments

Think how many royal bones
Sleep within this heap of stones . . .
For here they lie, had realms and lands,
That now want strength to stir their hands . . .

When Francis Beaumont (himself buried in the Abbey) wrote these lines, few had been buried here who were not of royal blood, but since then an extraordinary variety of people have been interred within its walls. Of royal graves those reputed to be of King Sebert, his queen and sister are the earliest. Edward the Confessor lies in the shrine in the chapel bearing his name behind the High Altar. The base of the shrine is all that remains of the magnificent structure of gold erected by Henry III, and ornately bejewelled. Near Edward lies Henry III in the elaborate marble tomb prepared for him by his son, Edward I, who, in his turn, was buried in this chapel, but in a very simple tomb-chest so that his body could be taken out at any time, and his flesh removed by boiling in case his bones were needed to carry before an army invading Scotland. Edward's beloved first wife, Eleanor of Castile – for whom 'Eleanor crosses' were erected between Nottinghamshire and London to mark the stopping-places of her funeral cortège – was buried in 1290, her tomb surmounted by an effigy by William Torel, the goldsmith who had also made Henry III's effigy. Edward III died in 1377 and his tomb, erected by his grandson Richard II, was by Henry Yevele. Nearby are the tombs of his queen, Philippa of Hainault, and their son, Thomas, Duke of Gloucester, youngest of 14 children. Richard II and his wife, Anne of Bohemia, lie in one tomb, their effigies once represented with holding hands, now, sadly, with the arms broken off. The king's jawbone was removed through a hole in the tomb by a boy of Westminster School in 1776 but was restored in 1916. Henry V has his own chantry chapel at the eastern

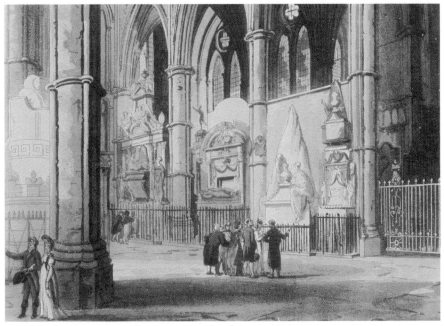

A guide showing visitors the monuments in the nave of Westminster Abbey in 1809.

end of St Edward's Chapel. The figure of the King was stripped of its decoration and even its head over the years, but a new one of polyester resin was installed in 1971. In the Abbey Museum are the shield, saddle and tilting helmet the King used at Agincourt in 1415. A riot of statuary depicting scenes from the King's life decorates every niche and surface of the tomb and the chantry chapel above it which are consequently among the principal sights of the Abbey. Henry's queen, Catherine de Valois, her body embalmed before burial, lay in an open tomb for 300 years. An entry in Pepys's diary for 23 February 1669 records that he 'did see by particular favour the body of Queen Catherine of Valois; and I had the upper part of her body in my hands, and I did kiss her mouth, reflecting upon it that I did kiss a queen, and that this was my birthday, 36 years old, that I did first kiss a queen.' In 1776 the Queen's body was hidden from sight beneath the Villiers monument in the chapel of St Nicholas.

After the building of Henry VII's chapel, royal burials regularly took place there. Elizabeth of York, Henry himself, Anne of Cleves, Edward VI, Queen Mary I and her half-sister, Queen Elizabeth, Mary Queen of Scots, all found resting-places here. They were later to be joined by James I, Anne of Denmark, James's daughter, Elizabeth of Bohemia, Charles II, Mary II, William III, Prince George of Denmark, Queen Anne, George II and Queen Caroline.

Richard II began the custom of burying great commoners in the Abbey when he ordered the burials here of John of Waltham, Bishop of Salisbury, and Sir John Galoppe. The Islip chantry chapels in the sanctuary commemorate Abbot John who supervised the building of Henry VII's chapel and the completion of the nave. One of the many statesmen to be honoured in the Abbey is Charles II's Lord Chancellor, Clarendon, buried here like Queen Mary and Queen Anne, Charles II's nieces and nearly 20 more of his relatives and descendants. Both Pitt the Elder and Younger are here, as well as many of the great figures of 19th-century political life: George Canning, Viscount Castlereagh, Sir Robert Peel, Lord Palmerston and W. E. Gladstone.

The first poet to be buried in the south transept commonly known as Poet's Corner was Geoffrey Chaucer in 1400 and, after this, other poets sought to be buried near him. But many poets, often because of the unconventional lives they led, were considered undesirable by successive Deans and have only been given memorials many years after their deaths. Shakespeare had to wait until 1740 for his memorial, Burns until 1885 and William Blake until the bicentenary of his birth in 1957, when a splendid Epstein memorial to him was erected. Keats, Byron and Shelley, too, had to wait a considerable time for recognition in the Abbey. Of 20th-century poets, T. S. Eliot has a memorial and John Masefield's ashes are beneath a stone near another commemorating W. H. Auden.

Many famous scientists and engineers have memorials. Sir Isaac Newton was buried in the Abbey and has a splendid monument against the choir screen, designed by Kent and executed by J. M. Rysbrack. Thomas Tompion and George Graham, the great clockmakers, are buried together, as are three great physicists, J. J. Thomson, Lord Rutherford and Lord Kelvin. Joseph Lister, the pioneer of antiseptic treatment, is also commemorated. The explorer David Livingstone was buried in the Abbey in 1874, his body having been brought back from Africa. The architects, Robert Adam, Sir William Chambers, Sir Charles Barry and Sir George Gilbert Scott are here along with Thomas Banks, the sculptor, and several actors and actresses are also buried here, among them David Garrick and Henry Irving.

One of the most famous and visited of all tombs is that in the nave, of the Unknown Warrior whose body was brought back from France after the 1st World War and buried on 11 November 1920 as a representative of the thousands of dead. The soil for his grave was brought from the battlefields and the marble slab from Belgium. On a pillar to the north is the Congressional Medal of Honour bestowed on the soldier in 1921 and above it is the Padre's Flag which had been use to cover the coffins of many soldiers buried in France and was laid over that of the Unknown Warrior at his burial. Winston Churchill, buried at Bladon, has a marble slab beside the Unknown Warrior and Franklin D. Roosevelt, one of the very few foreigners so honoured, a plaque on the wall of the nave nearby.

Many other great soldiers are buried or commemorated in the Abbey. One of the most splendid memorials is that by Roubiliac to Field-Marshal George Wade who died in 1748. Major-General James Wolfe has a colossal monument erected by the King and Parliament 13 years after his death; and General Gordon has a bronze bust given in 1892 by the Royal Engineers. Major-General Sir James Outram has a monument depicting scenes at the Residency during the siege of Lucknow and Field Marshal Allenby's ashes are buried in St George's Chapel, the Warriors' Chapel.

Some of the most interesting monuments are those commemorating whole families. The Duke of Buckingham, favourite of James I and Charles I, has a monument by Le Sueur which also commemorates his wife and children. The large and fine Norris family memorial is by Isaac James. As Elizabeth I's guardian while her sister Mary was Queen, Norris earned her respect and affection and was raised to the peerage in 1572. The monument has the figures of Lord and Lady Norris and the kneeling figures of six of their sons. Other notable family monuments are those of the Speaker of the House of Commons, Sir James Pickering, and the Percy family's private vault, the Percys still being the only family with the right to be buried in the Abbey. Baroness Burdett-Coutts was the last person to be buried there in 1906. Since then only ashes have been accepted.

The Abbey is open daily from 0800 to 1800 (to 2000 on Wednesdays). On Sundays, the nave and cloisters only are open between services. The Royal Chapels are open from 0900 to 1600 from Monday to Friday and from 0900 to 1400 and 1545 to 1700 on Saturdays. They are closed on Sundays. At the time of going to press the Treasure was closed for renovation. On weekdays there is a guided tour of the Abbey lasting one and a half hours. For details telephone 01-222 7110.

UNDERGROUND *Westminster, St James's Park* BUS ROUTES *3, 11, 12, 24, 29, 53, 70, 77, 77A, 88, 109, 159, 170, 184, 196.*

Westminster Abbey Gardens *College, Little Cloister and St Katherine's Chapel Gardens, SW1.* The College Garden, one of the oldest gardens in England, was once the infirmary garden of the ancient monastery and was originally planted with healing and culinary herbs. It is now a lawn with paved paths, and trees including planes and pink and white Japanese cherries. On the east and south side are herbaceous borders protected by the high original river boundary walls. To the north are two small gardens; the one known as the Little Cloister is approached through a Norman vaulted passage. In the centre of the garden are a small pool and fountain. A few yards away is St Katherine's Chapel Garden, consisting of a sunken lawn surrounded by flower-beds and overlooked by a clergy house on one side and the remains of the south aisle columns and arch face of the chapel on the other. A row of column bases stands out of the lawn.

The gardens are open to the public from 1000 to dusk on Thursdays.

176

Westminster Hall in 1738, housing the Law Courts and booksellers' stalls.

Westminster Hall   *Parliament Square, SW1.* The only surviving part of the original PALACE OF WESTMINSTER. The Hall was built as an extension of Edward the Confessor's palace in 1097 by William Rufus who originally intended to build an entire new palace. When the Hall was completed, William professed himself disappointed, saying it was a 'mere bedchamber' compared to what he had envisaged. The Hall, first used as a banqueting hall, then consisted of a central nave, divided from the aisles by timber posts. It was 240 ft long and nearly 40 ft high, with walls 6 ft 8 in thick. Along the plastered and painted walls was a row of Norman round-headed windows. A wide railed gallery ran around the Hall at a height of 20 ft. The building was damaged by fire in 1291 and restored by Edward II. Further alterations were made by Richard II, between 1397 and 1399, to the design of Henry Yevele. The walls were elevated by 2 ft and a stately porch installed. Richard II's motif, a white hart couchant, was incorporated into the moulding surround. The most striking addition was the oak hammer-beam roof by Hugh Herland; it springs to a height of 92 ft in the centre and has the widest unsupported span in the country.

The Hall became the centre of administrative life, outside the City walls. Grand Councils and, later, some early Parliaments were held here.

From the 13th century until 1882 the building housed the Law Courts. In the early days men were hired as witnesses here; the sign of their trade was a

177

Westminster Hall and the Abbey as seen from Westminster Bridge in 1819.

straw protruding from their shoe – hence the expression 'straw bail'. Later, in 1820–4, the courts were arranged by Sir John Soane along the west side of the Hall. These were the Court of Chancery, Court of the Queen's Bench, Court of Common Pleas and Court of Exchequer. From the time of Cromwell until the middle of the 18th century, justice lived alongside commerce here. Books, particularly law books, prints, toys, trinkets and the wares of seamstresses were sold in stalls inside the building.

The Hall has seen power change hands many times. In 1327 Edward II abdicated and presented his 14-year-old son, Edward III, as King. The barons interviewed Richard II here in 1387 after their rebellion, and in 1399 the Lords of the Council deposed Richard, then in the TOWER, and put Henry IV on the throne. Edward IV proclaimed himself King here in 1461. In 1649 Charles I was tried and condemned in the Hall; and Cromwell was installed as Lord Protector here in 1653. After the Restoration, Cromwell's head was placed, with those of Ireton and Bradshaw, on the roof; it remained there for 25 years before it was finally blown down.

Amongst those condemned here were Sir John Oldcastle (Shakespeare's Falstaff) in 1417; Sir Thomas More and Bishop Fisher in 1535; Queen Anne Boleyn in 1536; the Duke of Somerset, the Great Protector, in 1552; Robert Devereux, Earl of Essex, and Henry Wriothesley, Earl of Southampton, in 1601; Guy Fawkes in 1606; and the Earl of Strafford in 1641. The trials of Lord Melville in 1806 and Warren Hastings in 1788–95 were also held here. The bodies of Gladstone, Edward VII and Churchill lay in state here.

178

The Hall has witnessed happier events, too. Since 1099, when William Rufus celebrated the completion of the Hall with a banquet, English monarchs have held coronation festivals here. Traditionally the Royal Champion would ride to the centre of the Hall, throw down his gauntlet, and challenge any man denying the right of the sovereign to single combat. The last coronation festival held here was in celebration of George IV's coronation in 1821. Of this the Earl of Denbigh wrote, 'It exceeded all imagination and conception. Picture to yourself Westminster Hall lined beneath with the peers in their robes and coronets, the Privy Councillors, Knights of the Bath and a multitude of different attendants and chief officers of State in most magnificent dresses, and with a double row of galleries on each side above, filled with all the beauty of London, the ladies vying with each other in the magnificence of their apparel and the splendour of their head-dresses. Some of them being literally a blaze of diamonds.'

The Hall is now the vestibule of the House of Commons; it was retained by Sir Charles Barry in his design for the PALACE OF WESTMINSTER and is connected to the rest of the palace by St Stephen's Hall.

Tours of the Hall can be arranged with a Member of Parliament.

For directions *see* PALACE OF WESTMINSTER.

The Court of King's Bench in Westminster Hall in 1808, which housed the Law Courts from the 13th century until 1882.

The House of Commons, c. 1755, sitting in St Stephen's Chapel.

Westminster, Palace of   *Westminster, SW1.* The first Palace of Westminster was built for Edward the Confessor on land between the Thames and Westminster (now WESTMINSTER ABBEY), the comparatively modest monastery which he had renovated and enlarged. After he died in 1066 the Palace became the home of William the Conqueror and his Court. William's son, William Rufus, built WESTMINSTER HALL but his plans for further enlarging the Palace were not realised after his violent death in 1100. Nevertheless the Palace remained the main residence of the kings of England, and the home of the Court until Henry VIII abandoned it for WHITEHALL PALACE in 1512. Even after that it remained the administrative centre of the kingdom. In early times the King's Council had met in WESTMINSTER HALL, and there the 'Model' Parliament was summoned by Edward I; but soon after his death the Lords and Commons held their deliberations separately. After meeting in the presence of the King, usually in the Painted Chamber, where the Lord Chamberlain announced the reason for the summoning of Parliament, the Lords withdrew to the White Chamber. The Commons, however, had to meet wherever was convenient, sometimes in the Chapter House of the Abbey, or in the Refectory which the Abbot allowed them to use.

180

At the Reformation, under the Chantries Act of 1547, the Royal Chapel of St Stephen, like all other private chapels, was secularised, and by 1550 had become the meeting place of the Commons. This chapel, traditionally founded by St Stephen, had been burned down in 1298, rebuilt by Edward I, and finished in the reign of Edward III in 1347. The king had worshipped in St Stephen's, the courtiers in the crypt which had been built by Edward I in 1292. St Stephen's Chapel was a tall, two-storeyed building with high turrets at the four corners, and long stained-glass windows. As it had no aisle it was perfectly suitable for use as a debating chamber. The Members sat in the choir stalls on the north and south walls; the Speaker's chair was placed where the altar had been. (The tradition of Members bowing to the Speaker's chair probably derives from genuflexion to the altar.) The Mace, the Speaker's staff of office, was placed on a table where the lectern had been. The ante-chapel, separated from the main chapel by the choir-screen, served as a lobby in which Members registered their votes as Ayes, the Noes remaining in the Chapel. From the mid-16th century until its destruction by fire in 1834 St Stephen's was, in fact, the House of Commons.

After 1547 St Mary Undercroft, the crypt of St Stephen's, was used as a parliamentary store-house, as were the Cloisters. It survived the 1834 fire (*see below*), after which it was carefully restored by Barry for use as a chapel by Members of both Houses. It is 90 ft long by 26 ft wide, and comprises five vaulted bays with a fine groined roof and four carved bosses. In this chapel Members can be married and their children baptised, whatever their denomination, in the adjoining octagonal Baptistry, the work of Barry who also designed the font of alabaster and marble with its highly ornamented brass cover. The only other parts of the Palace to survive the fire of 1834 are WESTMINSTER HALL; the Cloisters, with their fine fan vaulting and carved bosses, built early in the reign of Henry VIII by Dr John Chamber, Dean of St Stephen's College; and the JEWEL TOWER, built in 1365–6 as a royal treasure house and used from 1621 as the Parliament Office and as a storage place for the House of Lords records.

After 1547 the canons of St Stephen's were dismissed and, as the Palace was no longer a royal residence, Members and officials of both Houses started to occupy the many vacant chambers. The Lords settled permanently in the White Chamber. In the cellars below, Guy Fawkes, a Roman Catholic convert, and his fellow conspirators were caught in their plot to blow up King James I and his ministers, and Members of both Houses on 5 November 1605. The cellars are searched to this day by the QUEEN'S BODYGUARD OF THE YEOMEN OF THE GUARD before each STATE OPENING OF PARLIAMENT, as if in confirmation of the nursery rhyme:

> I see no good reason
> Why Gunpowder Treason
> Should ever be forgot.

The Queen's Bodyguard of the Yeoman of the Guard making their traditional search of the Crypt of the Houses of Parliament in 1894, before the State Opening of Parliament.

Sixteen years later the King angered the Commons by tearing out the pages in their Journal in which they had asserted their right to deal 'with all matters of grievance and policy'. Relations between the Crown and the Commons deteriorated over the years until the day in January 1642 when Charles I burst into St Stephen's demanding the arrest of five Members. Replying to the King who asked where the missing Members were, the Speaker, William Lenthall, said, 'I have neither eyes to see, nor tongue to speak in this place, but as this House is pleased to direct me.' The King had no alternative but to withdraw. Since then no monarch can set foot in the Commons Chamber. The throne, which is occupied during the ceremony of the STATE OPENING OF PARLIAMENT, is in the Lords' Chamber, to which the Commons repair to hear the Monarch's Speech from the Throne.

In the reign of Queen Anne, Sir Christopher Wren, the Surveyor General, was commissioned to build galleries in the former St Stephen's Chapel to accommodate the new Scottish Members, and in 1800, because of the admission of Irish Members, the new Surveyor General, James Wyatt, was required to enlarge it further by reducing the thickness of the walls. At the same time the Lords moved from the White Chamber, which they were overcrowding, to the Hall, formerly used by the Court of Requests, next to the House of Commons kitchen.

In 1834 the House of Lords, the House of Commons and nearly all the conglomeration of buildings known as the Palace of Westminster burnt down, bringing to an end the makeshift accommodation in which the Lords and Commons had worked for almost 300 years; and the opportunity thus arose for buildings to be designed specifically to house Parliament. Architects were invited to submit plans 'in the Gothic or Elizabethan style'; 97 designs were submitted and of these Barry's was selected.

Charles Barry had travelled in Italy and had become deeply influenced by Renaissance architecture, but, conscious of his limitations as an architect in the Gothic style, he enlisted the help of Augustus Pugin who had been trained in the office of his father, the French architect, Auguste Pugin. He had spent much of his apprenticeship in making drawings for his father's books on Gothic architecture. Barry and Pugin made a perfect partnership, Barry providing the practical plans, Pugin the picturesque ornamentation. Construction began in 1837, Mrs Barry having the honour of laying the foundation stone. Ten years later the House of Commons was completed. The Clock Tower was not finished until 1858; it had presented even more problems than the extremely expensive heating and ventilation system which proved so inefficient that Lord Randolph Churchill once had no

A romantic view of the Palace of Westminster on a moonlit night in 1872.

difficulty in persuading the House to adjourn in mid-debate in protest against the foulness of the atmosphere.

When the Clock Tower reached a height of 150 ft, work on it had to be suspended as it was discovered that the mechanism of the clock could not be raised inside it. The clockmaker, not Barry's choice, was E. J. Dent, whose clock for the Royal Exchange was classed as 'the best public clock in the world'. In spite of his distinction and experience everything went wrong with the Westminster clock. When the Victoria Tower was roofed in 1860, however, and the Palace of Westminster was complete it was generally acclaimed as a building worthy to be the Houses of Parliament, and a splendid example of Perpendicular Gothic.

Prince Albert was greatly interested in art and ensured that the new buildings were richly furnished with painting and sculpture. In 1841, under his influence, a Select Committee was appointed 'to take into consideration the promotion of the Fine Arts . . . a connection with the rebuilding of the Houses of Parliament'. William Dyce was one of the winning artists of the resultant competitions, and his five huge frescoes of Arthurian legend can be seen in the Robing Room in which the Monarch assumes the Imperial Crown and Parliamentary Robes for the STATE OPENING OF PARLIAMENT.

The walls of the Royal Gallery, which leads from the Robing Room to the Prince's Chamber, are painted with two 45 ft long frescoes by Daniel Maclise, *The Death of Nelson* and *The Meeting of Wellington and Blücher*; the floor is patterned in buff, red and blue Minton tiles. In the Prince's Chamber is John Gibson's monument to Queen Victoria. The two fireplaces, with bronze bas relief panels by William Theed above them, are, like the one in the Robing Room, intricately patterned and ornamented.

There are more frescoes in the House of Lords by Dyce, Maclise, Charles Cope and John Calcott Horsley. Above the four doorways in the Central Lobby are mosaics of the patron saints of England, Scotland, Wales and Ireland by Sir Edward Poynter and Anning Bell, and there stand the life-size statues of four 19th-century statesmen, Earl Granville, William Ewart Gladstone, Earl Russell and the Earl of Iddesleigh by Sir Joseph Boehm, Sir William Hamo Thornycroft and Pomeroy. Barry's own statue in white marble by John Henry Foley is in the Lower Waiting Hall beneath a trefoiled window.

The whole interior of the Palace, except the part rebuilt after the bombing in 1941, is gorgeously and intricately ornamented to designs by Pugin, including panelled ceilings, tiled floors (the encaustic tiles by Herbert Minton), stained glass, wallpapers, clocks, fireplaces, door furniture and even umbrella stands and inkwells.

Barry's structure, described by James Pope-Hennessy as 'this great and beautiful monument to Victorian artifice', stood intact for nearly a century until 1940. Between September 1940 and May 1941 the Houses of Parliament were damaged 11 times during air raids, and on the night of 10 May 1941 the

House of Commons and the adjoining Lobby were reduced to a heap of smouldering rubble.

Sir Giles Gilbert Scott was commissioned to rebuild the House of Commons in the tradition of the old Chamber. This he did between 1945 and 1950, retaining Barry's general plan but simplifying Pugin's extreme Gothic decoration. (*See also* WESTMINSTER HALL *and* JEWEL TOWER.)

The Palace of Westminster may be visited only by arrangement with a Member of Parliament. When the House of Commons is sitting, debates may be heard from the Strangers' Gallery. Queues form at St Stephen's Entrance for admission at about 1615 from Monday to Thursday and at about 1000 on Friday. Queues for the House of Lords also form at St Stephen's Entrance for admission at about 1430 from Monday to Wednesday, at about 1500 on Thursday and (if the House is sitting) at about 1100 on Friday.

UNDERGROUND *Westminster* BUS ROUTES *3, 11, 12, 24, 29, 53, 70, 76, 77, 77A, 88, 109, 159, 170, 184, 196.*

𝖂𝖍𝖎𝖙𝖊𝖍𝖆𝖑𝖑 𝕻𝖆𝖑𝖆𝖈𝖊   When Walter de Grey, then Archbishop of York, gave 'our house in the street of Westminster' to the See of York, it became the Archbishop's official residence in London. At this time it was known as York House, but Wolsey, who became Archbishop of York in 1514, changed the name to York Place and began greatly to extend the house and grounds. He built a Great Hall in 1528, which enabled him to entertain King Henry VIII and his Court in a most lavish manner. One of his banquets was described as 'a most sumptuous supper, the like of which was never given by Cleopatra or Caligula'. But when Wolsey fell from the King's favour, Henry appropriated York Place for the Crown and decided to make it his main Palace in London. All memories of Wolsey were quickly obliterated, and the name changed to Whitehall Palace. This name may derive from the light stone that was used for some of the new buildings, but it is more likely that it comes from the term White Hall used in the early 16th century for any grand hall used for festivities. Shakespeare refers to the change of name in *Henry VIII* (Act IV, Scene 1):

> You must no more call it York Place, that's past:
> For since the Cardinal fell, that title's lost;
> 'Tis now the King's and called Whitehall.

Henry VIII carried out an extensive rebuilding programme. Splendid State Apartments were built along the river side; on the walls of the Privy Chamber Holbein painted his great celebration of the Tudor dynasty. The artist's preliminary study of the King, a life-sized cartoon drawing, can be seen today in the National Portrait Gallery. A turreted gateway, known as the Whitehall Gate, was built in 1531–2 to give access from the street, and two new sets of stairs led down to the River. On the other side of the road

Henry VIII and Anne Boleyn were married in 1533 in Whitehall Palace, which was then the Court's main residence in London.

(now Whitehall), which was a right of way between Charing Cross and Westminster, Henry acquired further land for his Palace and laid out tennis courts, a cockpit and a tilt-yard as well as further buildings. The new property was connected to the old by two large gatehouses; one, known as the Holbein Gate, immediately south of where the BANQUETING HOUSE now stands, the other, the King's Gate, about 50 yards south of the present Cenotaph.

Henry VIII celebrated his marriage to Anne Boleyn in Whitehall Palace in 1533, and that to Jane Seymour in 1536. The Palace was now the main London residence of the Court, and Henry issued a set of strict rules to govern the behaviour of those who lived there. They were to be 'loving together, of good unity and accord' and, most important, they were to avoid all 'grudging, rumbling or talking of the King's pastime'. Henry died at Whitehall Palace in 1547. Little remains to be seen today of the great Palace he had created, though his wine-cellar lies intact under the massive present-day Ministry of Defence. Henry's children continued the use of Whitehall Palace. There are accounts of Latimer preaching to Edward VI in the courtyard, and of the sick young king's 'white despairing face' looking from the window. Although Queen Elizabeth did not spend so much of her time at Whitehall, frequently removing the Court to Greenwich, HAMPTON COURT or RICHMOND, the Palace was still much in use. The Queen's bedroom contained two little silver cabinets where she kept her writing materials. Her bed was 'ingeniously composed' of woods of different colours, with quilts of silk, velvet, gold, silver and embroidery. A long gallery looked down on to the tilt-yard where jousting tournaments were held. The Great Hall was the scene of many dramatic performances.

The Stuart Kings restored Whitehall Palace to its importance as the main seat of the Court. James I found the Palace so dilapidated that he resolved to rebuild it on a magnificent scale. He enjoined Inigo Jones and John Webb to draw up plans for a huge new palace. Their designs allowed for a building with a river frontage of 1,152 feet, raised on piles running a great distance into the water. There were to be four fronts, the angles marked with square towers, a large central quadrangle and six smaller ones. But the new palace was never built, probably because of 'the vastness of its scale, for it was as far beyond the means, as beyond the wants, of James I'. So only the BANQUET- ING HOUSE was ever completed. Even so, by this time, the palace comprised some 2,000 rooms. Charles I built up a magnificent art collection in White- hall. He left more than 460 paintings, including 28 Titians and 9 Raphaels. Most of these were dispersed during the Commonwealth, when Oliver Cromwell lived in Whitehall as Lord Protector. He died there in 1658.

The Court returned after the Restoration, and Charles II restored masques and merrymaking to the Palace. He had a laboratory built and provided accommodation for two of his mistresses. Barbara Castlemaine took posses- sion of a suite over Holbein Gate, while the Duchess of Portsmouth's rooms were, according to John Evelyn, 'twice or thrice pulled down to satisfy her prodigal and expensive pleasures'. The Queen lived in a far simpler apartment overlooking the river. Another distinguished resident was James, Duke of Monmouth, who inhabited the converted tennis court, and was to return here as a defeated rebel during the reign of his uncle, James II, who replaced the old Privy Gallery with a three-storey building of brick, designed by Wren, and also added a Roman Catholic Chapel.

A plan of the Palace drawn in 1680 shows that at that time it covered an area of some 23 acres and stretched from the River Thames to the upper end of Downing Street. (The river then was much wider; its bank was near the base of the present Ministry of Defence.) The Bowling Green on the south covered Richmond Terrace, while apartments, galleries, gardens and recreation grounds stretched north on both sides of Whitehall to the BANQUETING HOUSE, with the tilt-yard extending over HORSE GUARDS PARADE. Along the river the Palace buildings continued as far as the present- day Horse Guards Avenue.

In 1688, after the arrival of William of Orange in England, James II 'stole away from Whitehall by the Privy Stairs'. The following year, in the last great ceremonial event at the palace, the crown was offered to William and Mary. The new rulers transferred their royal residence to KENSINGTON PALACE, as William found that the river air of Whitehall exacerbated his

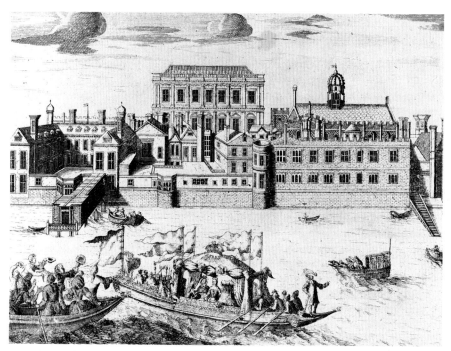

Whitehall Palace in the late 17th century before fire destroyed all but the Banqueting House, which can be seen in the background.

asthma. Also, Whitehall was liable to flooding. Pepys had noted in December 1663: 'At Whitehall I hear and find that there was the last night the greatest tide that ever was remembered in England to have been in this river; all Whitehall having been drowned, of which there was great discourse.' The old palace was damaged by fire in 1691. Wren designed the graceful new terrace which was built for Queen Mary in the same year. A reconstructed portion of this, together with part of a flight of steps which gave access from the Royal Apartments to the State Barge can still be seen.

On 2 January 1698, Evelyn wrote 'Whitehall burnt; nothing but walls and ruins left'. The day before, apparently due to the carelessness of a Dutch laundrymaid, fire had raged through the palace, consuming over 1,000 apartments. Only the BANQUETING HOUSE was saved.

A model of WHITEHALL PALACE as it was in the 17th century can be seen in the Museum of London, as Exhibit No. 126.

William I, the Conqueror (*1027–87*). Bastard son of Robert III, Duke of Normandy, he became Duke on his father's death in 1035. In January 1066 King Edward the Confessor died and was buried in WESTMINSTER ABBEY which he had founded; and on the same day his brother-in-law, Harold

Godwinson, became the first of the English monarchs to be crowned there. Duke William's claim to the throne, however, was genealogically stronger, as he was King Edward's cousin; and, having beaten the English on 14 October at the Battle of Hastings – in which King Harold was slain – on Christmas Day William, too, was crowned at the Abbey. Thereafter, when he was in London, he held court at the PALACE OF WESTMINSTER. To fortify and dominate London, the Conqueror ordered three strongholds to be built, the long-demolished Montfichat Tower, Castle Baynard and the TOWER OF LONDON.

Having rewarded his Norman lords with the lands of the Anglo-Saxon *thegns* who had fallen at Hastings and of those who had opposed him in 1085, William ordered a detailed survey of the whole country. This survey, Domesday Book, is housed in the Public Record Office in Chancery Lane. William died on one of his frequent sojourns in Normandy and is buried in his own foundation, Caen Cathedral.

William II (*d. 1100*). In 1087 his dying father, WILLIAM I, sent him from Normandy to England, where Archbishop Lanfranc crowned him in WESTMINSTER ABBEY. To distinguish him from his father, he was called Rufus because of his exceptionally ruddy complexion. He spent little time in

A mid-13th-century manuscript illustrating William I and his son Rufus holding models of churches they founded.

London, but he kept the first Christmas of his reign in the PALACE OF WESTMINSTER and at Pentecost 1099 'held his court for the first time in his new building at Westminster'. This was WESTMINSTER HALL, which he had intended as the first building in a complete reconstruction of the palace of Edward the Confessor. At Whitsuntide 1100 he was again at Westminster, but by August he was dead, killed – perhaps deliberately – by an arrow shot by one of his hunting companions. The *Anglo-Saxon Chronicle* describes him as 'loathsome to wellnigh all his people, and abominable to God.'

William III *(1650–1702)* and **Mary II Stuart** *(1662–94)*. At the request of Parliament, William of Orange, grandson of CHARLES I, invaded England in 1688; and in the BANQUETING HOUSE he and his wife, the Princess Mary, elder daughter of the deposed JAMES II, were offered joint sovereignty. They did not like WHITEHALL PALACE, partly because its proximity to the Thames exacerbated the King's asthma, so in 1689, the year of their coronation, they bought Nottingham House which they rebuilt as KENSINGTON PALACE. Both William and Mary were interested in gardens and they had the gardens to the south of the Palace laid out in the formal Dutch style.

William IV sitting beside Queen Mary, looking out at Whitehall Palace which he was to abandon in favour of Kensington because of his asthma.

Two more important building projects took place in their reign. Queen Mary ordered building to be undertaken at Greenwich to provide a Naval hospital for disabled seamen; this is now the ROYAL NAVAL COLLEGE. And much of HAMPTON COURT PALACE was rebuilt in a markedly French style, though the gardens around the palace are, like the gardens at Kensington, in the Dutch manner. The existing Maze was created for them. In nearby Bushy Park William ordered the planting of the splendid avenue of horse chestnut trees, while in ST JAMES'S PARK he had a little bird-watching house built on an island in the lake. The King and Queen both died at KENSINGTON PALACE, and are buried in the Henry VII Chapel in WESTMINSTER ABBEY.

William IV (*1765–1837*). Third son of GEORGE III, he succeeded his elder brother, GEORGE IV, in 1830. He was born at BUCKINGHAM PALACE (BUCKINGHAM HOUSE as it then was), a palace he never lived in as king. Much of his childhood was spent at Kew (*see* KEW PALACE). As Duke of Clarence he lived at Bushy Park House, BUSHY PARK, and in central London at 32 Mortimer Street. On the accession of GEORGE IV he was given CLARENCE HOUSE in the precincts of ST JAMES'S PALACE. As BUCKINGHAM PALACE was not finished on his own accession, and as he much preferred Clarence House, he lived there for the whole of his reign. He did, however, use ST JAMES'S PALACE for occasions of state. The ceiling of the CHAPEL ROYAL was redecorated in his reign with his and Queen Adelaide's names and cyphers. He is buried at Windsor Castle.

Windsor, Duke of, *see* EDWARD VIII.

York, Prince Andrew, Duke of (*b. 1960*). Second son of QUEEN ELIZABETH II and PRINCE PHILIP, DUKE OF EDINBURGH. Born at BUCKINGHAM PALACE, he has made a career in the Royal Navy. Prince Andrew was created Duke of York on the day of his wedding at WESTMINSTER ABBEY to Miss Sarah Ferguson, daughter of Major Ronald Ferguson and his first wife, now Mrs Hector Barrantes.

SOVEREIGNS OF
BRITAIN SINCE 1066

William I	1066–1087	*Commonwealth declared 1649*	
William II	1087–1100	Oliver Cromwell	
Henry I	1100–1135	Lord Protector	1653–1658
Stephen	1135–1154	Richard Cromwell	
Henry II	1154–1189	Lord Protector	1658–1659
Richard I	1189–1199	Charles II	1649–1685
John	1199–1216	James II	1685–1689
Henry III	1216–1272	William III	1689–1702
Edward I	1272–1307	and	
Edward II	1307–1327	Mary II	1689–1694
Edward III	1327–1377	Anne	1702–1714
Richard II	1377–1399	George I	1714–1727
Henry IV	1399–1413	George II	1727–1760
Henry V	1413–1422	George III	1760–1820
Henry VI	1422–1461	George IV	1820–1830
Edward IV	1461–1483	William IV	1830–1837
Edward V	1483	Victoria	1837–1901
Richard III	1483–1485	Edward VII	1901–1910
Henry VII	1485–1509	George V	1910–1936
Henry VIII	1509–1547	Edward VIII	1936
Edward VI	1547–1553	George VI	1936–1952
Jane Grey	1553	Elizabeth II	Succeeded 1952
Mary I	1553–1558		
Elizabeth I	1558–1603		
James I	1603–1625		
Charles I	1625–1649		

THE ORDER OF SUCCESSION

HRH The Prince of Wales (Heir Apparent)
HRH Prince William of Wales
HRH Prince Henry of Wales
HRH The Prince Andrew
HRH The Prince Edward
HRH The Princess Anne, Mrs Mark Phillips
Master Peter Phillips
Miss Zara Phillips
HRH The Princess Margaret, Countess of Snowdon
Viscount Linley
Lady Sarah Armstrong-Jones
HRH The Duke of Gloucester
Earl of Ulster
Lady Davina Windsor
Lady Rose Windsor
HRH The Duke of Kent
Earl of St Andrews
Lord Nicholas Windsor
Lady Helen Windsor
Lord Frederick Windsor
Lady Gabriella Windsor
HRH Princess Alexandra, the Hon Mrs Angus Ogilvy
Mr James Ogilvy
Miss Marina Ogilvy
The Earl of Harewood
Viscount Lascelles
Hon Alexander Lascelles
Hon Edward Lascelles
Hon James Lascelles
Master Rowan Lascelles

192

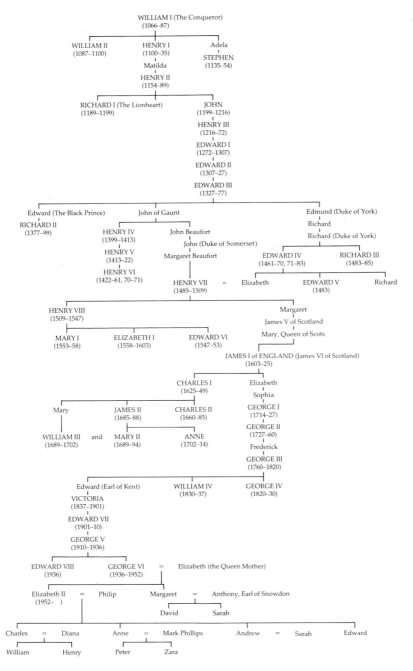

193

The Queen
The Duke of Edinburgh
The Prince of Wales
Prince William of Wales
Prince Henry of Wales
Prince Andrew
Prince Edward
Grandsons of the Sovereign
Brothers of the Sovereign
Uncles of the Sovereign
Nephews of the Sovereign (according to the seniority of their fathers)
Archbishop of Canterbury
Lord High Chancellor
Archbishop of York
The Prime Minister
Lord High Treasurer (no such office exists at present)
Lord President of the Council
The Speaker of the House of Commons
Lord Privy Seal
Ambassadors and High Commissioners

Above all Peers of their own degree:
Lord Great Chamberlain
Lord High Constable (no such office exists at present)
Earl Marshal (Duke of Norfolk)
Lord High Admiral (office held by HM the Queen)
Lord Steward of the Household (Duke of Northumberland)
Lord Chamberlain of the Household

Master of the Horse (Earl of Westmorland)
Dukes of England
———— Scotland (none created since 1707)
———— Great Britain (1707–1801)
Duke of Leinster (being the only Irish Duke existing at the time of the union)
Dukes of the United Kingdom (created since 1801)
Eldest sons of Dukes of the Blood Royal (when they are not brothers, grandsons, uncles, or nephews of the reigning sovereign)
Marquess of Cholmondeley (as Lord Great Chamberlain)
Marquesses of England (marq. of Winchester)
———— Scotland (none created after 1707)
———— Great Britain (1707–1801)
———— Ireland (created before 1801)
———— the United Kingdom (created since 1801)
Eldest sons of Dukes
Earls of England (anterior to 1707)
———— Scotland (none created after 1707)
———— Great Britain (1707–1801)
———— Ireland (created before 1801)
———— the United Kingdom (created since 1801)
Younger sons of Dukes of the Blood Royal (when they are not brothers, grandsons, uncles or nephews of the reigning sovereign)
Eldest sons of Marquesses
Younger sons of Dukes
Viscounts of England (visc. Hereford)
———— Scotland (anterior to 1707)
———— Great Britain (1707–1801)
———— Ireland (anterior to 1801)
———— the United Kingdom (created since 1801)
Eldest sons of Earls
Younger sons of Marquesses
Bishop of London
———— Durham
———— Winchester
English Bishops (according to date of consecration)
Bishops Suffragan (according to date of consecration)
Secretary of State (if a baron)
Baron Maclean (as Lord Chamberlain of HM's Household)

Barons of England
———— Scotland (none created since 1707)
———— Great Britain (1707–1801)
———— Ireland (anterior to 1801)
———— the United Kingdom (created since 1801)
Lords of Appeal in Ordinary
Commissioners of the Great Seal (those persons who execute the office of Lord High Chancellor when it happens to be vacant)
Treasurer of the Household
Comptroller of the Household
Vice-Chamberlain of the Household
Secretary of State (when not a baron)
Eldest sons of Viscounts
Younger sons of Earls
Eldest sons of Barons
Knights of the Garter
Privy Councillors
Chancellor of the Exchequer
———— Duchy of Lancaster
Lord Chief Justice
Master of the Rolls
President of the Family Division
Lords Justices of Appeal, ranking according to date of appointment
Judges of the High Court of Justice, ranking according to date of appointment
Vice-Chancellor of the County Palatine of Lancaster
Younger sons of Viscounts
———— Barons
———— Life Peers
Baronets
Knights of the Thistle
Knights Grand Cross of the Bath
Knights Grand Commanders of the Star of India
Knights Grand Cross of St Michael and St George
Knights Grand Commanders of the Order of the Indian Empire
Knights Grand Cross of the Royal Victorian Order
Knights Grand Cross of the British Empire
Knights Commanders of the Bath
Knights Commanders of the Star of India
Knights Commanders of St Michael and St George
Knights Commanders of the Order of the Indian Empire
Knights Commanders of the Royal Victorian Order
Knights Commanders of the British Empire
Knights Bachelor
Official Referees of the Supreme Court of Judicature
Circuit Judges
County Court Judges of England and Wales
Masters in Chancery
Master of Court of Protection
Companions of the Bath
Companions of the Star of India
Companions of St Michael and St George
Companions of the Indian Empire
Commanders of the Royal Victorian Order
Commanders of the British Empire
Companions of the Distinguished Service Order
Members of the Fourth Class of the Royal Victorian Order
Officers of the Order of the British Empire
Companions of the Imperial Service Order
Eldest sons of the younger sons of Peers
Eldest sons of Baronets
Eldest sons of Knights of the Garter
Eldest sons of Knights, according to the precedence of their fathers
Members of the Fifth Class of the Royal Victorian Order
Members of the Order of the British Empire
Younger sons of Baronets
Younger sons of Knights
Esquires
Gentlemen

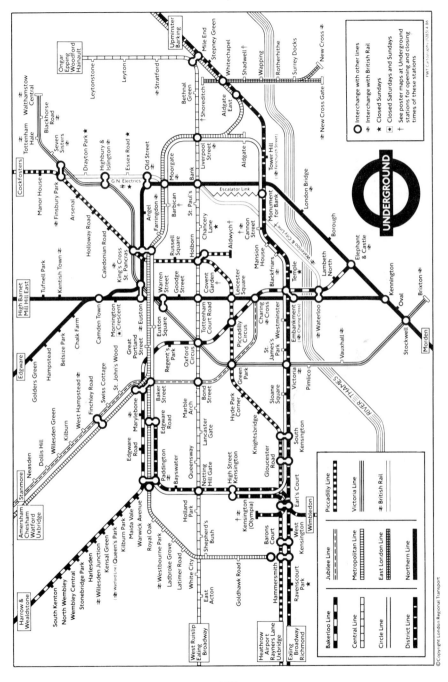

195

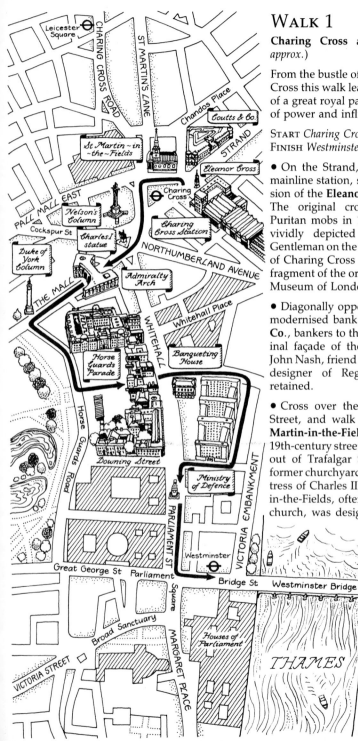

WALK 1

Charing Cross and Whitehall (*1 mile approx.*)

From the bustle of the Strand and Charing Cross this walk leads to Whitehall, the site of a great royal palace and now the centre of power and influence.

START *Charing Cross underground station*
FINISH *Westminster underground station*

● On the Strand, outside Charing Cross mainline station, stands the Victorian version of the **Eleanor Cross** (*see* Memorials). The original cross was destroyed by Puritan mobs in 1643. Its construction is vividly depicted in murals by David Gentleman on the Northern Line platforms of Charing Cross underground station. A fragment of the original is displayed in the Museum of London.

● Diagonally opposite, to the right, is the modernised bank building of **Coutts and Co.**, bankers to the royal family. The original façade of the building designed by John Nash, friend of the Prince Regent and designer of Regent Street, has been retained.

● Cross over the Strand to Duncannon Street, and walk along to the left of **St Martin-in-the-Fields**. This was one of the 19th-century streets created with the laying out of Trafalgar Square. It replaced the former churchyard where Nell Gwyn, mistress of Charles II, was buried. St Martin-in-the-Fields, often called the royal parish church, was designed by James Gibbs, a pupil of Wren. George I was churchwarden, the only British monarch to have held such a post. The royal pew is on the left of the sanctuary.

• Keeping Nelson's Column on your right, walk around the edge of Trafalgar Square to the splendid **equestrian statue of Charles I**, standing on its own traffic island (*see* Statues). The statue is original (1633), except for the sword which was replaced in the last century. An over-enthusiastic journalist trying to get a better vantage point during a royal procession knocked the sword into the crowd and it was not seen again.

• Walk on to **Admiralty Arch**, entrance to The Mall. The archway was designed by Sir Aston Webb as part of the Queen Victoria memorial scheme.

• Continue through the archway and down The Mall. On the right you will see the **Duke of York Column** (*see* Duke of York Column), erected in 1830. The memorial to the son of George III was paid for by a 'thankful army' which had a day's pay stopped to meet the cost.

• Leave The Mall when you have passed the ivy-covered citadel, bomb-proof extension to the Admiralty where vital wartime operations were planned. Beyond this building is **Horse Guards Parade** (*see* Horse Guards Parade; Trooping the Colour), the largest clear space in inner London.

Opposite the Admiralty can be seen the buildings of **Downing Street**, including No. 10, the Prime Minister's official office and residence. The Cabinet room is on the ground floor at the rear of the 17th-century building. The Cabinet was once a subcommittee of the Privy Council and began meeting without the King because the first Hanoverian, George I, could speak little English and became bored. It is unusual for the monarch to visit Downing Street, although George VI did so during the 2nd World War. The Prime Minister travels to Buckingham Palace each Tuesday at 1830 hours for an audience with the monarch.

• Cross over Horse Guards Parade and pass through the central arch (*see* Horse Guards; Household Division; Changing the Guard) on to Whitehall (*see* Whitehall Palace), where the **statue of the Duke of Cambridge** (*see* Statues) marks the approximate site of the turreted entrance to the former Whitehall Palace.

• Cross Whitehall to the **Banqueting House** (*see* Banqueting House). A small bust of Charles I at the main entrance marks the supposed position of the scaffold where he was beheaded, although contemporary drawings appear to dispute that.

Walk on past the **Ministry of Defence** building (*see* Henry VIII's Wine Cellar). Immediately round the corner are **Queen Mary's stairs**, part of Whitehall Palace, where the royal entourage formerly boarded river barges for journeys to Greenwich or Hampton Court. (The river's edge has been pushed back by 19th-century reclamation.)

• Continue through the Embankment Gardens to the far end of the Ministry of Defence, turn right again and left into Whitehall. Opposite is the entrance to Downing Street, now blocked to the public for security reasons.

• Continue down Whitehall to the **Cenotaph** ('empty tomb') in the middle of the road. Each year, on Remembrance Sunday, the Sunday closest to Armistice Day (November 11), members of the royal family attend the service to honour the dead of war. At 1059 the Queen and the Duke of Edinburgh, together with the Prince of Wales and the Duke of Kent, emerge from the nearby government office buildings. Other members of the royal family, including the King of Norway, watch from the balconies.

• Keep walking down Whitehall and Parliament Street and turn left at the traffic lights to conclude the walk at Westminster underground station.

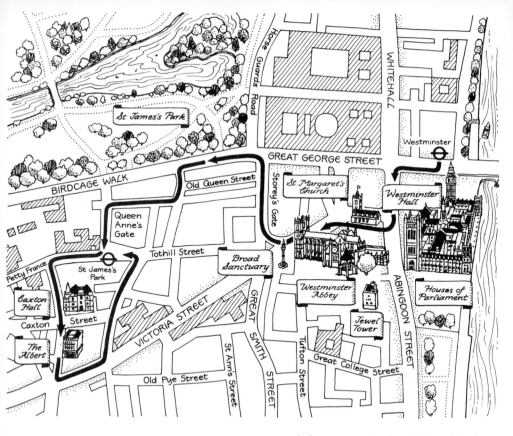

WALK 2

Westminster and Victoria (1¼ miles approx.)

This walk begins in the shadow of the Houses of Parliament, once the site of a great royal palace. It then leads to Westminster Abbey, a building with nine centuries of royal history, and on to the 18th-century elegance of Queen Anne's Gate. It makes its way towards Victoria, and finishes near St James's Park.

START *Westminster underground station*
FINISH *St James's Park underground station*

● Opposite Westminster underground station stand the **Houses of Parliament**, on the site of the old Palace of Westminster (*see* Westminster, Palace of; State Opening of Parliament). Although no longer a royal residence, the Houses of Parliament still retain the name of, and are officially regarded as, a royal palace. The original building is depicted in the Bayeux Tapestry.

● Take the subway from the underground station to cross under Bridge Street. Walk towards Parliament Square and turn left. Ahead, but inside the fence, is **Westminster Hall** (*see* Westminster Hall), the largest Norman hall in the country. Brass plates set in the floor of the building mark the sites of many of the great events that have occurred here, including the place where Charles I stood trial.

● Continue on to Old Palace Yard to the **equestrian statue of Richard the Lionheart** (Richard I) (*see* Statues). Reliefs on the base show how the King met his death. Badly wounded by an arrow, the King generously pardoned his assailant, but he died soon after and the archer was flayed alive.

• Across Abingdon Street is the **Jewel Tower** (*see* Jewel Tower), built in the 14th century for Edward III as the Privy Wardrobe. Personal treasure was stored here, and in Henry VIII's time even chessmen and the princesses' dolls were kept in the building.

• Return to the zebra crossing and walk over to the 15th-century **St Margaret's Church**, the parish church for the House of Commons. The east window commemorates the marriage between Prince Arthur, eldest son of Henry VII, and Catharine of Aragon. By the time the window was finished, Arthur was dead and his brother Henry VIII was married to his widow. By the altar is a statue of Charles I.

• Behind St Margaret's, and to the right, is **Westminster Abbey** (*see* Westminster Abbey; Coronations), which has been given an exterior facelift with the removal of centuries of grime.

Every coronation since 1066 has taken place here, although in that time two sovereigns have not actually been formally crowned: Edward V (one of the princes in the Tower of London, who was murdered in 1483, less than three months after his accession) and Edward VIII (who abdicated in 1936, after less than a year on the throne). Six kings and queens are buried behind the high altar.

In 1540, after Henry VIII dissolved the monasteries, the Abbey became a Royal Peculiar, directly responsible to the monarch and independent of any bishop or diocese.

Legend has it that John Bradshaw, who pronounced the death sentence on Charles I in 1649, haunts the Deanery.

• At the west end of the Abbey is **Broad Sanctuary**, called after the Sanctuary Tower which once stood to the north, and in which fugitives from justice were supposed to be safe. In 1483 Elizabeth Woodville, widow of Edward IV, fled here with her six children after Richard of Gloucester had taken her eldest son, Edward V, to the Tower of London. He later persuaded her to give him her other son, Richard, Duke of York, to be a companion to his brother. Both were murdered within two months. Elizabeth I restricted the right of sanctuary to debtors, and James I abolished it in 1623.

• Walk along Storey's Gate and turn left into Birdcage Walk, site of James I's aviary. Opposite is **St James's Park** (*see* St James's Park). Continue ahead and turn left into Cockpit Steps.

Turn right into Queen Anne's Gate, in which most of the houses, now smart offices, date from the early 18th century. Halfway along on the left is the weathered **statue of Queen Anne** (*see* Statues), the last of the Stuarts. She gave birth to 17 children, none of whom survived to adulthood. She was succeeded in 1714 by the Hanoverian George I who spoke little English and was always regarded as 'that foreigner'.

• Turn left and then right into Petty France, then left again into Palmer Street, and continue to Caxton Street. On the left is **Caxton Hall**, which displays **statues of Edward VII and Queen Victoria** (*see* Statues).

Continue along Palmer Street to Victoria Street and The Albert public house. Splendidly Victorian, complete with gas lamps, its name recalls Queen Victoria's consort, Prince Albert. He was one of the prime innovators of the Great Exhibition of 1851. On his death from typhoid fever in 1861 the Queen went into long-term mourning. She did not reappear in public for eight years, and then still dressed completely in black.

• Turn left into Victoria Street and walk to the small park on the corner of Broadway. Formerly a churchyard, this was the burial place of Colonel Blood, who attempted to steal the Crown Jewels from the Tower of London. Despite his crime, Charles II was so taken with Blood that he was pardoned and given land and a pension.

• Turn left into Broadway and finish the walk at St James's Park underground station.

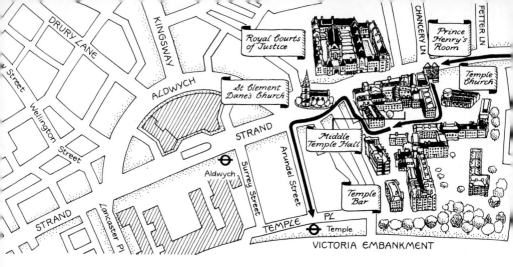

VICTORIA EMBANKMENT

WALK 3

St Paul's, Fleet Street and the Strand (1¼ miles approx.)

From Wren's great memorial this walk passes through ancient streets to Fleet Street and the Strand, and finishes near the historic Temple Bar.

START *St Paul's underground station*
FINISH *Temple underground station*

● Leave St Paul's underground station and walk round to the front of **St Paul's Cathedral**. This splendid tribute to the genius of Sir Christopher Wren has many royal associations. Ceremonies that have taken place here include a thanksgiving service in 1872 attended by Queen Victoria for the recovery of her son, the Prince of Wales, from typhoid fever. This event marked the end of republicanism as a political force in England. An inscription at the bottom of the steps at the front of the Cathedral recalls the service marking the 60th anniversary of Queen Victoria's accession on June 22, 1897.

In 1981 the heir to the throne, Prince Charles, and Lady Diana Spencer broke with usual royal tradition of weddings in Westminster Abbey by marrying in the Cathedral. The event was watched by one of the largest audiences in history – 700 million television viewers.

In front of the building stands a **statue of Queen Anne** (*see* Statues), sometimes wrongly described as being that of Queen Victoria.

● Cross St Paul's Churchyard and walk down Godliman Street to Carter Lane. Turn right and continue to **Wardrobe Place** (*see* King's Wardrobe) on the left. In 1603 William Shakespeare came here to collect 'four yards of scarlet cloth' for an outfit to wear in a procession for James I in the City of London. Shakespeare was one of the King's favourite players. Near Wardrobe Place is the site of Baynard Castle (now demolished), where Edward IV was proclaimed King in 1461.

● Continue down Carter Lane (its width is typical of many thoroughfares of old London). Turn left into Friar Street, and right into Ireland Yard. On the right, in a small courtyard, can still be found a pile of rubble, the only remains of **Blackfriars Monastery**. The Dominican Monks, the Blackfriars, built their priory in 1278 and became rich and powerful, their property extending down to the river. The Monastery was the scene of Cardinal Wolsey's court to try the divorce case of Henry VIII and Catharine of Aragon. Continue along past Playhouse Yard and down to Queen Victoria Street. Cross New Bridge Street (the route of the former Fleet River) and look for No. 14. The plaque on the wall

200

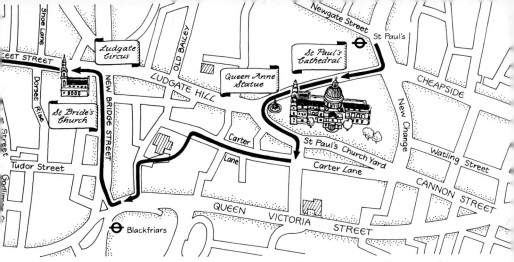

recalls the site of Bridewell Palace (*see* Bridewell) where Catharine of Aragon listened for the sound of footsteps on the bridge across the Fleet for news of the result of Henry's divorce application.

Continue up to Ludgate Circus and turn left into Fleet Street. On the left is **St Bride's Church**. George III was involved in a controversy about the safety of the lightning conductor at the top of the church's steeple.

● Further along Fleet Street, on the right, are the **statues of Mary Queen of Scots**, on the wall of No. 143 (above a restaurant), and **Queen Elizabeth I**, above the vestry door of the church of St Dunstan-in-the-West (*see* Statues). The second is 300 years old.

● Further along Fleet Street, on the left, is the half-timbered **Prince Henry's Room**, named after the popular son of James I (*see* Prince Henry's Room). Pass through the gateway beneath it and walk along Inner Temple Lane to the beautiful **Temple Church**. Built by the Knights Templar in the 12th century, the Temple today is a Royal Peculiar, like Westminster Abbey (*see* Westminster Abbey).

In 1608 King James I granted the Inner Templars, members of the legal fraternity that had taken over the area, limited ownership. In gratitude they gave him a 'stately cup' of pure gold. Later, the King's son, in need of money, pawned it.

● Walk through the cloisters to **Middle Temple Hall**, opened by Queen Elizabeth I in 1576. The Queen may also have been present at the hall in 1601 for a performance by Shakespeare of *Twelfth Night*. Portraits of six monarchs are displayed in the hall.

● Walk up Middle Temple Lane to Fleet Street and **Temple Bar** (*see* Ceremonies), which stands on the site of the original gateway. Many monarchs have been associated with Temple Bar. George III passed through it after attending a service of thanksgiving at St Paul's for recovering his sanity – perhaps optimistically.

● Continue along the Strand (as the road has now become). On the right stand the august **Royal Courts of Justice**, or Law Courts, which were opened in 1882 by Queen Victoria, whose bust is displayed inside the main hall. Walk around the **Church of St Clement Danes**. In front stands a statue of William Gladstone, Liberal Prime Minister in Queen Victoria's time. The Queen's relationship with Mr Gladstone was always difficult and she complained that in her audiences with him he was forever addressing her as if she were a public meeting.

● Turn left and finish the walk at Temple underground station.

WALK 4

Piccadilly, St James's, Buckingham Palace and Victoria (1½ miles approx.)

This walk leads from the bustle of Piccadilly to the elegance of St James's. It then leads into the complex of buildings that make up St James's Palace, passes Buckingham Palace and finishes at Victoria.

START *Piccadilly underground station*
FINISH *Victoria underground station*

• Leave Piccadilly Circus and, keeping to the left, walk along Piccadilly to **Hatchards**, one of the most celebrated bookshops in the English-speaking world. Established in 1797, today it displays its Royal Warrant, the symbol of royal patronage.

• Continue along the same side of Piccadilly to **Fortnum and Mason**, Grocers and Provision Merchants to HM the Queen. The original William Fortnum was a footman to Queen Anne who sold used candles from the royal household at Hugh Mason's grocery shop in Piccadilly. The two are depicted in the splendid clock above the entrance, and appear on the hour. Among the shop's former royal customers was Queen Victoria who on one occasion ordered 250lb of concentrated beef tea for Florence Nightingale in Scutari. Edward VII was a regular, ordering apricot pulp and cheese – Parmesan and Gruyère.

Turn left on Duke Street, St James's. At the corner of Jermyn Street is the modern Cavendish Hotel; inside are mementoes recalling its eccentric former proprietress, Rosa Lewis, who made her reputation by catering for royalty and the aristocracy. She also provided premises for a discreet rendezvous for Edward VII, when he was Prince of Wales, and his mistresses.

• Turn right along Jermyn Street to the corner of Bury Street where a mural above the street name shows Charles II presenting Henry Jermyn, Duke of St Albans, with the deeds for land in the area. This was a reward for his support while Charles was in exile during the republic of 1649–60.

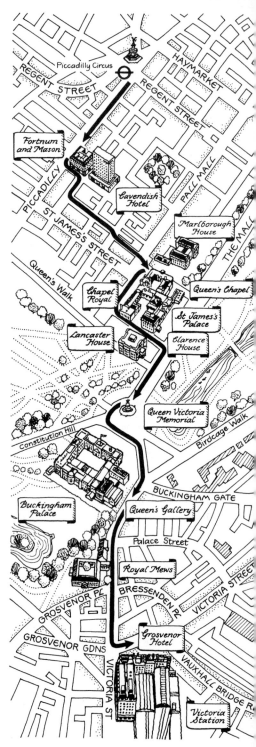

• Walk down Bury Street to King Street and enter Crown Passage opposite. The charming Red Lion public house was a favourite haunt of the Duke of Windsor when he was living in St James's Palace as Prince of Wales.

Cross Pall Mall to the red-brick **Marlborough House** (*see* Marlborough House), now headquarters of the Commonwealth Secretariat. This was the glittering centre of court life when it was the home of Edward, Prince of Wales, and his Princess in the latter half of the 19th century. They had nearly 100 servants, including four to clean the silver and two to look after the 300 bowls of fresh flowers. On the right hand side of Marlborough House is the unobtrusive **Queen's Chapel** with its entrance on Marlborough Gate (*see* Queen's Chapel).

• Opposite is the eastern side of **St James's Palace** (*see* St James's Palace), the main royal residence in London until 1837. From the balcony of **Friary Court**, the Garter King of Arms proclaims new monarchs. This ceremony also takes place before large crowds at Charing Cross, Temple Bar and at the Royal Exchange. In January 1936 Edward VIII and Mrs Simpson watched from the windows behind – an action thought at the time to have been ill-omened.

• Return to the front of St James's Palace and continue to the other end, passing the main clock tower and guard boxes. Turn left into Stable Yard Road. On the right is **Lancaster House** (*see* Lancaster House). To the left, but set back in a private area, is the ⌐hapel Royal (*see* Chapel Royal). On the Feast of Epiphany in January, offerings of gold, frankincense and myrrh are made on behalf of the Queen.

• Continue up Stable Yard Road to pass **Clarence House** (*see* Clarence House), the home of the Queen Mother. The Princess of Wales and the Duchess of York both stayed here before their weddings.

• Turn right into The Mall to approach Buckingham Palace. Ahead is the **Queen Victoria Memorial** (*see* Queen Victoria Memorial), unveiled in 1911 as a tribute to the long-reigning monarch. The Memorial is equipped with microphones for radio and television coverage of royal events.

Beyond is **Buckingham Palace** (*see* Buckingham House; Buckingham Palace; Changing the Guard). The large crowds that gather throughout the year can see little more than the stark façade of the Palace – a high brick wall surrounds the rest. However, good views of the extensive gardens at the rear can be gained from the top of a red double-decker bus travelling along Grosvenor Place towards Victoria.

• Walk to the left of the Palace along Buckingham Palace Road. Pass the Ambassadors' Entrance (used at the annual diplomatic reception in November) to reach the **Queen's Gallery** (*see* Queen's Gallery). This part of the Palace was damaged by bombing in 1940. Despite the danger, George VI and his wife, Queen Elizabeth, remained in the Palace during the height of the blitz, an example of devotion to duty much appreciated by besieged Londoners.

• Continue along the road to pass the **Royal Mews** (*see* Royal Mews). Until the time of Henry VIII, a 'mews' was where hunting birds such as falcons were housed during their loss of plumage – hence the word 'mewing'. When Henry's stables were burnt down, his horses were moved into the Mews, to the north of Whitehall Palace. The Royal Mews is now the home of carriage horses and coaches.

• Ahead is Victoria Station, a confusing jumble of buildings. The station is dwarfed by the Grosvenor Hotel (1861). The first and top floors are decorated with portrait busts set in medallions – most are too high to identify clearly – of eminent Victorians, including Queen Victoria and Prince Albert. Many of the state visits by foreign royalty and leaders begin officially at Victoria Station. The walk finishes at Victoria underground station.

WALK 5

Kensington High Street, Palace and Gardens and the Serpentine (1¾ miles approx.)

From London's second-busiest high street the walk passes homely Kensington Palace, through leisurely gardens and parks, and past imposing Victorian institutions and statues, to finish at Knightsbridge.

START *High Street Kensington underground station*
FINISH *Knightsbridge underground station*

• Leave High Street Kensington underground station and cross over the road to Kensington Church Walk, almost immediately opposite. Follow Kensington Church Walk round to **St Mary Abbots Church**; founded in the 12th century, the church is the fourth building on this site. William and Mary of Orange worshipped here before Kensington Palace (*see* Kensington Palace) had a chapel.

• Continue on to Holland Street and cross Kensington Church Street. Walk along

York House Place and take the passageway through Palace Green and by **Kensington Palace** (*see* Kensington Palace). The building is less imposing than other royal palaces and Leigh Hunt described it as a 'place to take tea in', whereas Windsor Castle was a 'place to receive monarchs in', and Buckingham Palace was a 'place to see fashion in'.

It was occupied by a succession of monarchs from William and Mary to George II. It was here that Victoria was roused from her bed in 1837 to hear the news of her accession to the throne.

• Turn left round the end of the Palace to see the **statue of Queen Victoria** in her night attire, dressed as she was when told of her new role (*see* Statues). Cross Broad Walk and **Kensington Gardens** (*see* Kensington Gardens) and walk towards Queen's Gate. Nearby is the **Albert Memorial** (*see* Albert Memorial), designed by Giles Gilbert Scott, champion of the Neo-Gothic revival.

Opposite is the **Royal Albert Hall** (*see* Royal Albert Hall), built – only after much debate and delay – in 1868–70 to the design

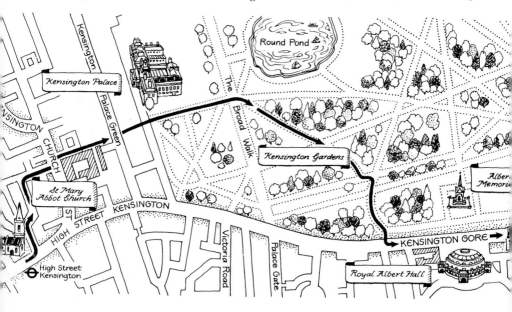

of Colonel H. Y. Darracott Scott. When Queen Victoria laid the foundation stone she unexpectedly announced that 'Royal Albert' was to be added to the existing title of 'Hall of Arts and Sciences'. The oval hall measures 272 ft by 238 ft and holds 7,000 people. For many years the acoustics were heavily criticised – Sir Thomas Beecham said the hall could be used for a hundred things, but music was not one of them. In 1968 the sound was improved by hanging saucer-like shapes from the roof.

• Continue along Kensington Gore to the **Royal Geographical Society** (an offshoot of the Travellers' Club, membership of which is restricted to those who have travelled a distance of 500 miles, measured in a straight line, outside the British Isles). The Society was granted a Royal Charter by Queen Victoria in 1859. Among expeditions it has sponsored and organised are those of Livingstone, Stanley, Scott and Hillary.

• Return to Hyde Park through the Alexandra Gate opposite, and continue on to **Rotten Row** (*see* Hyde Park; Kensington Gardens). One mile long, it is still the fashionable place to ride in London. As Prince of Wales, Edward VII announced his friendship with the beautiful Lillie Langtry by riding together there. Beyond Rotten Row is the **Serpentine** (*see* Hyde Park) which was dammed for George II's queen, Caroline, in 1730.

• Return to the Prince of Wales Gate at the bottom of Hyde Park. Near here the Crystal Palace was erected for the Great Exhibition of 1851 (*see* Hyde Park). The building was three times the length of St Paul's Cathedral and included 300,000 panes of glass. Prince Albert was so inspired by the success of the event that he developed the idea of a range of museums and colleges in the area. From this – and with the profits of the Exhibition – were established some of the great institutions that now dominate South Kensington.

• Continue along Knightsbridge past the Westminster Synagogue on the right. This stands on the site of Kent House, once the home of the Duke of Kent, Queen Victoria's father. Walk on to Knightsbridge underground station where the walk finishes.

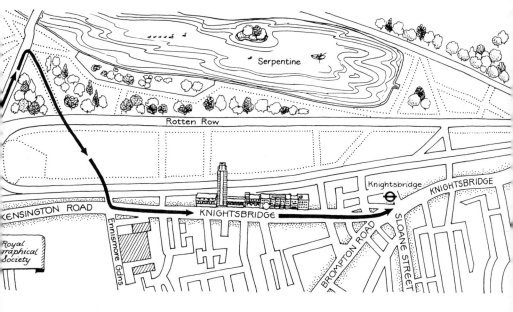

Royal Calendar

Daily Events

11.30 a.m. Changing the Guard at Buckingham Palace

11.15 a.m. Changing the Guard at St James's Palace

11.30 a.m. Changing the Guard at the Tower of London

11.00 a.m. Changing the Guard at Windsor Castle

9.50 p.m. Ceremony of the Keys at the Tower of London

January

6th Epiphany Service at the Chapel Royal, St James's Palace

February

6th Accession Day: Royal Salute in Hyde Park and at the Tower of London

19th Prince Andrew's birthday

March

10th Prince Edward's birthday
Royal Film Performance

April

Ceremony of the Garter at St George's Chapel, Windsor

21st The Queen's birthday: Royal Salute in Hyde Park and at the Tower of London

Badminton Horse Trials

May

early May Royal Mausoleum, Windsor open to the public

Chelsea Flower Show at the Royal Hospital, Chelsea

29th (or as near as possible) Founder's Day at the Royal Hospital (King Charles II)

late May (if not, June) Beating Retreat: the Royal Artillery at Horse Guards Parade

June

early June (if not, May) Beating Retreat: the Royal Artillery at Horse Guards Parade

early June Derby Day at Epsom

2nd Coronation Day: Royal Salute in Hyde Park and at the Tower of London

first Saturday The Queen's Official Birthday: Royal Salute in Hyde Park and at the Tower of London; Trooping the Colour, Horse Guards Parade

mid-June (Monday of Ascot week) Ceremony of the Garter, Windsor

Royal Ascot

10th Prince Philip's birthday: Royal Salute in Hyde Park and at the Tower

Lawn Tennis Championships at the All England Club, Wimbledon

The Lords Test Match

21st Prince William's birthday

July

1st Princess of Wales's birthday

Royal Tournament

Garden Parties at Buckingham Palace

Investitures at Buckingham Palace

Receptions at St James's Palace for the young who have reached Gold Standard in the Duke of Edinburgh's Award

Henley Royal Regatta

Swan Upping: annual marking and recording of the Queen's Swans at different points on the Thames

July–September Henry Wood Promenade Concerts at the Royal Albert Hall

August

4th Queen Elizabeth, the Queen Mother's birthday: Royal Salute in Hyde Park and at the Tower of London

15th Princess Anne's birthday

21st Princess Margaret's birthday

Cowes Week

September

Battle of Britain Service

Opening of Commonwealth Parliamentary Conference (if in London, it is held in Westminster Hall)

15th Prince Harry's birthday

October
Horse of the Year Show at Wembley
late October (if not, November) State
Opening of Parliament

November
early November (if not, October) State
Opening of Parliament
second Saturday Festival of
Remembrance at the Royal Albert Hall
second Sunday Remembrance Sunday:
service at the Cenotaph; Royal Salute
on Horse Guard Parade
14th Prince of Wales's birthday
15th Princess Andrew, Duchess of York's
birthday
The Lord Mayor's Show
Investitures at Buckingham Palace

late November Royal Command
Performance at Drury Lane Theatre or
London Palladium

December
Investitures at Buckingham Palace
Royal Smithfield Show

Also:
Thursday before Easter Royal Maundy
Distribution
Royal Visits to the City of London:
ceremony at Temple Bar
Ceremonies for the Order of St Michael
and St George, and also for the Order
of St John

ORGANISED TOURS IN AND AROUND LONDON

London Transport
Information Centres at Euston; King's
Cross; St James's Park; Oxford Circus;
Piccadilly Circus; Charing Cross;
Victoria; and Heathrow
General information – tel: 01–222 1234
Departures from Wilton Road Coach
Station

London Day Tour
whole day; Mon–Sat; incl. lunch
finishing point: Victoria
highlights: St James's, West End,
Westminster, City of London, St
Paul's, the Tower, Changing the
Guard, tour of Westminster Abbey

Westminster and Changing the Guard
morning; Mon–Sat
finishing point: Victoria
highlights: Changing the Guard, tour of
Westminster Abbey, Big Ben and the
Houses of Parliament, Downing Street

City and the Tower of London
afternoon; Mon–Sat
finishing point: Victoria
highlights: Mansion House, Bank of
England, Monument, St Paul's, tour of
Tower of London

Sunday London and Changing the Guard
summer season; morning; Sundays
finishing point: Victoria
highlights: Changing the Guard, the
Tower, St Paul's, City, Westminster,
Westminster Cathedral, Big Ben and
the Houses of Parliament

London Views and Lunch Cruise
morning; Sundays; incl. 4-course lunch
finishing point: Westminster Pier
highlights: St Paul's, the Tower,
Trafalgar Square, cruise to Greenwich,
Cutty Sark, Big Ben and the Houses of
Parliament

A Night on the Town
evenings; Mondays, Wednesdays and
Saturdays; incl. supper
finishing point: Victoria
highlights: St Paul's, the Tower,
Buckingham Palace, visit to 'a typical
pub'

London and the River by Night
summer season; evenings; Tuesdays and
Thursdays; incl. buffet supper
finishing point: Westminster Pier
highlights: St Paul's, the Tower, Buckingham Palace, Trafalgar Square, cruise

Greenwich and the Thames Barrier
whole day; Wednesdays; incl. lunch
finishing point: Victoria
highlights: Cleopatra's Needle, the
Tower, Tower Bridge, *Cutty Sark*, the
Thames Barrier, National Maritime
Museum, Royal Observatory

River Cruise and Royal Greenwich
afternoon; Mon–Fri
finishing point: Victoria
highlights: cruise to Greenwich,
Cleopatra's Needle, the Tower, Tower
Bridge, *Cutty Sark*, Royal Naval
College, Royal Observatory

*Royal Windsor and King Henry VIII's
Hampton Court Palace*
whole day; Wednesdays and Saturdays;
incl. lunch
finishing point: Victoria
highlights: tour of both royal homes and
gardens, pass Runnymede

King Henry VIII's Hampton Court Palace
afternoon; Sundays (Tuesdays and
Thursdays during summer season)
finishing point: Victoria
highlights: tour of the palace and garden

Royal Windsor and Runnymede
afternoon; Wednesday and Saturday
finishing point: Victoria
highlights: Runnymede and tour of
Windsor Castle

*Original London Transport Sightseeing
Tour*
takes about 1½ hours; daily with frequent
departures
departure and finishing points at
Piccadilly Circus; Marble Arch; Baker
Street Station; Victoria Street

London Tour Company
618 Linen Hall, 162/168 Regent Street,
London N1R 5TB. Tel: 01-734 3502/3
Departures from Lower Belgrave Street,
Victoria

London in a Day
whole day; Tuesdays, Thursdays and
Saturdays

finishing point: Lower Belgrave Street
highlights: Westminster Abbey,
St Paul's, the Tower, Changing the
Guard, Piccadilly Circus, Buckingham
Palace, Houses of Parliament, Bank of
England

The West End of London
morning; Tuesdays, Thursdays and
Saturdays
finishing point: Lower Belgrave Street
highlights: Changing the Guard, tour of
Westminster Abbey

The City and the Tower of London
afternoon; Tuesdays, Thursdays and
Saturdays
finishing point: Lower Belgrave Street
highlights: St Paul's, the Tower

*Morning Luncheon Cruise and London
Sights*
morning; Sundays; incl. lunch
finishing point: Westminster Pier
highlights: Changing the Guard,
Buckingham Palace, Big Ben and the
Houses of Parliament

Royal Windsor
afternoon; Saturdays
finishing point: Lower Belgrave Street
highlights: pass through Runnymede,
tour of Windsor Castle

Scenic Thames Cruise
afternoon; Wednesdays and Sundays
finishing point: Lower Belgrave Street
highlights: Richmond, cruise from
Richmond to Hampton Court, tour of
Hampton Court Palace

Leeds Castle–Greenwich–Thames Barrier
whole day; Wednesdays and Sundays
finishing point: Lower Belgrave Street
highlights: tour of Leeds Castle,
Greenwich, *Cutty Sark* and *Gypsy Moth
IV*, Royal Naval College, the Thames
Barrier

Windsor and Hampton Court
long afternoon; Mondays and Fridays
finishing point: Lower Belgrave Street
highlights: tour of Windsor and

208

Hampton Court; pass Kensington Palace, Runnymede and Kingston-upon-Thames

Evening Supper Cruise and London Sights
summer season; evening; Mondays and Wednesdays; incl. buffet supper
finishing point: Westminster pier
highlights: cruise down the Thames, pub visit

London by Sunset
evening; Fridays and Saturdays
finishing point: Lower Belgrave Street
highlights: tour of London and two pub visits

Frames Rickards Sightseeing and Coach Tours

11 Herbrand Street, London WC1N 1EX.
Tel: 01-837 3111
departure and finishing points at The Forum Hotel, Cromwell Road; 11 Herbrand Street, WC1; 60 Seymour Street, W1; Thomas Cook, Berkeley Street, W1

West End Daily Morning tour
also departs and finishes at Charles Dickens Hotel, Lancaster Gate
highlights: tour of Westminster Abbey, the Cenotaph, Trafalgar Square, Buckingham Palace and Changing the Guard

City Daily Afternoon tour
also departs and finishes at Charles Dickens Hotel, Lancaster Gate
highlights: the Law Courts and Fleet Street, tour of St Paul's, tour of the Tower

Day Tour of London
all day; daily
highlights: tour of Westminster Abbey, Buckingham Palace and Changing the Guard, St Paul's, tour of the Tower

Panoramic London with Thames River Cruise
summer season; morning or afternoon; daily
highlights: river view of St Paul's and the Tower, the City, Bank of England, Mansion House, Trafalgar Square, Buckingham Palace, Houses of Parliament and Westminster Abbey

Panoramic Tour of London
morning or afternoon; daily
highlights: the Houses of Parliament and Big Ben, Westminster Abbey, St Paul's

Sights of London and River Cruise with Luncheon
morning; Sundays; incl. 3-course lunch
finishing point: Westminster Pier

Elizabethan Banquet in the Old Palace at Hatfield House
evening; Tuesdays, Thursdays, Fridays and Saturdays
highlights: banquet with minstrels and ballad singers in the fifteenth-century palace of Queen Elizabeth I

Evening River Thames Cruise
no departure from Thomas Cook
summer season; Mondays, Wednesdays and Sundays; incl. light supper
finishing point: Westminster Pier

Windsor Castle and Runnymede
departs and finishes also from Charles Dickens Hotel, Lancaster Gate
afternoon; daily
highlights: walk in Windsor; tour of castle; pass Runnymede

Royal Windsor, Hampton Court and River Cruise
whole day; daily; incl. lunch
highlights: cruise from Maidenhead to Windsor, tour of castle, tour of Hampton Court Palace

Kew Gardens and Hampton Court Palace
summer season; afternoon; Mondays, Wednesdays, Fridays and Sundays
highlights: tour of Royal Botanic Gardens and tour of Hampton Court Palace

Greenwich and River Thames
departures only from 11 Herbrand Street, WC1, and from Thomas Cook, Berkeley Street, W1

summer season; afternoon; Tuesdays and Thursdays
finishing point: Westminster Pier
highlights: Houses of Parliament, Westminster Abbey, Lambeth Palace, Royal Naval College, Royal Observatory, visit to the National Maritime Museum and *Cutty Sark*, cruise to Westminster

Evans Evans Tours
27 Cockspur Street, Trafalgar Square, London SW1Y 5BT. Tel: 01–930 2377
departure and finishing points at: 25A Cockspur Street, SW1; 35–37 Woburn Place, WC1; Park Plaza Hotel, Bayswater Road, W2; 136 Wigmore Street, W1; 10 Ashburn Gardens, SW5

London Highlights and Thames Cruise
afternoon or morning; daily
finishing point: Trafalgar Square
highlights: river view of St Paul's and the Tower, Stock Exchange, Bank of England, Mansion House, St Paul's, Big Ben Houses of Parliament, Downing Street

Discovering London
whole day; daily; incl. lunch
highlights: tour of Westminster Abbey, Changing the Guard, 3-course cockney lunch, St Paul's, tour of Tower

The City of London, Crown Jewels and the Tower
afternoon; daily
highlights: Bank of England, Stock Exchange, Mansion House, Old Bailey, visit St Paul's, tour of the Tower

London's West End
morning; daily
finishing point: Trafalgar Square
highlights: Big Ben and the Houses of Parliament, visit to Westminster Abbey, Buckingham Palace, Changing the Guard, National Gallery, Scotland Yard, British Museum

London Night Out at the Cockney Tavern Music Hall, Charing Cross Road
Saturday nights
Cockney Cabaret and 4-course dinner

London Night Out at The Beefeater by the Tower, Ivory House, East Smithfield
Saturday nights
6-course feast and entertainment at the court of Henry VIII

London Night Out at the Talk of London Cabaret, Drury Lane
Saturday nights
International cabaret and dancing with a 4-course meal

Night Out at the Caledonian, Hanover Street
Saturday nights
5-course Scottish feast with Scottish cabaret and band

Shakespeare's Feast
Saturday nights
pageant and 6-course banquet attended by characters from Shakespeare's plays

Elizabethan Banquet at Hatfield House
departures only from 25A Cockspur Street, SW1, and 35–37 Woburn Place, WC1
evening; Tuesdays, Thursdays, Fridays and Saturdays
finishing points: Russell Square, Marble Arch, Bayswater Road, South Kensington, Trafalgar Square
highlights: 4-course feast with minstrels and ballad singers

Greenwich and Thames Cruise
departs and finishes only at 136 Wigmore Street, W1, 35–37 Woburn Place, WC1 and 25A Cockspur Street, SW1
summer season; afternoon; Tuesdays, Wednesdays, Fridays, Saturdays and Sundays
highlights: cruise to Greenwich past the Tower and St Paul's, Royal Observatory, *Cutty Sark* and *Gypsy Moth IV*, Royal Naval College

Hampton Court and Kew Gardens
summer season; morning; Tuesdays, Thursdays, Saturdays and Sundays
highlights: tour of Hampton Court Palace and visit to the Royal Botanic Gardens

Windsor Castle and the Royalty and Empire Exhibition
summer season; afternoon; every day except Monday
highlights: tour of Windsor Castle and visit to the Exhibition at Windsor and Eton Railway Station

Windsor, Hampton Court and Thames Cruise
whole day; daily; incl. tea
highlights: Changing the Guard at Windsor Castle and tour of castle, tour of Hampton Court Palace and cruise to Kingston-upon-Thames

London Pride/Culture Bus
60 St James's Street, London SW1A 1LE. Tel: 01–629 4999

London Pride Guided Tour
bus journey through the heart of London buses leave frequently all day from the Trocadero, Coventry Street

Culture Bus Sightseeing
buses all day, stopping at twenty different places of interest in London; you may get off and rejoin buses at each stop
includes: London Museums and Art Galleries, Madame Tussauds and the Planetarium, St Paul's, the Barbican, HMS *Belfast*, the Tower, Westminster, Royal Albert Hall, Kensington Palace

London Cityrama
Silverthorne Road, Battersea, London SW8. Tel: 01–720 6663
1½–2 hour tour of London; daily
departures every half hour from: Piccadilly Circus; Grosvenor Gardens; Victoria; Trafalgar Square; Westminster Abbey
syncronised tape-recorded commentaries in eight different languages across London from the Royal Albert Hall to the Tower of London

Go-By-Guide Ltd
67 Clapham Common Northside, London SW4. Tel: 01–350 2408
daily tours in private cars for up to four

people with driver/guide
the departure point is your choice

Full-Day London
highlights: Big Ben and the Houses of Parliament, Buckingham Palace, Changing the Guard, Westminster Abbey, the Tower, St Paul's, the Royal Parks, Museums and Galleries, Shopping Districts

Half-Day London
3 hours
highlights: the major sights of the City and West End with visits to two of the following – the Tower, Westminster Abbey, St Paul's

London and Windsor
whole day
highlights: the major sights of London, tour of Windsor Castle

Half-Day Windsor, Eton and Runnymede
highlights: tour of Windsor Castle, Eton College, pass Runnymede

Half-Day Hampton Court/Kew Gardens
highlights: tour of Hampton Court Palace and optional extended tour to the Royal Botanic Gardens

London Waterbus Company
Camden Lock, London NW1 8AF. Tel: 01–482 2550
special day trips with full commentary one Saturday each month
departure and finishing point: Camden Lock
cruise through twelve locks and seven miles of little-seen London, through the Islington Tunnel and Victoria Park, and past the Three Mills on the River Lea; one-hour stop to see London's dockland area and return via the Hertford Union Canal and Regent's Canal

Charing Cross River Services
Charing Cross Pier, Victoria Embankment, London WC2N 6NU. Tel: 01–930 0971

Historic Greenwich
one hour
departures from Charing Cross Pier
every half hour
highlights: *Cutty Sark* and *Gypsy Moth IV*,
the Royal Observatory, Royal Naval
College, National Maritime Museum,
Greenwich Park, Blackheath

The Tower of London
one hour
departures from Charing Cross Pier
every half hour
highlights: the Tower, Tower Bridge and
Walkway, HMS *Belfast*, St Katharine's
Yacht Marina

Evening Cruise
summer season; twice every evening
departures from Charing Cross Pier
river sightseeing with bar facilities

Jason's Trip
60 Blomfield Road, Little Venice, London
W9. Tel: 01–286 3428
cruises daily for 1½ hours
departures from opposite the offices
several times a day
the original London canal cruise in a
narrow boat along Regent's Canal

The Thames Floating Entertainers
River Ride Ltd, Westminster Pier,
London SW1. Tel: 01-839 2349

Music Hall Showboat
summer season; evening; Sundays
departs and finishes at Westminster Pier
3-course dinner, music hall show and
dancing

Sunday Luncheon Cruise
departs and finishes at Westminster Pier
cruise to Greenwich and back with
traditional Sunday lunch and
commentary

Luncheon Cruise
summer season; Saturdays and
Wednesdays
departs and finishes at Westminster Pier
cruise to Greenwich and back with lunch
and commentary

Floodlit and Supper Cruise
summer season; every evening except
Saturday
departs and finishes at Westminster Pier
cruise between Chelsea and the Tower
with optional supper

Disco Cruise
every night
supper and dancing

Green Line Buses
Green Line Information Office, Eccleston
Bridge, Victoria. Tel: 01-668 7261

*Bus Service to Royal Windsor and the
Royalty and Railways Exhibition (if
available)*
departs daily from Eccleston Bridge

Bus Service to Hampton Court
departs daily from Eccleston Bridge

Also worth visiting

The London Experience
The sights and sounds of London old
and new at the Trocadero, Piccadilly
Circus, London W1
daily from 1020 hours and every 40
minutes thereafter until 2220; multi-
screen audio-visual entertainment
allowing an audience to experience
London from Roman times up to the
present day

TOURIST INFORMATION SERVICES

In advance, write to:
Central Information Unit,
London Visitor and Convention Bureau,
26 Grosvenor Gardens, London SW1W 0DU

For personal callers:
Tourist Information Centre (LVCB)
Victoria Station Forecourt, SW1
Open daily 0900–2030 (July and August:
extended hours)
Telephone Information Service
(LVCB)
01-730 3488
Open Mon–Fri 0900–1730 (automatic
queueing system)
Harrods Tourist Information Desk
(LVCB)
Harrods, Knightsbridge, SW1
Open during store hours
Heathrow Tourist Information Centre
(LVCB)
Heathrow Central Station, Heathrow
Airport, Middlesex
Open daily 0900–1800
Selfridges Tourist Information Centre
(LVCB)
Selfridges, Oxford Street, W1
Open during store hours
HM Tower of London Tourist
Information Centre (LVCB)
West Gate, HM Tower of London, EC3
Open (April–October) daily 1000–1800
British Travel Centre (BTA)
Lower Regent Street, W1
Open Mon–Sat 0900–1830, Sun
1000–1600

Local Information Centres:
City of London Information Centre
St Paul's Churchyard, EC4
Tel: 01-606 3030
Clerkenwell Heritage Centre
33 St John's Square, EC1. Tel: 01-250
1039
Croydon Tourist Information Centre
Katharine Street, Croydon, Surrey
Tel: 01-688 3627 ext 45/46
Greenwich Tourist Information Centre
Cutty Sark Gardens, SE10. Tel: 01-858
6376

Hillingdon Tourist Information
Centre
22 High Street, Uxbridge, Middlesex
Tel: Uxbridge (0895) 50706
Kingston-upon-Thames Tourist
Information Centre
Heritage Centre, Fairfield West,
Kingston-upon-Thames, Surrey
Tel: 01-546 5386
Lewisham Tourist Information Centre
Borough Mall, Lewisham Centre, SE13
Tel: 01-318 5421/2
Richmond Tourist Information Centre
Central Library, Little Green, Richmond,
Surrey. Tel: 01-940 9125
Tower Hamlets Tourist Information
Centre
88 Roman Road, E2. Tel: 01-980 3749
Twickenham Tourist Information
Centre
District Library, Garfield Road,
Twickenham, Middlesex. Tel: 01-892 0032

Royal Warrant Holders in London

The lists that follow are not exhaustive lists of Royal Warrant holders; they are selections of shops and businesses in London that hold Royal Warrants and most of which are open to the public.

Royal Warrants of Appointment to HM Queen Elizabeth II

Department of Her Majesty's Privy Purse

Ainsworths Homoeopathic Pharmacy	*Chemists*
Amies, Hardy, Ltd	*Dressmakers*
Army & Navy Stores Ltd	*Suppliers of Household and Fancy Goods*
Asprey plc	*Goldsmiths, Silversmiths and Jewellers*
Billings & Edmonds Ltd	*Tailors and Outfitters*
Bridger & Kay Ltd	*Postage Stamp Dealers*
Buckley, Anthony & Constantine Ltd	*Photographers*
Burberrys Ltd	*Weatherproofers*
Calman Links (Trading) Ltd	*Furriers*
Carrington & Co. Ltd	*Silversmiths and Jewellers*
Cartier Ltd	*Jewellers and Goldsmiths*
Collingwood of Bond Street Ltd	*Jewellers and Silversmiths*
Cyclax Ltd	*Manufacturers of Beauty Preparations*
Daniel, Neville, Ltd	*Hairdressers*
Devlin, Stuart, Ltd	*Goldsmiths and Jewellers*
Forces Help Society, The, and Lord Roberts Workshops	*Manufacturers of Fancy Goods*
Fox, Frederick, Ltd	*Milliners*
General Trading Co. (Mayfair) Ltd, The	*Suppliers of Fancy Goods*
Gibbons, Stanley, plc	*Philatelists*
Goodyear, Edward, Ltd	*Florists*
Grima, Andrew, Ltd	*Jewellers*
Halcyon Days Ltd	*Suppliers of Objets d'Art*
Hamblin, Theodore, Ltd	*Opticians*
Hamleys of Regent Street Ltd	*Toy and Sports Merchants*
Hartnell, Norman, Ltd	*Dressmakers*
Hatchards	*Booksellers*
Heaton, Wallace, Ltd	*Suppliers of Photographic Equipment*
John, C., (Rare Rugs), Ltd	*Suppliers of Carpets*
Johnson, Herbert, (Bond Street) Ltd	*Hatters*
Lillywhites Ltd	*Outfitters*
Lock, S., Ltd	*Embroiderers*
Longmire, Paul, Ltd	*Suppliers of Jewellery and Leather Goods*
Mappin & Webb Ltd	*Silversmiths*
Maxwell, Henry, & Co. Ltd	*Bootmakers*
Mirman, Simone	*Milliner*
Page, J. & E., (Sales) Ltd	*Florists*
Purdey, James, & Sons Ltd	*Gun and Cartridge Makers*
Rayne, H. & M., Ltd	*Shoemakers and Handbag Manufacturers*
Remploy Ltd	*Manufacturers of Knitwear*
Rigby, John, & Co. (Gunmakers) Ltd	*Rifle and Cartridge Makers*
Rigby and Peller	*Corsetières*

Simpson (Piccadilly) Ltd	*Outfitters*
Smythson, Frank	*Stationers*
Spink & Son Ltd	*Medallists*
Steinway & Sons	*Pianoforte Manufacturers*
Tate, Anthony	*Chemists*
Thomas, Ian	*Dressmakers*
Trumper, Geo. F.	*Hairdressers*
Wartski Ltd	*Jewellers*
Weatherill, Bernard, Ltd	*Riding Clothes Outfitters and Livery Tailors*

Department of the Master of the Household

Arden, Elizabeth, Ltd	*Manufacturers of Cosmetics*
Benoist, V., Ltd	*Purveyors of Table Delicacies*
Berry Bros. & Rudd Ltd	*Wine and Spirit Merchants*
Broadwood, John, & Sons Ltd	*Pianoforte Manufacturers*
Bronnley, H., & Co. Ltd	*Toilet Soap Makers*
Charbonnel et Walker Ltd	*Chocolate Manufacturers*
Christopher & Co. Ltd	*Wine Merchants*
Cole and Son (Wallpapers) Ltd	*Suppliers of Wallpapers*
Coney & Barrow Ltd	*Wine Merchants*
De Blank, Justin, (Provisions) Ltd	*Bakers*
Dewhurst, J. H., Ltd	*Butchers*
Ferrari, S., & Sons (Soho) Ltd	*Suppliers of Kitchen Equipment*
Findlater Mackie Todd & Co. Ltd	*Wine and Spirit Merchants*
Fitch & Son Ltd	*Provision Merchants*
Floris, J., Ltd	*Perfumers*
Fortnum & Mason plc	*Grocers and Provision Merchants*
Foster, John, & Co. Ltd	*Suppliers of Furnishing Fabrics*
Goode, Thomas, & Co. Ltd	*Suppliers of China and Glass*
Harrods Ltd	*Suppliers of Provisions and Household Goods*
Harvey Nichols Ltd	*Linen Drapers*
Heal & Son Ltd	*Upholsterers and Suppliers of Bedding*
Higgins, H. R., (Coffee-man) Ltd	*Coffee Merchants*
Horne Brothers plc	*Livery Tailors*
Jones, Yarrell, & Co. Ltd	*Newsagents*
Justerini & Brooks Ltd	*Wine Merchants*
Lidstone, John	*Butchers*
Mayfair Trunks Ltd	*Suppliers of Luggage*
Morny Ltd	*Manufacturers of Soap*
Newbery, Henry, & Co. Ltd	*Suppliers of Furnishing Trimmings*
H. A. Percheron Ltd	*Suppliers of Furnishing Fabrics*
Prestat Ltd	*Purveyors of Chocolates*
Price's Patent Candle Company Ltd	*Candlemakers*
Saccone & Speed Ltd	*Wine Merchants*
Sandeman, Geo. G., Sons & Co. Ltd	*Wine Merchants*
Sekers Fabrics Ltd	*Manufacturers of Furnishing Fabrics*
Sproston, W. F., Ltd	*Suppliers of Fish*
Szell, Michael, Ltd	*Suppliers of Furnishing Fabrics*
Thresher & Glenny Ltd	*Shirtmakers*
Tissunique Ltd	*Suppliers of Furnishing Fabrics*

Turner, G. J., & Co. (Trimmings) Ltd	*Manufacturers of Furnishing Trimmings*
Twining, R., & Co. Ltd	*Tea and Coffee Merchants*
Warner & Sons Ltd	*Suppliers of Silks and Furnishings Fabrics*
Woodhouse Hume Ltd	*Suppliers of Meat and Poultry*
Yardley & Co. Ltd	*Manufacturers of Soap*

Lord Chamberlain's Office

Atlantis Paper Co. Ltd	*Fine Art and Archival Suppliers*
Connolly Bros. (Curriers) Ltd	*Leather Tanners and Curriers*
Cooper, A. C., Ltd	*Fine Art Photographers*
Dege, J., & Sons Ltd	*Tailors*
Ede & Ravenscroft Ltd	*Robe Makers*
Fine Arts Valets Ltd	*Fine Art Services*
Garrard & Co. Ltd	*Goldsmiths and Crown Jewellers*
Maggs Bros Ltd	*Purveyors of Rare Books and Manuscripts*
Plowden & Smith Ltd	*Restorers of Fine Art Objects*
Rogers, T., & Co. (Packers) Ltd	*Packers and Transporters of Works of Art*
Seaby, B. A., Ltd	*Numismatists*
Skinner, A. E., & Co.	*Jewellers and Silversmiths*
Tortoiseshell and Ivory House Ltd, The	*Restorers of Objets d'Art*
Toye, Kenning & Spencer Ltd	*Suppliers of Gold and Silver Laces, Insignia and Embroidery*
Wiggins, Arnold, & Sons Ltd	*Picture Frame Makers*

Royal Mews Department

Allen, J. A., & Co. Ltd	*Suppliers of Equine and Equestrian Literature*
Gardiner & Co.	*Suppliers of Protective Clothing*
Gidden, W. & H., Ltd	*Saddlers*
Godfrey Davis Europcar Ltd	*Motor Vehicle Hirers*
Lobb, John, Ltd	*Bootmakers*
Owen, Charles, & Co. (Bow) Ltd	*Protective Headwear Manufacturer*
Patey, S., (London) Ltd	*Manufacturers of Hats*
Poole, Henry, & Co. (Savile Row) Ltd	*Livery Outfitters*
Swaine, Adeney, Brigg & Sons Ltd	*Whip and Glove Makers*

Royal Warrants of Appointment to HM Queen Elizabeth, the Queen Mother

Ackerman's Chocolates Ltd	*Confectioners*
Ainsworths Homoeopathic Pharmacy	*Chemists*
Amor, Albert, Ltd	*Suppliers of Fine Porcelain*
Aquascutum Ltd	*Makers of Weatherproof Garments*
Arden, Elizabeth, Ltd	*Manufacturers of Cosmetics*
Army and Navy Stores Ltd	*Suppliers of Household and Fancy Goods*
Asprey and Co. plc	*Jewellers*
Benoist, V., Ltd	*Purveyors of General Groceries*
Bronnley, J. & Co Ltd	*Toilet Soap Makers*
Burberrys Ltd	*Weatherproofers*
Burton Group plc	*Tailors*
Calman Links (Trading) Ltd	*Furriers*
Carrington & Co. Ltd	*Jewellers and Silversmiths*
Cartier Ltd	*Jewellers and Goldsmiths*
Chess, Mary, Ltd	*Perfumers*

Collingwood of Bond Street Ltd	*Jewellers*
Dipré, D., & Son	*Cutlery Services, Knifegrinders and Suppliers of Kitchen Equipment*
Ede & Ravenscroft Ltd	*Robemakers*
Fortnum & Mason plc	*Suppliers of Leather and Fancy Goods*
Foster, John, & Co.	*Suppliers of Furnishing Fabrics*
Garrard & Co. Ltd	*Jewellers and Silversmiths*
General Trading Co. (Mayfair) Ltd, The	*Suppliers of Fancy Goods*
Goode, Thomas, & Co. Ltd	*Suppliers of China and Glass*
Goodyear, Edward, Ltd	*Florists*
Halcyon Days Ltd	*Suppliers of Objets d'Art*
Hamblin, Theodore, Ltd	*Opticians*
Hancocks and Co. (Jewellers) Ltd	*Goldsmiths and Silversmiths*
Harris, D. R., & Co. Ltd	*Chemists*
Harrods Ltd	*Suppliers of China, Glass and Fancy Goods*
Hartnell, Norman, Ltd	*Dressmakers*
Harvey Nichols & Co. Ltd	*Drapers*
Hatchards	*Booksellers*
Heaton, Wallace, Ltd	*Suppliers of Photographic Equipment*
Jones, Peter, Ltd	*Drapers and Furnishers*
Levy, M., (London Wall) Ltd	*Fruiterers and Greengrocers*
Liberty & Co. plc	*Silk Mercers*
Lidstone, John	*Butchers*
Longmire, Paul, Ltd	*Supplier of Silver and Presentation Gifts*
Maurice & Robert	*Hairdressers*
Mayfair Trunks Ltd	*Suppliers of Luggage*
Mirman, Simone	*Milliners*
Morny Ltd	*Manufacturers of Soap*
Moyses Stevens Ltd	*Florists*
Paxton & Whitfield Ltd	*Cheesemongers*
Phillips, S. J., Ltd	*Antique Dealers*
Prowse, Keith, & Co. Ltd	*Theatre Ticket Agents*
Rayne, H. and M., Ltd	*Shoemakers and Handbag Manufacturers*
Riché of Hay Hill Ltd	*Manicurists*
Rudolf	*Milliners*
Smith, H. Allen, Ltd	*Wine Cooper and Merchant*
Sproston, W. F., Ltd	*Fishmongers*
Steiner Products	*Cosmeticians*
Stowells of Chelsea	*Wine and Spirit Merchants*
Swaine, Adeney, Brigg & Sons Ltd	*Umbrella Makers*
Thorn Lighting Ltd	*Manufacturers of Electric Lamps*
Thresher & Glenny Ltd	*Shirtmakers*
Twining, R., & Co. Ltd	*Tea and Coffee Merchants*
Warner & Sons Ltd	*Suppliers of Silks and Furnishing Fabrics*
Wartski Ltd	*Jewellers*
Weatherill, Bernard, Ltd	*Livery Tailors*
Wiggins, Arnold, & Sons Ltd	*Picture Frame Makers*
Woodhouse Hume Ltd	*Suppliers of Meat and Poultry*
Yardley and Co. Ltd	*Perfumers and Manufacturers of Soap*

Royal Warrants of Appointment to HRH the Duke of Edinburgh

Ashley and Blake Ltd	*Shirtmakers*
Buckley, Anthony & Constantine Ltd	*Photographers*
Ede & Ravenscroft Ltd	*Robe Makers*
General Trading Co. (Mayfair) Ltd, The	*Suppliers of Fancy Goods*
Goodyear, Edward	*Florists*
Hamblin, Theodore, Ltd	*Opticians*
Harrods Ltd	*Outfitters*
Hatchards	*Booksellers*
Hawes & Curtis (Tailors) Ltd	*Tailors*
Heaton, Wallace, Ltd	*Suppliers of Photographic Equipment*
Holland & Holland Ltd	*Rifle Makers*
Jones, Yarrell, & Co. Ltd	*Newsagents*
Kenning (London)	*Motor Car Distributors*
Lobb, John, Ltd	*Bootmakers*
Lock, James, & Co. Ltd	*Hatters*
Penhaligon's Ltd	*Manufacturers of Toilet Requisites*
Purdey, James, & Sons Ltd	*Gunmakers*
Simpson (Piccadilly) Ltd	*Outfitters*
Stephens Brothers Ltd	*Shirt Makers and Hosiers*
Weatherill Ltd, Bernard	*Livery Tailors*

Royal Warrants of Appointment to HRH the Prince of Wales

Asprey and Co. plc	*Jewellers, Goldsmiths and Silversmiths*
Benoist, V., Ltd	*Purveyors of Fine Foods and General Groceries*
Coney and Barrow Ltd	*Wine Merchants*
Exemious Ltd	*Manufacturers of Monogrammed Accessories*
Farlow, C., and Co. Ltd	*Suppliers of Fishing Tackle and Waterproof Clothing*
Floris, J., Ltd	*Manufacturers of Toilet Preparations*
General Trading Co. (Mayfair) Ltd., The	*Suppliers of Fancy Goods*
Gieves & Hawkes Ltd	*Tailors and Outfitters*
Goodyear, Edward, Ltd	*Florists*
Harrods Ltd	*Outfitters and Saddlers*
Harvey Nichols Ltd	*Suppliers of Household and Fancy Goods*
Hatchards Ltd	*Booksellers*
Heaton, Wallace, Ltd	*Suppliers of Photographic Equipment*
Johns & Pegg Ltd	*Tailors*
Johnson, Herbert, (Bond Street) Ltd	*Hatters*
Jones, Yarrell, & Co. Ltd	*Newsagents*
Lobb, John, Ltd	*Bootmakers*
Luxford, Keith, (Saddlery) Ltd	*Saddlers and Horse Clothiers (Teddington)*
Mappin & Webb Ltd	*Silversmiths*
Purdey, James, & Sons Ltd	*Gun and Cartridge Makers*
Simpson (Piccadilly) Ltd	*Outfitters*
Sproston, W. F., Ltd	*Suppliers of Fish*
Turnbull & Asser Ltd	*Shirtmakers*
Woodhouse Hume Ltd	*Suppliers of Meat and Poultry*

INDEX

Numbers in bold type indicate main entries.

219

Picture Acknowledgements Reproduced by gracious permission of Her Majesty the Queen: 23 (detail), 54 (detail), 166–7 (detail). The Royal Library, Windsor Castle, © 1986 Her Majesty the Queen: 15, 16 (detail), 45. Reproduced by permission of the Worshipful Company of Barbers: 63 (detail). The British Library, London; photo Bridgeman Art Library: 14. Reproduced by courtesy of the Trustees of the British Museum: 189. The Builder, 1863: 8. The Thomas Coram Foundation for Children, London; photo Bridgeman Art Library: 26, 27. Reproduced by kind permission of Viscount De L'Isle VC, KG, from his collection at Penshurst, Kent: 56. The Fitzwilliam Museum, Cambridge: 106–7 (detail). The Forbes Magazine Collection, New York; photo Bridgeman Art Library: 162 (detail). The Fotomas Index, London: 21, 29, 30, 31, 32, 49, 67, 85, 88, 116, 121, 137, 146, 150, 157, 159 (detail), 161, 174 (detail), 177, 179 (detail), 188, 190. The Guildhall Library, City of London; photo Bridgeman Art Library: 2 (detail), 34, 102 (detail), 111, 115 (detail), 118, 127 (detail), 130, 134 (detail), 178 (detail). The Guildhall Library, City of London: 19, 65, 80, 89, 91, 92, 143, 145. Macmillan Archives: 4, 11, 35, 98, 99, 100, 108. The Mansell Collection, London: 114. Roy Miles Fine Paintings, London; photo Bridgeman Art Library: 50–1 (detail). The Museum of London: 12, 68, 69, 70 (detail), 71 (detail), 72, 75, 77, 82, 87, 90, 96, 97, 101, 113, 119 (detail), 120, 122, 124, 125, 128, 132, 139 (detail), 158, 165, 169, 171 (detail), 180, 182 (detail), 183 (detail). The National Maritime Museum, London: 94 (detail). The National Portrait Gallery, London: 24 (detail), 38, 39 (detail), 42 (detail), 47, 55 (detail), 73 (detail), 79 (detail), 104 (detail), 133 (detail), 135 (detail), 155 (detail), 186 (detail). Private Collections: 41, photo Bridgeman Art Library: 18, 59, 123. Royal Botanic Gardens, Kew; photo Bridgeman Art Library: 110 (detail). By courtesy of the Board of Trustees of the Victoria and Albert Museum, London: 7 (detail), photo Bridgeman Art Library: 66 (detail), 126 (detail). Reproduced by permission of the Trustees, The Wallace Collection, London: 37 (detail). The Christopher Wood Gallery, London; photo Bridgeman Art Library: 163. The Zoological Society of London: 103.